Cisco Networking Academy Program
Fundamentals of Wireless LANs
Lab Companion

D1105412

Cisco Systems, Inc.
Cisco Networking Academy Program

Cisco Press
800 East 96th Street
Indianapolis, IN 46240 USA

Cisco Networking Academy Program
Fundamentals of Wireless LANs Lab Companion

Cisco Systems, Inc.
Cisco Networking Academy Program

Published by:
Cisco Press
800 East 96th Street
Indianapolis, IN 46240 USA

Printed in the United States of America   1 2 3 4 5 6 7 8 9 0

First Printing   March 2004

ISBN: 1-58713-121-8

Warning and Disclaimer

This book is designed to provide information based on content from the Cisco Networking Academy Program *Fundamentals of Wireless LANs* course. Every effort has been made to make this book as complete and as accurate as possible, but no warranty or fitness is implied.

The information is provided on an "as is" basis. The author, Cisco Press, and Cisco Systems, Inc., shall have neither liability nor responsibility to any person or entity with respect to any loss or damages arising from the information contained in this book or from the use of the programs that may accompany it.

The opinions expressed in this book belong to the author and are not necessarily those of Cisco Systems, Inc.

This book is part of the Cisco Networking Academy® Program series from Cisco Press. The products in this series support and complement the Cisco Networking Academy Program curriculum. If you are using this book outside the Networking Academy program, then you are not preparing with a Cisco trained and authorized Networking Academy provider.

For information on the Cisco Networking Academy Program or to locate a Networking Academy, please visit www.cisco.com/edu.

Trademark Acknowledgments

All terms mentioned in this book that are known to be trademarks or service marks have been appropriately capitalized. Cisco Press or Cisco Systems, Inc., cannot attest to the accuracy of this information. Use of a term in this book should not be regarded as affecting the validity of any trademark or service mark.

Corporate and Government Sales

Cisco Press offers excellent discounts on this book when ordered in quantity for bulk purchases or special sales. For more information please contact: U.S. Corporate and Government Sales 1-800-382-3419 corpsales@pearsontechgroup.com
For sales outside the U.S. please contact: International Sales international@pearsoned.com

Feedback Information

At Cisco Press, our goal is to create in-depth technical books of the highest quality and value. Each book is crafted with care and precision, undergoing rigorous development that involves the unique expertise of members of the professional technical community.

Readers' feedback is a natural continuation of this process. If you have any comments regarding how we could improve the quality of this book, or otherwise alter it to better suit your needs, you can contact us at networkingacademy@ciscopress.com. Please be sure to include the book title and ISBN in your message.

We greatly appreciate your assistance.

Publisher	John Wait
Editor-in-Chief	John Kane
Executive Editor	Mary Beth Ray
Cisco Systems Representative	Anthony Wolfenden
Cisco Press Program Manager	Nannette M. Noble
Production Manager	Patrick Kanouse
Senior Development Editor	Chris Cleveland
Senior Project Editor	Sheri Cain
Copy Editor	Marcia Ellett

CISCO SYSTEMS

Corporate Headquarters
Cisco Systems, Inc.
170 West Tasman Drive
San Jose, CA 95134-1706
USA
http://www.cisco.com
Tel: 408 526-4000
     800 553-NETS (6387)
Fax: 408 526-4100

European Headquarters
Cisco Systems Europe
11 Rue Camille Desmoulins
92782 Issy-les-Moulineaux
Cedex 9
France
http://www-europe.cisco.com
Tel: 33 1 58 04 60 00
Fax: 33 1 58 04 61 00

Americas Headquarters
Cisco Systems, Inc.
170 West Tasman Drive
San Jose, CA 95134-1706
USA
http://www.cisco.com
Tel: 408 526-7660
Fax: 408 527-0883

Asia Pacific Headquarters
Cisco Systems Australia,
Pty., Ltd
Level 17, 99 Walker Street
North Sydney
NSW 2059 Australia
http://www.cisco.com
Tel: +61 2 8448 7100
Fax: +61 2 9957 4350

Cisco Systems has more than 200 offices in the following countries. Addresses, phone numbers, and fax numbers are listed on the Cisco Web site at www.cisco.com/go/offices

Argentina • Australia • Austria • Belgium • Brazil • Bulgaria • Canada • Chile • China • Colombia • Costa Rica • Croatia • Czech Republic • Denmark • Dubai, UAE • Finland • France • Germany • Greece • Hong Kong • Hungary • India • Indonesia • Ireland Israel • Italy • Japan • Korea • Luxembourg • Malaysia • Mexico • The Netherlands • New Zealand • Norway • Peru • Philippines Poland • Portugal • Puerto Rico • Romania • Russia • Saudi Arabia • Scotland • Singapore • Slovakia • Slovenia • South Africa • Spain Sweden • Switzerland • Taiwan • Thailand • Turkey • Ukraine • United Kingdom • United States • Venezuela • Vietnam • Zimbabwe

Table of Contents

Foreword

Throughout the world, the Internet has brought tremendous new opportunities for individuals and their employers. Companies and other organizations are seeing dramatic increases in productivity by investing in robust networking capabilities. Some studies have shown measurable productivity improvements in entire economies. The promise of enhanced efficiency, profitability, and standard of living is real and growing.

Such productivity gains aren't achieved by simply purchasing networking equipment. Skilled professionals are needed to plan, design, install, deploy, configure, operate, maintain, and troubleshoot today's networks. Network managers must assure that they have planned for network security and for continued operation. They need to design for the required performance level in their organization. They must implement new capabilities as the demands of their organization, and its reliance on the network, expands.

To meet the many educational needs of the internetworking community, Cisco Systems established the Cisco Networking Academy Program. The Networking Academy is a comprehensive learning program that provides students with the Internet technology skills essential in a global economy. The Networking Academy integrates face-to-face teaching, web-based content, online assessment, student performance tracking, hands-on labs, instructor training and support, and preparation for industry-standard certifications.

The Networking Academy continually raises the bar on blended learning and educational processes. All instructors are Cisco Certified Academy Instructors (CCAIs). The Internet-based assessment and instructor support systems are some of the most extensive and validated ever developed, including a 24/7 customer service system for Networking Academy instructors and students. Through community feedback and electronic assessment, the Networking Academy adapts the curriculum to improve outcomes and student achievement. The Cisco Global Learning Network infrastructure designed for the Networking Academy delivers a rich, interactive, and personalized curriculum to students worldwide. The Internet has the power to change the way people work, live, play, and learn, and the Cisco Networking Academy Program is in the forefront of this transformation.

This Cisco Press title is one of a series of best-selling companion titles for the Cisco Networking Academy Program. Designed by Cisco Worldwide Education and Cisco Press, these books provide integrated support for the online learning content that is made available to academies all over the world. These Cisco Press books are the only authorized books for the Networking Academy by Cisco Systems, and provide print and CD-ROM materials that ensure the greatest possible learning experience for Networking Academy students.

I hope you are successful as you embark on your learning path with Cisco Systems and the Internet. I also hope that you will choose to continue your learning after you complete the Networking Academy curriculum. In addition to its Cisco Networking Academy Program titles, Cisco Press also publishes an extensive list of networking technology and certification publications that provide a wide range of resources. Cisco Systems has also established a network of professional training companies—the Cisco Learning Partners—who provide a full range of Cisco training courses. They offer training in many formats, including e-learning, self-paced, and instructor-led classes. Their instructors are Cisco certified, and Cisco creates their materials. When you are ready, please visit the Learning & Events area on Cisco.com to learn about all the educational support that Cisco and its partners have to offer.

Thank you for choosing this book and the Cisco Networking Academy Program.

Kevin Warner
Senior Director, Marketing
Worldwide Education
Cisco Systems, Inc.

Introduction

Cisco Networking Academy Program Fundamentals of Wireless LANs Lab Companion supplements your classroom and laboratory experience in the Fundamentals of Wireless LANs course within the Cisco Networking Academy Program.

The labs in this book are designed to further train you on the topics covered in the Cisco Wireless LAN Design Specialist certification exam. Most of the labs are hands-on and require access to a Cisco router lab or a simulator. Additional paper-based labs, which are practice exercises for complex topics, are included to supplement the online curriculum.

The Audience of This Book

Anyone who wants to learn about wireless networking technologies can use this book. The intended audience is students in high schools, community colleges, or four-year institutions, particularly those enrolled in the Fundamentals of Wireless LANs course in a Cisco Networking Academy Program.

How This Book Is Organized

Table I-1 outlines all the labs in this book by Target Indicator (TI) in the online curriculum, the time it should take to do the lab, and the difficulty rating (1 to 3, with 3 being the most difficult).

Table I-1   Master Lab Overview

Lab TI	Title	Difficulty	Estimated Time (Minutes)
Lab 1.2.7	Wireless Components and Media Identification	1	30
Lab 1.4.7	Wireless Lab Setup	1	30
Lab 1.6.1	Challenges of Wireless Regulations	1	20
Lab 1.6.8	Challenges of Wireless Media	1	20
Lab 2.4.3	Install a WLAN Adapter Card	1	15

Lab TI	Title	Difficulty	Estimated Time (Minutes)
Lab 2.5.2	Install Aironet Client Utility (ACU)	2	30
Lab 2.5.5	Configure Auto Profiles	2	25
Lab 2.6.5.1	ACU Utilities	1	10
Lab 2.6.5.2	Creating an Adhoc Network	2	30
Lab 3.2.3	Wireless Mathematics	2	25
Lab 3.4.1	Signals in Time	1	30
Lab 3.7.6	Wave Propagation	1	30
Lab 4.5.3	Topology Design with Cisco Network Designer (CND)	2	60
Lab 5.2.2	Configuring Basic AP Settings	1	30
Lab 5.2.4	Using Features of the Internetworking Operating System (IOS) Command-Line Interface (CLI)	2	30
Lab 5.2.5	Manage AP Configuration and Image Files	2	30
Lab 5.3.5	Configure Ethernet/FastEthernet Interface	2	15
Lab 5.4.4	Configure Radio Interfaces through the GUI	2	20
Lab 5.4.5	Configure Radio Interfaces through the IOS CLI	2	30
Lab 5.4.8	Configure an AP as a Repeater through the IOS CLI	2	30
Lab 6.3.6	Configure Site-to-Site Wireless Link	2	60

Lab TI	Title	Difficulty	Estimated Time (Minutes)
Lab 6.4.4	Configure Bridge Services	1	30
Lab 6.5.3	Manage Bridge Configuration and Image Files	1	20
Lab 6.5.5	Configure Layer 3 Site-to-Site Wireless Link (Optional Challenge Lab)	3	45
Lab 7.1.4	Antenna Setup	1	15
Lab 7.1.8.1	Configure AP Diversity Settings	1	15
Lab 7.1.8.2	Configure Bridge Diversity Settings	1	15
Lab 7.2.6	OmniDirectional Antennas	1	15
Lab 7.3.4	Directional Antennas	1	15
Lab 8.2.4	Wireless Attacks and Countermeasures	1	25
Lab 8.3.1.1	Configure Basic AP Security via GUI	2	30
Lab 8.3.1.2	Configure Basic AP Security via IOS CLI	2	30
Lab 8.3.2	Configure Filters on AP	1	25
Lab 8.3.3.1	Configure WEP on AP and Client	1	20
Lab 8.3.3.2	Configure an AP as a Repeater Using WEP	2	30
Lab 8.4.5.1	Configuring LEAP/EAP Using Local RADIUS Authentication	3	40
Lab 8.4.5.2	Configuring LEAP/EAP Using Cisco Secure ACS (Optional)	3	60
Lab 8.5.4.1	Configure Enterprise Security on AP	2	30
Lab 8.5.4.2	Configuring Site-to-Site Wireless Link Using Enterprise Security	3	45
Lab 8.6.2	Configure VLANs on the AP	2	40

Lab TI	Title	Difficulty	Estimated Time (Minutes)
Lab 9.3.9	WLAN Design	2	Time varies
Lab 9.5.5	Link Status Meter and Preferences	1	5
Lab 9.6.2	Using the Bridge Range Calculation Utility	1	15
Lab 10.2.7.1	Site Survey Active Mode	1	20
Lab 10.2.7.2	Survey the Facility	3	Time varies depending on site
Lab 10.3.6	Mounting and Installation	2	Time varies depending on availability of equipment
Lab 10.4.2.1	Request for Proposal	2	Time varies depending on scope of project
Lab 10.4.2.2	RFP Response	2	Time varies depending on scope of project
Lab 10.4.2.3	Review of RFP Response	2	Time varies depending on scope of project
Lab 11.1.4	Basic Troubleshooting on AP	2	10
Lab 11.2.6	Troubleshooting TCP/IP Issues	2	20
Lab 11.5.6.1	Configure Syslog on AP	2	25
Lab 11.5.6.2	Configure SNMP on AP	2	20

Lab TI	Title	Difficulty	Estimated Time (Minutes)
Lab 11.5.6.3	Configure Syslog and SNMP on the Bridge	2	25
Lab 12.4.8.1	Wireless Case Study of a School	2	Time varies depending on scope of project
Lab 12.4.8.2	Wireless Case Study of an Organization	2	Time varies depending on scope of project

This Book's Features

Many of this book's features help facilitate a full understanding of WLANS covered in this book:

- **Objectives**—The goal or goals that are to be accomplished in the lab.

- **Scenario**—The scenarios provided allow students to relate the lab exercises to real-world experiences.

- **Topology**—The topology diagrams provided for each lab show the students the network topology that is required to complete the lab.

- **Preparation**—This section details any setup that is necessary before beginning the steps listed in the lab exercise.

- **Tools and Resources**—Any tools or outside resources that are needed or are helpful to the completion of the lab exercise are listed here.

- **Steps 1-X**—These are the actual steps that students take to complete the lab exercise and fulfill the objectives of the lab.

- **Questions Within the Labs**—To demonstrate an understanding of the concepts covered, you have a reflection question at the end of the lab as appropriate. In addition, labs include questions that are designed to elicit particular points of understanding. These questions help verify your comprehension of the technology being implemented.

- The conventions used to present command syntax in this book are the same conventions used in the *Cisco IOS Command Reference*:

- **Bold** indicates commands and keywords that are entered literally as shown (for example, a **show** command).

- *Italic* indicates arguments for which you supply values.

- Braces ({ }) indicate a required element.

- Square brackets ([ ]) indicate an optional element.

- Vertical bars (|) separate alternative, mutually exclusive elements.

- Braces and vertical bars within square brackets (such as [x {y | z}]) indicate a required choice within an optional element. You do not need to enter what is in the brackets, but if you do, you have some required choices in the braces.

Chapter 1

Introduction to Wireless LANs

Lab 1.2.7: Wireless Components and Media Identification

Estimated Time: 30 Minutes

Number of Team Members: 5 teams with 2 students per team

Objectives

This lab covers the following objectives:

- Identify the basic media characteristics of wireless LANs.

- Identify the components of a wireless LAN.

- Describe the functions of the wireless components.

Scenario

Wireless local-area networks (WLANs) have become a popular choice in network installations. A WLAN is simple because installation is generally limited to installing building mounted antennas and placing the access points (APs). Figure 1-1 shows the Cisco Aironet WLAN product line.

Figure 1-1   Aironet WLAN Product Line

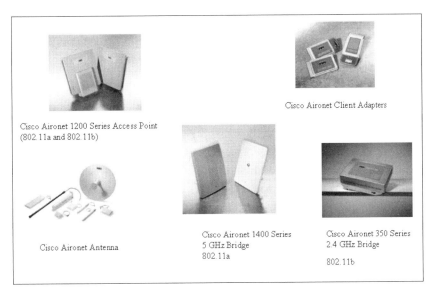

LANs can quickly become a mixture of wired and wireless systems depending on the network needs and design constraints.

In larger enterprise networks, the core and distribution layers continue as wired backbone systems. Enterprise systems are typically connected by fiber optics and unshielded twisted-pair (UTP) cabling. Even in many smaller networks, a wired LAN still remains at some level.

Preparation

The instructor will set up four equipment stations, as listed in Table 1-1.

Table 1-1   Equipment Station Setup

	Wireless	Wired
Station 1	Access point(s)	Hub or switch
Station 2	Bridge(s)	Fiber optic, modem, WAN switch
Station 3	Client adapter(s)	Wired Ethernet NIC
Station 4	Antenna(s)	Ethernet cable

The instructor allows the students to examine the equipment and compare the equipment to wired networking equipment.

The following tools and resources are required to complete the lab:

- A conventional PCI and PCMCIA Network Interface Card(s) for wired networking connections

- Physical media, such as UTP, coax, and fiber

- A conventional wired network hub or switch

- The Cisco Wireless course equipment bundle

Safety

Do not handle any wireless devices while they are powered. A general rule is to not touch or come within several inches of any powered antenna. Also, make sure to power down any device before removing a PC or PCMCIA card. Most important, do not remove antennas from a wireless access point or bridge while powered. This can damage the unit.

Station 1: Access Point

The access point station contains at least one model of a wireless access point. Depending on the academy equipment inventory, there may be multiple models and vendors. There are also some wired equivalent devices.

1. What models of Cisco access points are currently listed at Cisco.com?

    _____

2. What is the model of the AP at the station?

    _____

3. What is the frequency range(s) of the access point provided?

    _____

4. Does the access point have a detachable antenna, or is the antenna built in?

    _____

5. What wired ports are available?

    _____

6. What is the wired equivalent to the access point that is located at Station 1?

    _____

7. What are the advantages and disadvantages of the wired and wireless access devices?
    Document your answer in Table 1-2.

Table 1-2   Wired Versus Wireless Access Devices

Device	Advantage	Disadvantage

8. Draw and label the appropriate icons for the access point, hub, and switch in the
    following space.

Station 2: Bridge

The bridge station contains at least one model of wireless bridge. Depending on the academy equipment inventory, there may be multiple models and vendors. There are also some wired equivalent devices or media.

1.   What models of Cisco bridges are currently listed at cisco.com?

_____

2.   What is the model of the bridge at the station?

_____

3.   What is the frequency range of the bridge provided?

_____

4.   Does the bridge have a detachable antenna, or is the antenna built in?

_____

5.   What wired ports are available?

_____

6.   What is the wired equivalent to the bridge that is located at Station 2?

_____

7.   What are the advantages and disadvantages of the wired and wireless bridge devices? Document your answer in Table 1-3.

Table 1-3   Wired Versus Wireless Bridge Devices

Device	Advantage	Disadvantage

8.   Draw and label the appropriate icons for the bridge, modem, and serial line in the following space.

Station 3: Client Adapters

The client adapter station contains several models of wired and wireless adapters. Depending on the academy equipment inventory, there may be multiple models and vendors. There are also some wired equivalent devices.

1.   What models of client adapters are currently listed at cisco.com?

     _____

2.   What are the models of the client adapters at the station?

     _____
     _____
     _____
     _____

3.   Does the client adapter have a detachable antenna, or is the antenna built in?

     _____

4.   At what frequency range does the client adapter operate?

     _____

5.   What is the wired equivalent to the wireless client adapter that is located at Station 3?

     _____

6.   What are the advantages and disadvantages of the wired and wireless client adapter? Document your answer in Table 1-4.

Table 1-4   Wired Versus Wireless Client Adapters

Device	Advantage	Disadvantage

7.   Draw and label the appropriate icons for the client adapter in the following space.

Station 4: Antenna

The antenna station contains at least one antenna model. Depending on the academy equipment inventory, there may be multiple models and vendors. There are also some wired equivalent devices or media.

1. What is the model of the antenna?

    _____

2. What is the frequency range of the antenna provided?

    _____

3. What is the wired equivalent to the antenna that is located at Station 4?

    _____

4. What are the advantages and disadvantages of the antenna devices? Document your answer in Table 1-5.

Table 1-5   Advantages of Antennas

Device	Advantage	Disadvantage

5. Draw and label the appropriate icons for the antenna, wireless signal, and Ethernet line in the following space.

Lab 1.4.7: Wireless Lab Setup

Estimated Time: 30 Minutes

Number of Team Members: Instructor-led classroom demonstration

Objectives

This lab covers the following objectives:

- Learn the topologies for the basic WLAN design.

- Learn the topology in the basic metropolitan area design.

Scenario

WLAN technology has two functions. First, a WLAN can take the place of a traditional wired network. Second, a WLAN can extend the reach and capabilities of a traditional wired network.

Much like wired LANs, in-building WLAN equipment consists of a PC Card (PCMCIA), a personal computer interface (PCI) or industry-standard architecture (ISA), client adapters, and APs. APs perform functions similar to wired networking hubs.

WLANS are also similar to wired LANs for small or temporary installations. A WLAN can be arranged in a peer-to-peer or ad hoc topology using only client adapters. For added functionality and range, access points can be incorporated to act as the center of a star topology, and function as a bridge to an Ethernet network.

With a wireless bridge, networks located in buildings miles away from each other can be integrated into a single local-area network. Figure 1-2 shows a WLAN topology.

Figure 1-2   Wireless LAN Topology

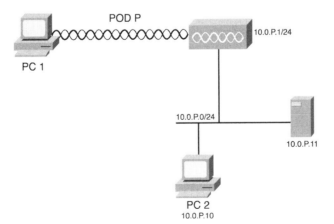

Note: The topology figures and lab examples contain P and Q values. The P value in the addressing and naming scheme refers to *your* assigned Pod number.

The following are examples of determining P values:

- Pod2 is looking at a topology figure and is trying to determine the **P** values in the figure. In this scenario, the **P** values equals **2**. 10.0.**P**.12 becomes 10.0.**2**.12, 172.30.**P**.2 becomes 172.30.**2**.2, and so on.

- Pod1 is looking at a topology figure and is trying to determine the **P** values in the figure. In this scenario, the **P** values equals **1**. 10.0.**P**.12 becomes 10.0.**1**.12, 172.30.**P**.2 becomes 172.30.**1**.2, and so on.

In both examples, the **P** values are directly related to the Pod number of the team.

The **Q** value in the naming and addressing scheme is used when testing the security or connectivity with the "peer" team.

The following are examples of determining Q values:

- In a lab, Pod2 has been asked to test connectivity to their peer inside host at IP address 10.0.**Q**.12. In this scenario, 10.0.**Q**.12 equals 10.0.**1**.12.

- In a lab, Pod1 has been asked to test connectivity to their peer inside host at IP address 10.0.**Q**.12. In this scenario, 10.0.**Q**.12 equals 10.0.**2**.12.

In both examples, the **Q** value is the directly related to the peer Pod number.

Preparation

The instructor needs at least one laptop computer, at least one desktop computer, and the equipment in the Cisco Wireless course equipment bundle. The instructor should attempt to have as many wireless computers as possible to display the concepts involved in the wireless network.

The following tools and resources are needed for this lab:

- Wireless networking course equipment bundle

- Laptop computers with the PCMCIA NIC inserted

- Desktop computers with the PCI NIC inserted

- A switch or hub for a wired connection

- A computer to act as a server on the wired network

The instructor might compile any variety of equipment on the wired network to depict the wired network in a more realistic setting.

Step 1: Setting Up a Basic WLAN

1.   The instructor has a variety of PCs or servers cabled into the wired network infrastructure without wireless devices.

2.   The instructor distributes the various computers with the wireless NICs around the classroom in a similar fashion to a basic WLAN topology.

3.   The instructor introduces one AP as the root hub in the classroom.

4.   The instructor introduces a cable from the AP to a switch connected to the wired network. The wired network is now being extended with the wireless AP to the various wireless clients that were assembled.

5.   The instructor is assembling a basic wireless networking topology.

6.   List the devices in this topology configuration:

_____

_____

_____

_____

_____

_____

_____

Step 2: Setting Up a Site-to-Site WLAN (Optional)

The instructor introduces a second AP or bridge into the topology and introduces the various antennas that can bridge wireless signals across to another building.

1.   What type of antenna distributes wireless signals in all directions and can be used in a point-to-multipoint wireless bridge topology?

_____

_____

2.   What type of antenna distributes wireless signals in one general direction and can be used in a point-to-point topology?

_____

_____

Lab 1.6.1: Challenges of Wireless Regulations

Estimated Time: 20 Minutes

Number of Team Members: Each team consists of two students

Objectives

The students learn the future direction and technologies associated with wireless regulations.

Scenario

There is continual development in wireless LAN technologies. One primary challenge is to conform to local, state, and national regulations related to wireless LAN emissions. Our focus is on wireless emissions that occur in the 2.4-GHz and 5-GHz radio frequency spectrums. In this lab, each team is assigned a topic to investigate.

Preparation

The instructor should compile a list of wireless regulatory bodies.

This lab requires a computer with a connection to the Internet for online research purposes.

The student teams should be encouraged to research resources, such as trade publications, magazines, and vendor literature, that are applicable to current and future trends in the area of WLANs.

Step 1: Assigning Each Team a Regulatory Agency to Research

The research should include guidelines regulating the operation in both radio frequency spectrums (2.4 GHz and 5 GHz):

- United States (FCC)

- Europe (ETSI)

- Japan (JST)

- Australia/New Zealand (ANZ)

- Other

Record the assignments in Table 1-6.

Table 1-6   Regulatory Agency Assignments

Team	Agency Assigned
Team 1	
Team 2	
Team 3	
Team 4	
Team 5	
Team 6	

Step 2: Researching Sources

List at least three different websites that were visited for the research information:

_____

_____

_____

Step 3: Presentations

1.   Give a brief summary of the regulatory agencies researched.

_____

_____

2.   What is the future trend of this agency's regulations in the 2.4-GHz RF spectrums?

_____

_____

3.   What is the future trend of this agency's regulations in the 5-GHz RF spectrums?

_____

_____

4.   How does this body differ from the others?

_____

_____

5.   What officials comprise the regulatory agency or body?

_____

_____

6.   How do companies comply with the regulations?

_____

_____

7.   How do the regulatory agencies police the airwaves?

_____

_____

8.   What action(s) do they take for violations?

_____

_____

9.   What penalties are imposed for violations?

_____

_____

Lab 1.6.8: Challenges of Wireless Media

Estimated Time: 20 Minutes

Number of Team Members: Each team consists of two students

Objectives

The students research a topic involved with the future direction and technologies associated with wireless networking.

Scenario

There is continual development in the WLAN community. One emerging standard is 802.11g. 802.11g operates at higher speeds than 802.11b in the 2.4-GHz range. 802.11g, like 802.11a, supports OFDM modulation with speeds up to 54 Mbps. 802.11g is designed to be backwards-compatible with 802.11b clients. If additional speed is needed, 802.11g might become a good choice. If the 2.4-GHz frequency is noisy at a given locale, 802.11a 5-GHz technology might be a better option.

Preparation

The instructor should compile a list of current trends in the area of wireless local-area networking, or use the topics given in Step 1 of the lab.

This lab requires a computer with a connection to the Internet for online research purposes.

Utilize resources such as trade publications, magazines, and vendor literature that are applicable to current and future trends in the area of WLANs.

Step 1: Assigning Each Group a Specific Topic from the Following List to Research

- WLAN security

- WLAN frequency ranges

- WLAN devices

- WLAN connection speeds

- WLAN applications

- WLAN vendors

Record the assignments in Table 1-7.

Table 1-7   WLAN Topic Assignments

Team	Topic Assigned
Team 1	
Team 2	
Team 3	
Team 4	
Team 5	
Team 6	

Step 2: Researching Sources

List at least three different websites that you visited for the research information:

_____
_____
_____

Step 3: Presentations

1.   Give a brief summary of the wireless local-area networking topic researched.

_____
_____
_____

2.   What is the future trend of this topic for wireless local-area networking?

_____
_____
_____

3.   What companies are involved in the development of the wireless networking topic?

_____
_____
_____

4.	Is there an IEEE standard for the topic researched? If so, what is it?

_____
_____
_____

Chapter 2

IEEE 802.11 and Network Interface Cards

Lab 2.4.3: Install a WLAN Adapter Card

Estimated Time: 15 Minutes

Number of Team Members: Six teams with two students per team

Objectives

The students learn the procedures for installing the client adapter in the PC for wireless networking.

Scenario

Install a wireless LAN adapter card in a laptop, desktop, or both. Figure 2-1 shows Cisco wireless LAN adapter cards.

Figure 2-1   Wireless LAN Adapter Cards

Preparation

This lab requires the following materials:

- Desktop or laptop PC

- Appropriate wireless client adapter card

- One Cisco Aironet PCI352, CB20A, or PCM 352 Client Adapter network interface card (NIC).

- One PC with a Microsoft Operating System installed

- One screwdriver for PCI card installation

Step 1: Installing the Client Adapter Card in a Laptop

Before installing a new adapter card into the laptop, the laptop may need to have an integrated wireless NIC disabled. To disable an integrated wireless NIC, click on the **Start** button and select the **Control Panel** option. If in Classic View, select **Network Connections** or the appropriate Network Control panel. If in Category View, select the **Network and Internet Connections** category and select **Network Connections**. Right-click on the integrated wireless adapter and select **Disable**.

Note: When inserting a wireless NIC into a PCMCIA slot on a laptop, the power can be on or off.

Insert the Cisco Aironet PCM 352 Client Adapter into the PCMCIA slot. The CB20A installs into the laptop PC CardBus slot. A CardBus adapter will not fit completely into a PCMCIA laptop slot. This might be a problem on older laptops. A PCMCIA adapter, however, will fit in a PCMCIA slot or a CardBus slot. Figure 2-2 is a comparison of the cards.

Figure 2-2   Card Comparison

Notice the different shape on the right-hand side of the cards. The top card in Figure 2-2 is a PCMCIA adapter, and the bottom card is a CardBus adapter

Step 2: Installing the Client Adapter Card in a Desktop

1.   Turn off the PC and all the components.

2.   Remove the computer cover.

3.   Remove the screw from the top of the CPU back panel above an empty PCI expansion slot. This screw holds the metal bracket on the back panel.

4.   Examine the client adapter. The antenna connector and the LEDs face out of the computer and are visible when the cover is placed back on.

5.   Tilt the adapter to allow the antenna connector and LEDs to slip through the opening in the CPU back panel.

6.   Make sure the rubber duck antenna is not attached.

7.   Press the client adapter into the empty slot until the connector is firmly seated. Install the screw. Figure 2-3 shows the result of these steps.

Figure 2-3   Client Adapter Installed in PCI Slot

8.   Reinstall the screw on the CPU back panel and replace the computer cover.

9.   Attach the 2-dB dipole antenna to the adapter antenna connector until it is finger-tight, as illustrated in Figure 2-4.

Figure 2-4   Completed Installation

10.   For optimal reception, position the antenna so it is straight up.

11.   Boot up the computer and proceed to Step 3. Install the drivers for Windows.

Step 3: Installing the Drivers for Windows

1.   After the client adapter is installed into the computer, Windows automatically detects it
       and briefly opens the Found New Hardware window.

2.   The Found New Hardware Wizard window opens and indicates that the wizard will help
       to install the driver.

3.   Click **Next**. Another window opens and asks what the wizard should do.

4.   Select the recommended **Search for a suitable driver for my device** and click **Next**.

5.   Select **CD-ROM drives**. Deselect all other options. Insert the Cisco Aironet Series
       Wireless LAN Adapters CD into the computer CD-ROM drive. Click **Next**.

6.   The wizard finds the installation files on the CD and displays the search results.

7.   When the client adapter driver is displayed, click **Next** to copy the required files.

8.   When Windows has finished the installation, click **Finish**.

9.   Remove the CD from the computer CD-ROM drive.

Step 4: Configuring the SSID Through Windows

1.   Double-click **My Computer**, **Control Panel**, and **System**.

2.   In the System Properties window, click the **Hardware** tab.

3.   Click **Device Manager**.

4.   In the Device Manager window, double-click **Network Adapters**.

5.   Right-click the **Cisco Systems 350 Series PCMCIA Wireless LAN Adapter**, or the applicable **Aironet Card**.

6.   Click **Properties**.

7.   In the client adapter Properties window, click the **Advanced** tab.

8.   In the Advanced window, select **Client Name**. Type the unique client name of the computer in the Value dialog box.

9.   Select **SSID**. Type the RF network SSID, as assigned by the instructor, in the Value dialog box. Remember that the SSID is case-sensitive. Click **OK**.

Step 5: Completing the Driver Installation Without a DHCP Server

1.   Double-click **My Computer**, **Control Panel**, and **Network and Dial-up Connections**.

2.   Right-click **Local Area Connection**.

3.   Click **Properties, Internet Protocol (TCP/IP)**, and **Properties**.

4.   Click **Use the following IP address** and enter the IP address, subnet mask, and default gateway address of the computer, which you can obtain from the instructor. Click **OK**.

5.   In the Local Area Connection Properties window, click **OK**.

6.   If prompted to restart the computer, click **Yes**.

7.   The driver installation is complete.

Step 6: Verifying the TCP/IP Settings

1.   Select **Start** > **Run** and enter the following:

2.   On Win2000 or XP, enter **cmd** to bring up the command prompt. While at the command prompt, type in **ipconfig /all** to verify the IP settings.

3.   On Win9x, enter the **winipcfg** command from **Start** > **Run** and press **Enter**.

Step 7: Installing the Aironet Client Adapter Card on Other Operating Systems (Optional)

The following URLs provide information for installing the Aironet Client Adapter card on non-Windows operating systems:

- http://www.cisco.com/en/US/products/hw/wireless/ps4555/products_installation_and _configuration_guides_list.html

- http://www.cisco.com/en/US/products/hw/wireless/ps4555/ps448/index.html

Lab 2.5.2: Install Aironet Client Utility (ACU)

Estimated Time: 30 Minutes

Number of Team Members: Six teams with two students per team

Objectives

The students learn the procedures for installing the Aironet Client Utility. Also, students configure, select, and manage profiles.

Scenario

ACUs allow a user to easily configure, manage, and monitor wireless connections.

Topology

Figure 2-5 shows the topology that will be used in this lab.

Figure 2-5   Completed Installation

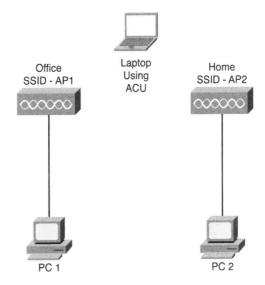

Preparation

This lab requires the following materials:

- Desktop or laptop PC

- Appropriate wireless client adapter card

- One Cisco Aironet PCI352, CB20A, or PCM 352 Client Adapter NIC

- Aironet Client Utility installer

- Two configured access points (instructor must set up)

- Office Profile: AP1 – SSID of AP1

- Home Profile: AP2 – SSID of AP2

Resources

http://www.cisco.com/en/US/products/hw/wireless/ps4555/products_installation_and_ configuration_guide_book09186a0080184b6e.html

Step 1: Configuring XP to Use the ACU

To configure the client adapter through the ACU instead of through Windows XP, follow these steps:

1. Double-click **My Computer**, **Control Panel**, and **Network Connections**.

2. Right-click **Wireless Network Connection** and click **Properties**.

3. Select the **Wireless Networks** tab.

4. Deselect the **Use Windows to configure my wireless network settings** checkbox.

5. Follow the instructions in the "Installing ACU" section to install the ACU.

Note: If you are planning to configure the client adapter through Windows XP but you want to use ACU's diagnostic tools, install the ACU but do not create any profiles.

Step 2: Installing the Aironet Client Utilities (ACU)

After the appropriate driver is installed for the computer's operating system and for the client adapter type, follow these steps to install the ACU, shown in Figure 2-6.

If EAP-TLS, EAP-MD5, PEAP, or EAP-SIM authentication is going to be used on a computer running Windows 2000, Service Pack 3 for Windows 2000 and the Windows 2000 Wireless 802.1X hot fix must be installed before installing the ACU.

Figure 2-6   The Aironet Client Utility

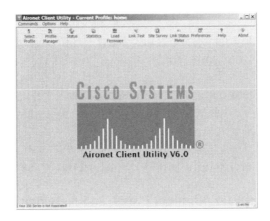

Follow the below procedure if the ACU has never been installed on the computer or if ACU version 4.13 or greater is currently installed. If a version of ACU prior to 4.13 is installed on the computer, uninstall it; then, follow the steps below to install the latest version. Cisco does not recommend uninstalling ACU version 4.13 or greater before installing the latest version of ACU.

ACU version 5.05.001 or greater must be used with one of the following software combinations:

- PCM/LMC/PCI card driver version 8.2 or greater and firmware version 4.25.30 or greater

- Mini PCI card driver version 3.4 or greater and firmware version 5.00.03 or greater

- PC-CardBus card driver version 3.4 or greater and firmware version 4.99 or greater

Note: You can obtain the most recent version of the ACU through the Software Center at Cisco.com.

1.   To install or use the client utilities on Windows NT or Windows 2000 systems, a user must log onto the system as a user with administrative privileges. The utilities do not install or operate correctly for users not logged in with administrative rights.

2.   Select **Start** > **Run**, and enter the path for the downloaded ACU setup.exe file.

   To use the CD, go to **d:\Utilities\ACU\setup.exe**. "d" is the letter of the CD-ROM drive.

3.   Execute the ACU setup.exe file. When the Welcome screen appears, click **Next**.

4.   In the Authentication Method screen, select **None,** the default value, because server-based authentication is not enabled for a client adapter. Click **Next**.

Note: See the hyperlink noted earlier in the "Resources" section to find out more about the authentication choices.

5.   After the client utilities are installed, a user can elect not to implement any security features, or a user can activate some level of security by using WEP keys.

6. In the Select Components screen, make sure the client utilities are selected. Make sure that any undesired utilities are deselected. Click **Next**.

7. In the Select Program Folder screen, click **Next** to allow icons for the client utilities to be placed in the Cisco Systems, Inc. folder.

8. If no server-based authentication was selected in Step 3, select **Launch the Aironet Client Utility** and click **Finish**. The ACU opens so that the client adapter can be configured.

Step 3: Completing the Driver Installation Without a DHCP Server

1. Double-click **My Computer**, **Control Panel**, and **Network and Dial-up Connections**.

2. Right-click **Local Area Connection**.

3. Click **Properties, Internet Protocol (TCP/IP)**, and **Properties**.

4. Click **Use the following IP address** and enter the IP address, subnet mask, and default gateway address of the computer, which you can obtain from the instructor. Click **OK**.

5. In the Local Area Connection Properties window, click **OK**.

6. If prompted to restart the computer, click **Yes**.

7. The driver installation is complete.

Step 4: Verifying the TCP/IP Settings

1. Select **Start** > **Run** and enter the following:

2. On Win2000 or XP, enter **cmd** to bring up the command prompt. While at the command prompt, type in **ipconfig /all** to verify the IP settings.

Step 5: Installing the Aironet Client Adapter Card on Other Operating Systems (Optional)

The following URLs provide information for installing the Aironet Client Adapter card on non-Windows operating systems:

- http://www.cisco.com/en/US/products/hw/wireless/ps4555/products_installation_and_configuration_guides_list.html

- http://www.cisco.com/en/US/products/hw/wireless/ps4555/ps448/index.html

Step 6: Using the Profile Manager

1. Double-click the **Aironet Client Utility (ACU)** icon on your desktop to open the ACU's profile manager, shown in Figure 2-7.

Figure 2-7   Profile Manager

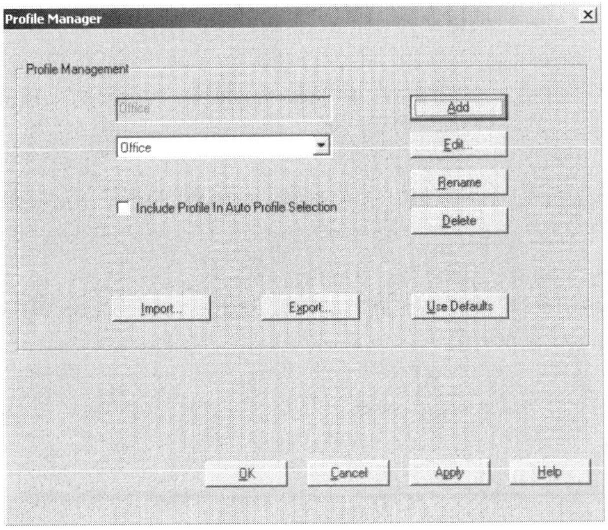

2.   Click the **Profile Manager** icon or select **Profile Manager** from the Commands drop-down menu. The Profile Manager screen appears.

What tasks does the Profile manager allow?

Step 7: Creating a New Profile

Follow these steps to create a new profile, as shown in Figure 2-8.

Figure 2-8   Creating a Profile

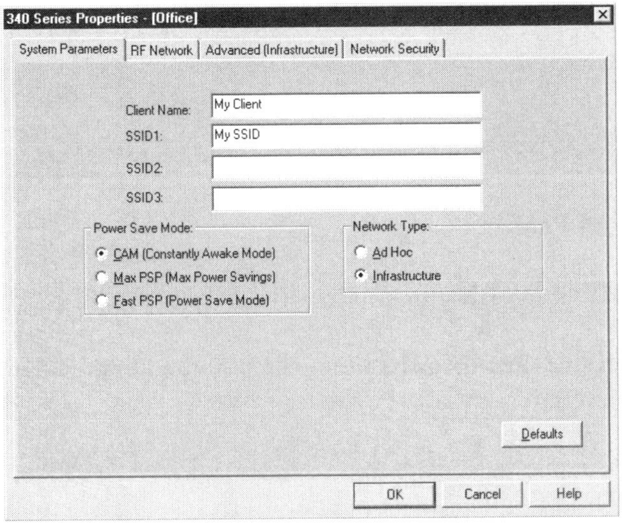

1.   Click **Add**. A cursor appears in the Profile Management edit box.

2.   Enter the name for the first new profiles named "Office."

3.   Press **Enter**. The Properties screens appear with the name of the new profile in parentheses.

Note: To use the default values, click **OK**. The profile is added to the list of profiles on the Profile Manager screen.

4.   Configure the client name and SSID for the Office profile, as directed by the instructor, to connect to the access point.

5.   Click **OK** or **Apply** to save your profile.

6.   Create profiles named Home and Airport.

Step 8: Selecting the Active Profile

Follow these steps to specify the profile that the client adapter is to use:

1.   Open the ACU; click the **Select Profile** icon or select **Select Profile** from the Commands drop-down menu, shown in Figure 2-9. The Select Profile screen appears.

Figure 2-9   Creating a Profile

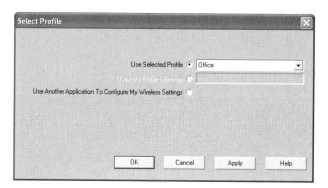

2.   Select **Use Selected Profile**.

3.   Now select the **Office Profile**.

4.   Click **OK** or **Apply** to save the selection. The client adapter starts using a profile based on the option selected.

Note: If the client adapter cannot associate to an access point (AP) or loses association while using the selected profile, the adapter does not attempt to associate using another profile. To associate, a different profile must be selected, or select **Use Auto Profile Selection**. This option causes the client adapter's driver to automatically select a profile from the list of profiles that were set up to be included in auto profile selection. The **Use Another Application To Configure My Wireless Settings** option allows an application other than ACU to configure the client adapter. Examples of such applications include Windows XP and Boingo. You must select this option if you are configuring your card through Windows XP or 2000 but want to use ACU's diagnostic tools.

Step 9: Using the Aironet Client Monitor (ACM)

ACM is an optional application that provides a small subset of the features available through the ACU. Specifically, it enables you to access status information about your client adapter and perform basic tasks. ACM is accessible from an icon in the Windows system tray, making it easily accessible and convenient to use.

The profile can also be quickly switched through the system tray using ACM. Figure 2-10 shows the icon in the system tray.

Figure 2-10   The ACM Icon in the System Tray

1. Left-click on the ACU icon and go to **Select Profile**, as shown in Figure 2-11, and choose the **Home** profile.

2. The client now associates to the second AP. Observe the ACM icon.

3. Select the **Airport** profile. Observe the ACM icon turn gray.

4. Finally, reselect the **Office** profile to connect to the first AP. The ACM icon should turn green.

Figure 2-11   Select Profile

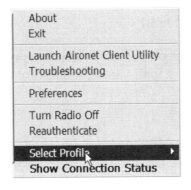

The appearance of the ACM icon indicates the connection status of your client adapter, as listed in Table 2-1. ACM reads the client adapter status and updates the icon every 2 seconds.

Table 2-1   ACM Icon Descriptions Based on Color

Icon Color	Description
White	The client adapter's radio is turned off.
Dark gray	The client adapter is not associated to an access point.
Light gray	The client adapter is associated to an access point, but the user is not authenticated.
Green	The client adapter is associated to an access point, and the link quality is excellent or good.
Yellow	The client adapter is associated to an access point, and the link quality is fair.
Red	The client adapter is associated to an access point, and the link quality is poor.

What is the status of the client adapter?

Step 10: Modifying a Profile (Optional)

This section provides instructions for modifying an existing profile. Follow the steps in the corresponding section to edit, set to default values, rename, or delete a profile.

Editing a Profile

1.   Open ACU; click the **Profile Manager** icon or select **Profile Manager** from the Commands drop-down menu. The Profile Manager screen appears.

2.   From the Profile Management drop-down box, select the profile that you want to edit.

3.   Click **Edit**. The Properties screens appear with the name of the profile in parentheses.

4.   Change any of the configuration parameters for this profile.

5. If you want this profile to be included in auto profile selection, make sure the **Include Profile in Auto Profile Selection** checkbox on the Profile Manager screen is selected.

6. Click **OK** or **Apply** to save your configuration changes.

Setting a Profile to Default Values

1. Open ACU; click the **Profile Manager** icon or select **Profile Manager** from the Commands drop-down menu. The Profile Manager screen appears.

2. From the Profile Management drop-down box, select the profile that you want to set to default values.

3. Click **Use Defaults**.

4. When prompted, click **Yes** to confirm your decision.

5. Click **OK** or **Apply** to save your change. The profile is saved with default values.

Renaming a Profile

1. Open ACU; click the **Profile Manager** icon or select **Profile Manager** from the Commands drop-down menu. The Profile Manager screen appears.

2. From the Profile Management drop-down box, select the profile that you want to rename.

3. Click **Rename**. The Profile Management edit box becomes enabled.

4. Enter a new name for the profile.

5. Click **OK** or **Apply** to save your change. The profile is renamed and added to the list of profiles.

Deleting a Profile

1. Open ACU; click the **Profile Manager** icon or select **Profile Manager** from the Commands drop-down menu. The Profile Manager screen appears.

2. From the Profile Management drop-down box, select the profile that you want to delete.

3. Click **Delete**.

4. When prompted, click **Yes** to confirm your decision.

5. Click **OK** or **Apply** to save your change. The profile is deleted.

Step 10: Importing and Exporting Profiles

This section provides instructions for importing and exporting profiles. You might want to use the import/export feature for the following reasons:

- To back up profiles before uninstalling the client adapter driver or changing radio types

- To set up your computer with a profile from another computer

- To export one of your profiles and use it to set up additional computers

Follow the steps in the corresponding section to import or export profiles.

Exporting a Profile

1.   Insert a blank floppy disk into your computer's floppy drive if you wish to export a profile to a floppy disk, or save the file to the PC hard disk.

2.   Open ACU; click the **Profile Manager** icon or select **Profile Manager** from the Commands drop-down menu. The Profile Manager screen appears.

3.   From the Profile Management drop-down box, select the profile that you want to export.

4.   Click **Export**. The Save Profile As screen appears. The default filename is *ProfileName*.pro, where *ProfileName* is the name of the selected profile, and the default directory is the directory in which ACU was installed.

5.   If you want to change the profile name, enter a new name in the File name edit box.

6.   Select a different directory (for example, your computer's floppy disk drive or a location on the network) from the Save in drop-down box.

7.   Click **Save**. The profile is exported to the specified location.

Importing a Profile

1.   If the profile that you want to import is on a floppy disk, insert the disk into your computer's floppy drive.

2.   Open ACU; click the **Profile Manager** icon or select **Profile Manager** from the Commands drop-down menu. The Profile Manager screen appears.

3.   Click **Import**. The Import Profile screen appears.

4.   Find the directory where the profile is located.

5. Click the profile so it appears in the File name box at the bottom of the Import Profile screen.

6. Click **Open**. The imported profile appears in the list of profiles on the Profile Manager screen.

Step 11: Denying Access to Non-Administrative Users

By default, ACU allows regular-class users to modify and save profiles to the registry. However, if you have administrative rights, you can prevent regular-class users from saving profiles on computers running Windows NT, 2000, or XP. (This option is not available for Windows 95, 98, or Me, because these versions of Windows do not support different classes of users.)

Follow these steps if you want to prevent users without administrative rights from modifying and saving profiles (or to allow regular-class users to save profiles if permission was denied previously).

1. Open ACU by double-clicking the **Aironet Client Utility (ACU)** icon on your desktop.

2. Click the **Preferences** icon or select **Preferences** from the Options drop-down menu. The Aironet Client Utility Preferences screen, shown in Figure 2-12, appears.

Figure 2-12   ACU Preferences Screen

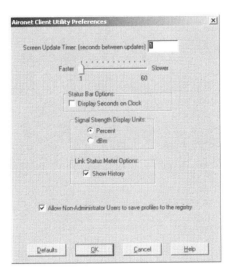

3. Deselect the **Allow Non-Administrator Users to save profiles to the registry** checkbox (or select this checkbox if you want to allow regular-class users to save profiles).

4. Click **OK** to save your changes.

Step 12: Uninstalling the Aironet Client Utilities (Optional)

Note: If this step is performed, you have to reinstall the ACU before the next lab.

1. Uninstall the Client Utilities.

2. Close any Windows programs that are running.

3. Insert the Cisco Aironet Series Wireless LAN Adapters CD into the computer CD-ROM drive.

4. Select **Start** then **Run**, and enter the following path: **d:\Utilities\ACU\setup.exe**. "d" is the letter of the CD-ROM drive.

5. When the Welcome screen appears, select **Remove** and click **Next**.

6. When asked if selected applications should be completely removed, click **Yes**.

7. If a message appears indicating that a file was detected that may no longer be needed by any application but deleting the file may prevent other applications from running, click **Yes**.

8. If a message is received indicating that locked files were detected, click **Reboot**.

9. In the Maintenance Complete screen, click **Finish**.

10. If prompted to restart the computer, remove the CD from the computer CD-ROM drive and click **Yes**.

Lab 2.5.5: Configure Auto Profiles

Estimated Time: 25 Minutes

Number of Team Members: Six teams with two students per team

Objectives

The students learn the procedures for configuring ACU to use Auto Profiles.

Scenario

The **Use Auto Profile Selection** option causes the client adapter's driver to automatically select a profile from the list of profiles that were set up to be included in auto profile selection. The name of the profile that is being used appears in the box to the right of the Use Auto Profile Selection option.

If the client adapter loses association for more than 10 seconds (or for more than the time specified by the LEAP authentication timeout value on the LEAP Settings screen, if LEAP is enabled), the driver switches automatically to another profile that is included in auto profile selection. The adapter will not switch profiles as long as it remains associated or reassociates within 10 seconds (or within the time specified by the LEAP authentication timeout value). To force the client adapter to associate to a different access point, you must disable auto profile selection and select a new profile.

Topology

Figure 2-13 shows the topology that will be used in this lab.

Figure 2-13   Lab Topology

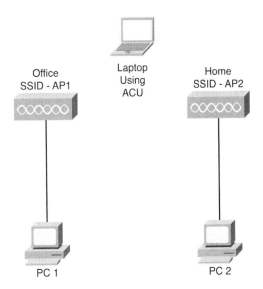

Preparation

This lab requires the following materials:

- Three desktop or laptop PCs

- Appropriate wireless client adapter card

- One Cisco Aironet PCl352, CB20A, or PCM 352 Client Adapter NIC

- Aironet Client Utility installer

- Two configured access points (instructor must set up)

- AP1 – SSID of AP1

- AP2 – SSID of AP2

- AP3 – SSID of AP3 (optional)

Resources

http://www.cisco.com/en/US/products/hw/wireless/ps4555/products_installation_and_configuration_guide_chapter09186a008007f869.html#1091568

Step 1: Creating Multiple Profiles

1.   Remove any existing profiles.

2.   Now create four profiles based on Table 2-2.

Table 2-2   Profiles

Profile	Profile Name	Client Name	SSID
1	Office1	StudentP1	AP1
2	Home	StudentP2	AP2
3	Office2	StudentP3	AP3
4	Airport	StudentP4	AP4

(Where StudentP is the student name.)

Step 2: Including a Profile in Auto Profile Selection

After creating three profiles for the client adapter, the profile manager's auto profile selection feature can be used. When auto profile selection is enabled, the client adapter automatically selects a profile from the list of profiles that were included in auto profile selection and uses it to establish a connection to the network.

Take the following steps to include the profiles in auto profile selection and to establish the order in which the profiles will be selected for use.

Open ACU; click the **Select Profile** icon or select **Select Profile** from the Commands drop-down menu. The Select Profile screen, shown in Figure 2-14, appears.

Figure 2-14   Select Profile Screen

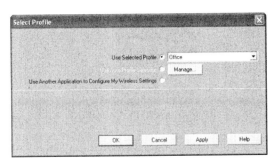

Step 3: Managing and Adding Profiles

The following rules apply to the auto profile selection:

- At least two profiles must be included in the Auto Selected Profiles Box.

- The profiles must specify an SSID; otherwise, they cannot be selected in the Available Profiles box.

- Profiles cannot specify multiple SSIDs; otherwise, they cannot be selected in the Available Profiles box.

- Each profile that is included in auto profile selection must have a unique SSID. For example, if Profile A and Profile B both have "ABCD" as their SSID, only Profile A or Profile B can be included in auto profile selection.

1. Click the **Manage** button next to the Use Auto Profile Selection option. The Auto Profile Selection Management screen appears.

2. All the created profiles are listed in the Available Profiles box, as shown in Figure 2-15. Highlight each one to include in auto profile selection and click the **Add** button. The profiles move to the Auto Selected Profiles box.

3. The first profile in the Auto Selected Profiles box has the highest priority, while the last profile has the lowest priority. To change the order (and priority) of your auto-selectable profiles, highlight the profile that you want to move and click the **High Priority** or **Low Priority** arrow to move the profile up or down, respectively.

Figure 2-15   Available Profiles

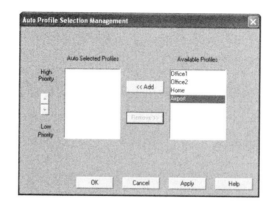

4.   Click **OK** to save the changes.

When auto profile selection is enabled, the client adapter scans for an available network. The profile with the highest priority and the same SSID as one of the found networks is used to connect to the network. If the connection fails, the client adapter tries the next-highest priority profile that matches the SSID, and so on.

To remove a profile from auto profile selection, highlight the profile in the Auto Selected Profiles box and click the **Remove** button. The profile moves to the Available Profiles box.

Step 4: Connecting to the Highest-Priority Access Point

Connecting to APs in various venues becomes very easy. Follow these instructions to observe the auto profile feature.

1.   With the **Select Profile** window open, select the **Use Auto Profile Selection**.

2.   Click **OK**.

3.   As soon as the changes are made in Step 3, a connection to the first AP in the list should be established. If not, turn off the client radio and then turn the radio back on.

4.   After connecting to the highest-priority AP, turn off the AP. Observe the ACM icon status.

5.   Turn off the radio on the client NIC.

6.   Turn on the radio on the client NIC. Because the Highest-Priority AP is down, the Auto Profile will attempt to connect to the AP. After an unsuccessful attempt, the Profile Manager will try to connect using the second highest profile in the list.

Lab 2.6.5.1: ACU Utilities

Estimated Time: 10 Minutes

Number of Team Members: Two students per team

Objectives

Students use the ACU utilities to complete the following tasks:

- Assess the performance of the Radio Frequency (RF) link.

- View the status of the wireless network.

- View the statistics of the wireless network.

- View the link status of the wireless network.

Topology

Figure 2-16 shows the topology that is used in this lab.

Figure 2-16   Lab Topology

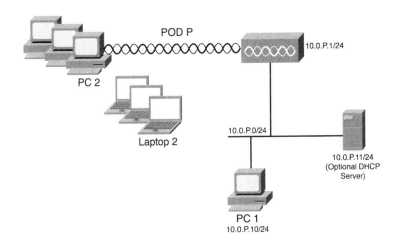

Note: The topology figures and lab examples contain **P** and **Q** values. The **P** value in the addressing and naming scheme refers to *your* assigned Pod number. No **Q** values are used in this lab.

The following are examples of determining P values:

- Pod2 is looking at a topology figure and is trying to determine the **P** values in the figure. In this scenario, the **P** values equal **2**. 10.0.**P**.12 becomes 10.0.**2**.12, 172.30.**P**.2 becomes 172.30.**2**.2, and so on.

- Pod1 is looking at a topology figure and is trying to determine the **P** values in the figure. In this scenario, the **P** values equal **1**. 10.0.**P**.12 becomes 10.0.**1**.12, 172.30.**P**.2 becomes 172.30.**1**.2, and so on.

In both examples, the **P** values are directly related to the Pod number of the team.

Scenario

ACU, as shown in Figure 2-17, provides tools that enable a wireless technician to assess the performance of the client adapter and other devices on the wireless network. ACU diagnostic tools perform the following functions:

- Display the current status and configured settings of the client adapter.

- Display statistics pertaining to the transmission and reception of data of the client adapter.

- Display a graphical image of the client adapter RF link.

- Run an RF link test to assess the performance of the RF link between the client adapter and its associated access point.

Figure 2-17   Aironet Client Utility

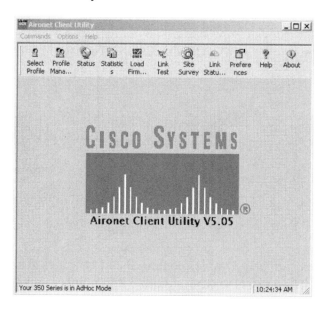

Preparation

The instructor prepares one access point that will be used by the entire class to perform this lab exercise. An IP address and SSID must be configured for the AP, or a Bridge can be used in root AP mode.

Step 1: Running an RF Link Test

The ACU link test tool sends out pings to assess the performance of the RF link. The test is performed multiple times at various locations throughout the lab area. The test is designed to run at the data rate set in the Edit Properties - RF Network section of ACU.

The results of the link test can be used to determine the RF network coverage and, ultimately, the required number and placement of APs in the network. The test also helps installers avoid areas where performance is weak. Therefore, the test helps to eliminate the risk of a lost connection between the client adapter and its associated AP.

Because the link test operates above the RF level, it does more than test the RF link between two network devices. It also checks the status of wired sections of the network and verifies that TCP/IP and the proper drivers have been loaded.

Select the **Link Test** button from the Aironet Client Utility screen, as shown in Figure 2-18. The Link Test Screen appears on the desktop.

Figure 2-18   Link Test Button

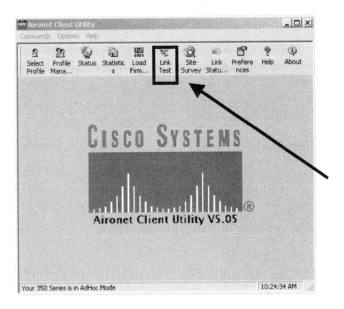

Step 2: Setting Up the Link Test Screen

Notice that, by default, in the IP Address of Access Point field, the IP address is the AP to which the wireless NIC is associated, as shown in Figure 2-19. This IP address could be changed to another wireless device IP address.

Figure 2-19   Link Test Screen

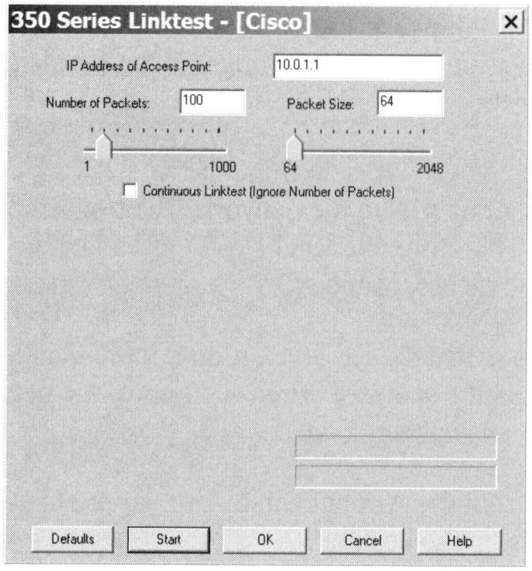

The link test can be set up to run until it has attempted to send a specific number of packets, or to run until it is stopped. Choose one of the following steps to determine how long the link test will run:

1. Select the number of packets that the link test should attempt to send. You can enter a number in the Number of Packets field or use the slider to select this value. (The Number of Packets parameter is ignored if the Continuous Linktest checkbox is selected.)

    Range: 1 to 1000

    Default: 4

2. Select the Continuous Linktest checkbox to allow the link test to run continuously:

    Default: Deselected

3. Select the size of the data packet that is to be sent. Using the ACU, enter a number in the Packet Size field, or use the slider to select this value.

    Range: 64 to 2048

    Default: 100

4. Leave all options on the default settings.

Step 3: Running the Link Test

Click the **Start** button to run the link test, as shown in Figure 2-20. While the test is running, statistics are displayed and updated periodically.

Figure 2-20   Run the Link Test

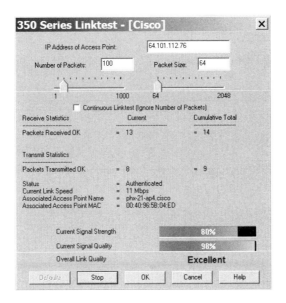

1.   What is the Cumulative Total of the AP Receive Statistics (Packets)?

_____

2.   What is the Cumulative Total of the AP Transmit Statistics (Packets)?

_____

Step 4: Viewing the Status Screen

From the Aironet Client Utility screen, select the **Status** button.

Complete the following list of information about the wireless infrastructure status that is displayed on this page:

1.   Firmware version

_____

2.   Is WEP enabled or disabled?

_____

3.   IP address

_____

4.   Current link speed

_____

5.   Current power level

_____

6.   Channel or frequency

_____

7.   Status

_____

8.   SSID

_____

9.   Power save mode

_____

10.   Associated AP address

_____

11.   Associated AP MAC address

_____

Step 5: Viewing the Statistics Screen

From the Aironet Client Utility screen, select the **Statistics** button. Figure 2-21 shows the Statistics screen.

Figure 2-21   Statistics Screen

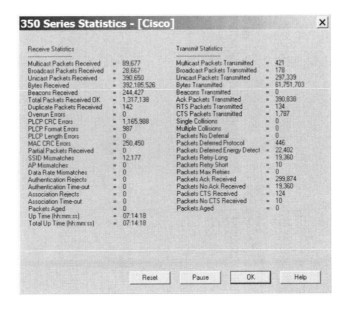

1.   Which statistics are incrementing greater, transmit or receive? Why?

_____

_____

_____

_____

2.   Define the following terms from the Statistics screen:

   A.   RTS

   _____

   B.   CTS

   _____

   C.   ACK

   _____

Step 6: Viewing the Link Status Meter

1.   Bring up the Link Status Meter (see Figure 2-22) by clicking the **Link Status Meter** button on the ACU.

Figure 2-22   Link Status Meter

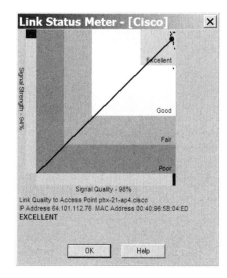

2.   Observe the signal quality over a period of 30 seconds.

3.   What is the signal quality of the AP?

_____

4.   What is the signal strength of the AP?

_____

Lab 2.6.5.2: Creating an Ad Hoc Network

Estimated Time: 30 Minutes

Number of Team Members: Students work in teams of two for this lab process

Objectives

Each team configures several personal computers to communicate with each other without an access point or cables.

Scenario

Several PCs equipped with Cisco Aironet Client Adapters are needed. They should be installed and set up. Configure the ACU to allow them to connect together as a network without an access point. Perform some of the diagnostics included in the ACU for Ad Hoc mode.

Passive mode differs from Active mode in wireless LANs. The diagnostics tests performed in Passive mode can help determine the best placement and coverage for the network's access point. Instead of using an access point, the other PC becomes the wireless client that can provide similar information.

Active mode performs these diagnostics with the use of an access point. This lab familiarizes students with gathering some of this valuable information.

Topology

Figure 2-23 shows the topology that is used in this lab.

Figure 2-23   Lab Topology

10.0.P.11/24   10.0.P.10/24

Note: The topology figures and lab examples contain **P** and **Q** values. The **P** value in the addressing and naming scheme refers to *your* assigned Pod number. No **Q** values are used in this lab.

The following are examples of determining **P** values:

- Pod2 is looking at a topology figure and is trying to determine the **P** values in the figure. In this scenario, the **P** values equal **2**. 10.0.**P**.12 becomes 10.0.**2**.12, 172.30.**P**.2 becomes 172.30.**2**.2, and so on.

- Pod1 is looking at a topology figure and is trying to determine the **P** values in the figure. In this scenario, the **P** values equals **1**. 10.0.**P**.12 becomes 10.0.**1**.12, 172.30.**P**.2 becomes 172.30.**1**.2, and so on.

In both examples, the **P** values are directly related to the Pod number of the team.

Preparation

Prior to this lab, all the PCs should be equipped with working Cisco Aironet Client Adapters. The ACU should be installed on the computers.

It is important for the instructor to assign team numbers. Also, unique IP addresses should be assigned to each client adapter or personal computer within each team to avoid IP conflicts.

Each team should use the same unique SSID to ensure that the computers associate to each other. The SSID to be used for all PCs is adhocP (where P is the group number assigned by the instructor).

The instructor should help students understand the addressing scheme. Using the information in the Table 2-3, configure the host computers. Note that no default gateway is needed. By assigning unique IP addresses and SSIDs, the students avoid conflict with other teams.

Table 2-3   Client Addressing Scheme

Team	Client Name	SSID	Client Address
1	Client1a	Adhoc1	10.0.1.10/24
	Client1b	Adhoc1	10.0.1.11/24
2	Client2a	Adhoc2	10.0.2.10/24
	Client2b	Adhoc2	10.0.2.11/24
3	Client3a	Adhoc3	10.0.3.10/24
	Client3b	Adhoc3	10.0.3.11/24

You need two PCs equipped with the Cisco Aironet Client Adapter per group to complete this lab. One of the computers should be a laptop for mobility purposes.

Step 1: Creating a Profile Named adhocP (Where P Is the Team Number)

1.   Open the Cisco Aironet Client Utility.

2.   Click the **Profile Manager** icon.

3.   Click the **Add** button.

4.   Click the **OK** button.

5.   From the System Parameters tab, type **adhoc#** (where # is the group number assigned by the instructor) in the SSID1: box.

6.   In the Network Type section, select the **Ad Hoc** radio button.

Power Save mode can be left as the default Constantly Awake Mode (CAM) setting at this time.

7.   Click the **OK** button.

8.   Exit Profile Manager by clicking on the **OK** button.

Step 2: Selecting the Profile Named adhocP (Where P is the Team Number)

1.   From the Aironet Client Utility, click on **Select Profile** icon.

2.   From the Use Selected Profile drop-down box, select **adhoc**.

3.   Click the **OK** button.

Notice that a message appears on the status line at the bottom of the ACU that the wireless NIC is in Ad Hoc mode.

Step 3: Obtaining the PC's MAC Address

Click the **Status** button on the ACU. Figure 2-24 shows the Status screen. Provide this MAC address to one of the other students for site survey and other diagnostic purposes.

Figure 2-24   Status Screen

1.   What is the computer's MAC address? Provide this information to your team partner so diagnostics can be performed.

---

2.   Write your partner's MAC address.

Step 4: Establishing Ad Hoc Site Survey Passive Mode

1.   Click the **Site Survey** button. This starts the Site Survey Passive mode, as shown in Figure 2-25.

Figure 2-25   Site Survey Passive Mode

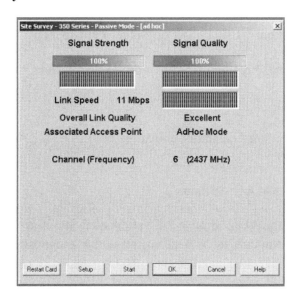

2.   Click the **Setup** button to start the Site Survey Setup mode.

3.   Type in the destination MAC address of the other group's PC that was obtained. Their PC will be used for an ad hoc site survey. Try this a few different times with different members of the class.

4.   Click the **OK** button to go back to the Ad Hoc Passive Mode screen.

5.   Click the **Start** button to initiate an Active mode site survey.

      What additional information was added to the Ad Hoc Site Survey screen?

Step 5: Displaying the Ad Hoc Status Screen

Figure 2-26 shows the Ad Hoc Status screen.

Figure 2-26   Ad Hoc Status Screen

1.   What is the status of the PC?

_____

2.   What is the PC's SSID?

_____

3.   What is the PC's network type?

_____

4.   What is the Power Save mode of the PC?

_____

Note: (Optional) Walk around the class and note the change in signal strength and signal quality.

Step 6: Displaying the Ad Hoc Statistics Screen

Figure 2-27 shows the Ad Hoc Statistics screen.

Figure 2-27   Ad Hoc Statistics Screen

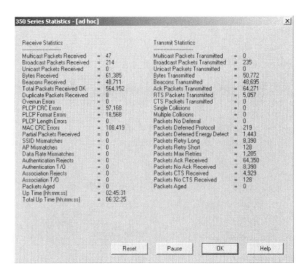

1.   How many broadcast packets were received?

_____

2.   How many broadcast packets were transmitted?

_____

Exit from the Ad Hoc Statistics screen by selecting **OK**.

Step 7: Displaying the Link Status Meter Screen

After Ad Hoc mode is configured properly on the computer, click on the **Link Status Meter** (LSM) icon with the ACU to activate the Link Status Meter, as shown in Figure 2-28. Note the position of the signal strength and signal quality indicator line on the meter.

Figure 2-28   Link Status Meter

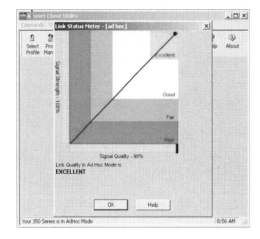

If using a laptop (or a mobilized desktop on a rolling cart with an extension cord), answer the following questions.

1.   Move the laptop around the area. Note how the Link Status Meter behaves. What is the approximate distance that the two computers can be apart before they disassociate?

_____

2.   Move one of the computers behind a metal bookcase or file cabinet. Was there a noticeable change in signal quality or signal strength?

_____

3.   Try this same experiment with other materials, such as a glass window, walls, desks, and plastic objects. Which of the materials had the greatest effect on the signal quality or signal strength?

_____

4.   If a 2.4-GHZ phone is available, activate the talk button near one of the computers. Note the Link Status Meter. What happens to the signal quality or signal strength?

_____

5.   Move the computer behind a wooden door and note the Link Status Meter. Did the wooden door have any effect on the signal quality or signal strength?

_____

Optional Lab Addendum: Set Up File Share in Ad Hoc Mode

Scenario 1: Set up a window file share, a web page, or an FTP server program on each PC. Transfer files from one PC to the other. Open a web browser and enter the IP address of the peer team member. If web services are enabled on the peer PC, a web page should be displayed. Try to transfer a file by FTP between PCs.

Scenario 2: Set up a network game or program that requires network connectivity between PCs. Determine if any performance issues exist. Have other teams change to the ad hoc network by matching the SSID and moving into the same IP subnet. Determine if there is a point at which network performance is an issue. Remember that network connectivity is more than ping or telnet traffic. Network application and user demands must always be tested to ensure proper network performance after any wireless installation.

Scenario 3: Set up a PC as an mp3 file server and stream music across the wireless ad hoc network. Determine if any performance issues exist. Have other teams change to the ad hoc network by matching the SSID and moving into the same IP subnet. Determine if there is a point at which network performance is an issue.

Optional Lab Addendum: Create an Ad Hoc Network with Internet Connection Sharing

Is it necessary to purchase an access point in order to share the fast broadband connection at home? This step of the lab is similar to using a cross-connect cable for a small PC network, as shown in Figure 2-29, but without the use of the router or additional cables.

Figure 2-29   Small PC Network

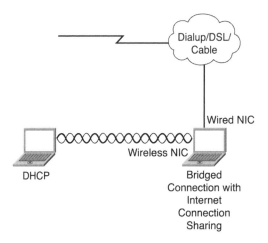

Step 1: Bridging the Connection on the Desktop PC

Select Bridge Connections, as shown in Figure 2-30.

Figure 2-30   Bridge the Connection

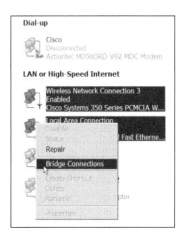

Step 2: Sharing an Internet Connection

Share the Internet connection using the Network Setup Wizard, as shown in Figure 2-31.

Figure 2-31   Network Setup Wizard

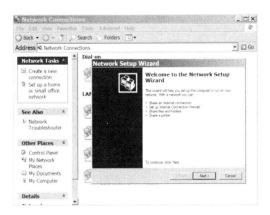

Step 3: Configuring Wireless NICs on both PCs in Ad Hoc Mode

Both computers will need to be configured to operate in ad hoc mode. Detailed instructions for setting up an ad hoc network can be found at the beginning of this lab activity.

Chapter 3

Wireless Radio Technology

Lab 3.2.3: Wireless Mathematics

Estimated Time: 25 minutes

Number of Team Members: Students work in teams of two or individually

Objectives

In this lab, students learn the importance of the output power of the transmitting wireless device. The overall output power of the transmitting wireless device is affected by two important features. First, the importance of the gain and loss features of the wireless transmitting device affect the outcome. Second, is the importance of the radio frequency (RF) signal on the outcome. Finally, students calculate the amount of power actually transmitted from a wireless transmitting device. This is done through the antenna element, the Effective Isotropic Radiated Power (EIRP), based on the type of antenna, cabling, connectors, and the transmitting device setting being used.

Scenario

Upon completion of this lab, students will understand the potential range of the radiated wave signal transmitted by wireless devices.

Students will also have a better understanding of how to calculate the power gain or loss from the various device selections. As a result, wireless device placement and selection placements will benefit with this knowledge of.

Learn to convert all radio frequency (RF) signal ratings into a common decibel (dB) unit to calculate power gain or loss.

Preparation

Prior to the lab, the instructor should have the technical specifications for a variety of wireless transmitting devices, wireless antenna devices, and wireless device connectors.

Tools and Resources

- Technical specifications of the power output in decibels (milliwatts) of the wireless devices used. Access points and client adapters are examples of these devices.

- Technical specifications of the gain in decibels (dBi) of various wireless device antennae.

- Technical specifications of the gain/loss in decibels (dB) of various wireless device cables.

- Technical specifications of the gain/loss in decibels (dB) of various wireless device connectors. These connectors are necessary when cables have to be joined for longer cable lengths.

Additional Materials

The instructor provides a variety of Flash simulated calculators for wireless networking that can assist with the calculations.

Step 1: Calculating the Decibel Rating

A *decibel (dB)* is a unit for measuring ratios in terms of gain and loss. Radio waves are measured by db. The formula to calculate decibels is dB = 10 log10 (Pfinal/Pref), as shown in Figure 3-1.

Figure 3-1   Calculate the Decibel Rating

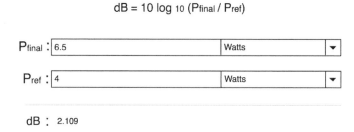

The following breaks down the terms of the calculation:

- **dB** is the amount of decibels.

- **10** indicates that this is a power measurement.

- **log10** describes the fact that the number in parenthesis is transformed using the base 10 logarithm rule.

- **Pfinal** is the delivered power.

- **Pref** is the original power.

Calculate the decibel (dB) rating given the **Pfinal** of 6.5 watts and a **Pref** of 4 watts.

Step 2: Calculate the Delivered Power

Another way to look at this formula is where Pfinal = Pref * 10 (dB/10), as shown in Figure 3-2. Choose dB and Pref and see what the resulting power is.

Figure 3-2   Calculate the Delivered Power

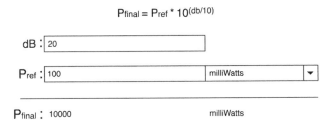

What is the Pfinal value given a dB of 20 and a Pref of 100mw?

Step 3: Calculating the Total Power Output of the Wireless Device

Calculate the amount of power actually transmitted from a wireless transmitting device. This is done through the antenna element, the effective isotropic radiated power (EIRP) based on the type of antenna, cabling, connectors, and the transmitting device setting being used.

Adding or subtracting the decibel values of the components involved in the transmitting wireless device easily calculates the EIRP.

Review the following example:

Access Point output: 25 dBm

Amplifier gain: 10 dB

Antenna gain: 8 dBi

Amplifier Cable loss: -6 dBi

Antenna Cable loss: -3 dBi

25dBm + 10dB + 8dBi – 6dBi – 3dBi = 34dBm

EIRP = 34dBm

Step 4: Calculating the EIRP

Calculate the EIRP for the values in Table 3-1.

Table 3-1   EIRP Calculations

Access Point Output	Antenna Gain	EIRP
20-dBm	2.2 dBi	
17-dBm	2.2 dBi	
15-dBm	2.2 dBi	
13-dBm	2.2 dBi	
7-dBm	2.2 dBi	
0 dBm	2.2 dBi	

Lab 3.4.1: Signals in Time

Estimated Time: 30 minutes

Number of Team Members: Students work in teams of two

Objectives

In this lab, students use a spectrum analyzer to examine a familiar radio system and to understand how WLANs work. This activity also examines the complexities of radio waves by examining how analog signals vary with time and frequency. Most complex waves in time can be represented by an appropriate combination of pure sine waves. Next, students examine the connection between analog and digital and how an analog wave can be converted into binary digits representing that analog wave. Finally, students completely represent this wave, with its continuous variation in voltages, into a set of binary numbers (bits). Digital computers and communications networks can transmit the stream of bits quickly and with few errors. This process is called *analog-to-digital (A to D)* conversion.

Scenario

One of the most important facts of the Information Age is that data can be represented electrically by voltage patterns on wires and in electronic devices.

This is important for in this study of WLANs because they are electronic devices. Data, represented by voltage patterns, can be converted to radio waves, and radio waves can be converted into data.

An understanding of voltage patterns can be very helpful in the study of WLANs. This is because voltages are much easier to measure than directly measuring the radio waves.

Tools and Resources

WLAN course Flash simulation programs.

Step 1: Understanding the Relationship of Power Versus Frequency

Use the amplitude, frequency, and phase simulation to examine how changes in amplitude and frequency can affect wave signals. Figure 3-3 shows the simulation.

Figure 3-3 Amplitude, Frequency, and Phase Simulation

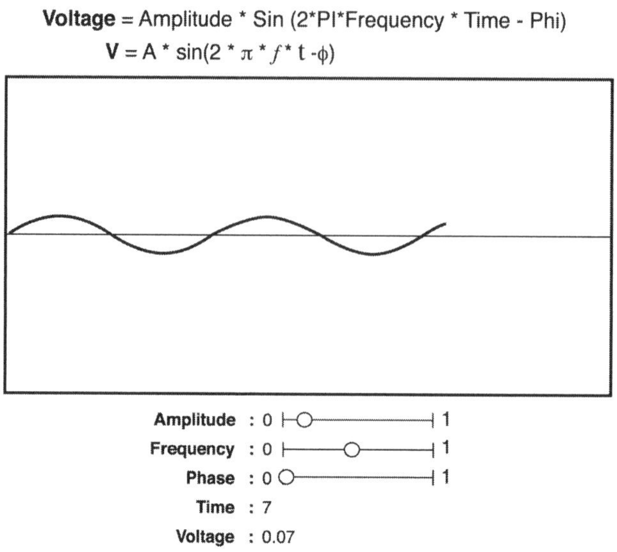

Voltage = Amplitude * Sin (2*PI*Frequency * Time - Phi)
V = A * sin(2 * π * f * t -φ)
Amplitude : 0 1
Frequency : 0 1
Phase : 0 1
Time : 7
Voltage : 0.07

1. What shape does the signal take when the amplitude is increased?

___

2. What shape does the signal take when the frequency is increased?

___

Step 2: Examining Sine Wave Behavior

Use the Amplitude and Frequency simulation, shown in Figure 3-4, to examine the behavior of the sine wave.

Figure 3-4 Amplitude and Frequency of the Sine Wave

- A M P L I T U D E +
- F R E Q U E N C Y +

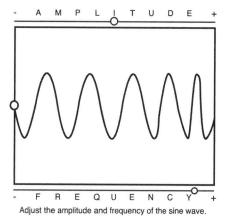

Adjust the amplitude and frequency of the sine wave.

Use the Analog to Digital Conversion simulator, shown in Figure 3-5, to examine the wave signal.

Figure 3-5   Converting Analog Signals to Digital Signals

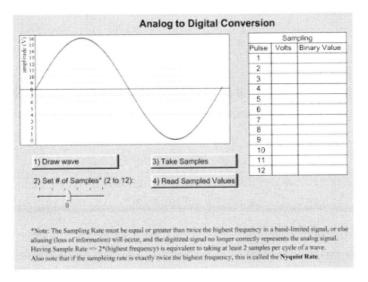

Why is this tool useful?

Lab 3.7.6: Wave Propagation

Estimated Time: 30 Minutes

Number of Team Members: Students work in teams of two or individually

Objectives

In this lab, students learn about objects that refract, reflect, diffract, and scatter radio waves in a WLAN. Students also examine objects that cause multipath problems in a WLAN. Finally, students calculate a path loss value of the radio wave for various wave propagation effects.

Scenario

It is important to understand how radio waves are propagated from one device to another. Radio wave propagation is an important issue regarding the availability and reliability of a WLAN.

When setting up and troubleshooting WLANs, it is useful to be able to identify possible obstructers in a WLAN environment. It is also useful to know how these obstructers affect the behavior of the WLAN network.

A crucial factor in the success or failure of a communications system is how much power that comes from the transmitter actually gets to the receiver.

RF waves can be refracted, reflected, diffracted, scattered, or affected in many ways by multipath problems.

These many different effects can be combined and described by what is known as *path loss*.

Preparation

The instructor provides the Flash simulation tools for radio wave propagation to each student team.

The instructor might need various obstructers for actual in-class demonstration.

Tools and Resources

As an option to using actual equipment, the instructor provides the student with the WLAN course Flash program simulation tools.

Safety

Use the proper safety precautionary measures associated with any of the equipment in this lab.

Step 1: Demonstrating Reflection of a Signal

Demonstrate the behavior of a wave through a reflective medium. Figure 3-6 shows the Reflection Simulator. Set up two PCs in Wireless Ad Hoc mode for a passive site survey, as in the Lab 2.6.5.2 in Chapter 2.

Figure 3-6   Reflection Simulator

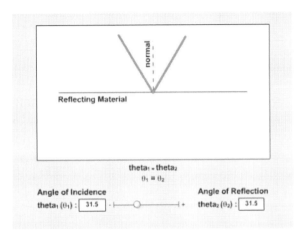

A radio wave has a tendency to bounce off of its course when coming in contact with a reflective medium. These bouncing signals can cause an effect known as *multipath*.

Place a metal cabinet between the two PCs to act as a reflective medium.

What happens to the signal quality and strength when it passes through a reflective medium?

Step 2: Demonstrating Diffraction of a Signal

Demonstrate the behavior of diffraction of a signal. Figure 3-7 illustrates diffraction. Set up two PCs in Wireless Ad Hoc mode for a passive site survey, as in Lab 2.6.5.2 in Chapter 2.

Figure 3-7   Diffraction

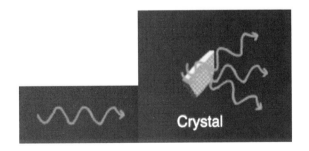

A radio wave has a tendency to be obstructed when coming in contact with a diffractive medium. A portion of the wave does not pass through most diffractive mediums, and can cause a high degree of signal loss.

Place an irregular rough surface, such as a rooftop, between the two PCs to act as a diffractive medium. Diffractive surfaces are more commonly found outside.

What happens to the signal quality and strength when it passes through a diffractive medium?

Step 3: Demonstrating Scattering of a Signal

Demonstrate the behavior of "scattering of a signal." Set up two PCs in Wireless Ad Hoc mode for a passive site survey, as in Lab 2.6.5.2 in Chapter 2.

The radio wave has a tendency to scatter when coming in contact with a scattering-causing medium.

Place a large plant, a street sign, or a lamppost between the PCs to act as a scattering medium, as shown in Figure 3-8.

Figure 3-8   Scattering of a Signal

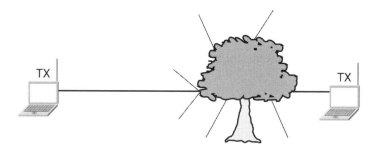

What happens to the signal quality and strength when it passes through a scattering medium?

Step 4: Demonstrating Signal Multipath Problems

Demonstrate the behavior of signal multipath problems, as shown in Figure 3-9. Set up two or more PCs in Wireless Ad Hoc mode for a passive site survey, as in Lab 2.6.5.2 in Chapter 2.

Radio waves have a tendency to bounce off reflective mediums and can cancel each other. This condition is considered multipath.

Figure 3-9   Multipath Distortion Problems

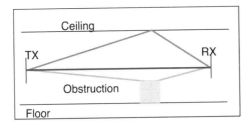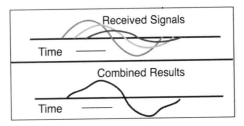

Try adding more than two wireless LAN clients in a small area with several reflective surfaces, such as windows, smooth textured walls, and so on. Look at what happens to the site survey meter.

What happens to the signal quality and strength when it passes through a refractive medium?

Step 6: Calculating Free Space Path Loss

Use the Free Space Path Loss Flash program simulator, shown in Figure 3-10, to calculate different path loss values.

Figure 3-10   Free Space Path Loss Calculation

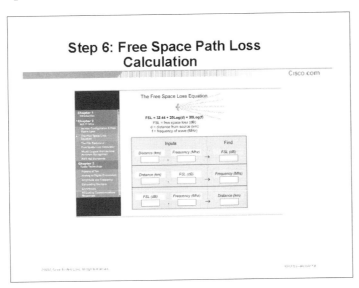

Which frequency is affected by distance more, the 2.4GHz or 5GHz?

Chapter 4

Wireless Topologies

Lab 4.5.3: Topology Design with Cisco Network Designer (CND)

Estimated Time: 60 minutes

Number of Team Members: Students work in teams of two or individually

Objectives

Design the following network topologies with the Cisco Network Design (CND) software:

- Ad Hoc network

- Basic Service Set (BSS) network

- Extended Service Set (ESS) network

- Basic home network

- Enterprise network (optional)

Scenario

Network architecture is a roadmap and guide for ongoing network planning, design, and implementation. It provides a logical framework that unifies disparate solutions onto a single foundation.

After an organization has developed network architecture, it then has a framework in place for more informed decision-making. This includes appropriate investments in network technologies, products, and services.

Preparation

The instructor will provide each student team with a copy of the CND software.

(Optional: This lab can be performed with any other graphical application software or drawing materials the instructor has available.)

The student must review and understand Chapter 4 of the *Cisco Networking Academy Program Fundamentals of Wireless LANs Companion Guide* before doing the lab.

Tools and Resources

- Cisco Network Design (CND) software

- Personal computers for each student or group, which are compatible with the CND software.

Step 1: Loading the CND or Designer Software, If It Has Not Been Loaded on the PC

Open the Cisco Network Design software, shown in Figure 4-1. Use the **help** feature to get acquainted with the software's configuration settings.

Figure 4-1   Cisco Network Designer

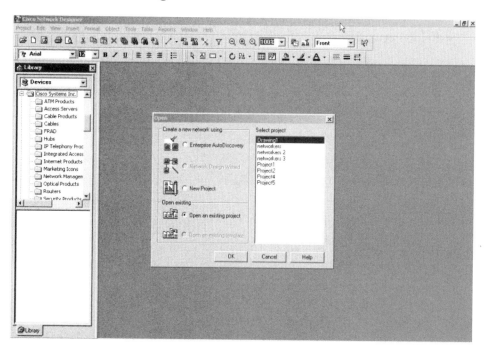

Step 2: Designing the Ad Hoc Topology

Figure 4-2 shows the topology design for this lab.

Figure 4-2   Topology Design

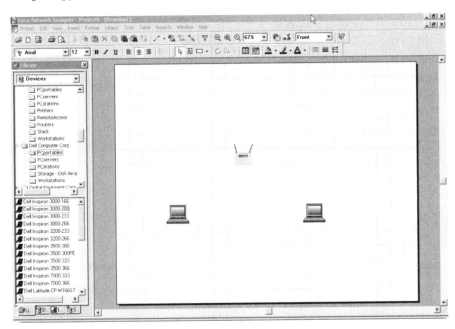

Sketch the Ad Hoc design in the space provided before creating the design using the software tool. Make sure to show the radio frequency (RF) signal from the access point.

Step 3: Designing the BSS Topology

Sketch the BSS design in the space provided before creating the design using the software tool. Make sure to include the following for the BSS topology:

- One DHCP server

- Network segments

- One wireless access point (show the RF signal)

- Several wireless clients

- Two laptops

- Two desktops

Step 4: Designing the ESS Topology

Sketch the ESS design in the space provided before creating the design using the software tool. Make sure to include the following for the ESS topology:

- One DHCP server

- Three wireless access points

Make sure to indicate the channels of each access point and show the RF signal from the access point.

Step 5: Designing a Home Network Topology

Sketch the design in the space provided before creating the design using the software tool. Make sure to include the following for the topology:

- One or more PCs

- Network segments

- One wireless access point (show the RF signal)

- Router

- Switch

- One or more laptop(s)

- One handheld (PDA)

- Connection to the Internet via modem (DSL, cable, dialup, wireless ISP)

Step 6: Designing an Enterprise Network Topology

Choose a type of enterprise network such as a school, hospital, transportation, manufacturing, and so on. Based on the type of business, design a network. Sketch the design in the space provided before creating the design using the software tool. Make sure to include the following for the enterprise network topology:

- Numerous PCs and laptops

- Workgroups

- Servers

- Network segments

- Numerous wireless access points

- Router(s)

- Switches

- Firewalls

- IP phones

- Handheld devices applicable to the business, and so on

Step 7: Creating a PowerPoint Presentation or Posters

Assemble all five topologies within a PowerPoint presentation or display posters. Each group or individual can present their topologies to the class or create a wall display.

Chapter 5

Access Points (APs)

Lab 5.2.2: Configuring Basic AP Settings

Estimated Time: 30 minutes

Number of Team Members: Students work in teams of two

Objective

In this lab, students assign basic parameters to the access point via GUI and IOS CLI. The Express Setup page is also accessed through a web browser to assign the IP address, subnet mask, default gateway, and SSID to the access point.

Scenario

Basic configuration of an access point can be done via GUI or IOS CLI.

Topology

Figure 5-1 shows the topology used in this lab.

Figure 5-1   Lab Topology

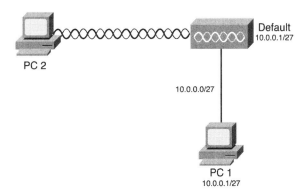

Preparation

The student's PC should be connected to the AP via an isolated wired network or crossover cable. The access point should be set to factory defaults.

Tools and Resources

Each team needs the following:

- One AP

- The AP power supply or source

- A PC (PC1) that is connected to the same wired network as the access point

- A wireless PC or laptop (PC2)

Additional Materials

http://www.cisco.com/en/US/products/hw/wireless/ps430/products_installation_and_configuration_guide_book09186a0080147d69.html

Command List

In this lab, the following commands are used. Refer to Table 5-1 if you need assistance during the lab.

Table 5-1   Command Reference

Command	Description
configure terminal	Enter global configuration mode.
hostname	Set the hostname on the device.
interface bvi1	Enter the virtual interface for the AP.
ip address	Set the IP address and subnet mask on the device.
interface dot11radio 0	Enter the device radio interface.
station role repeater | root [fallback { shutdown | repeater }]	Set the access point role. Set the role to repeater or root. (Optional) Select the radio's fallback role. If the access point's Ethernet port is disabled or disconnected from the wired LAN, the access point can either shut down its radio port or become a repeater access point associated to a nearby root access point.

Command	Description
ssid ssid-string	Create an SSID and enter SSID configuration mode for the new SSID. The SSID can consist of up to 32 alphanumeric characters. SSIDs are case sensitive. *Note*: Do not include spaces or underscore characters in SSIDs.
enable password *password*	The default password is Cisco. This commands allows an administrator to change the password.
enable secret *password*	The default enable password is *Cisco*.
enable password level *level password*	The default is Level 15 (privileged EXEC level). The password is encrypted before it is written to the configuration file.
show dot11 associations	View the connected wireless clients.
show running-config	Display the current configuration of the device.
show startup-config	Display the startup configuration of the device.
copy running-config startup-config	Save the entries in the configuration file.
show interfaces	Display interface information of the device.

Step 1: Connecting to the AP via the Console

1. Connect a Cisco rollover cable (console cable) between PC1 and the AP, as shown in Figure 5-2.

2. Open a terminal emulator, as shown in Figure 5-3.

Figure 5-2   Console Cable

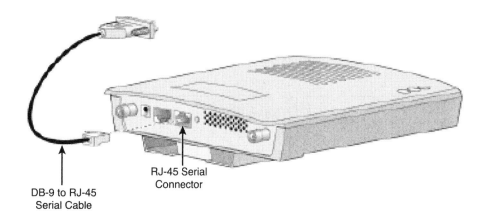

Figure 5-3   Opening a Terminal Emulator

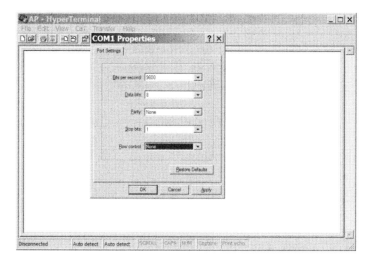

3.   Enter these settings for the connection:

- Bits per second (baud rate): 9600

- Data bits: 8

- Parity: none

- Stop bits: 1

- Flow control: none

4. Press **Enter** to get started.

5. Unplug the AP power by removing the power supply cable or powered Ethernet cable. Hold the MODE button until the Status LED turns amber (approximately 1 to 2 seconds), and release the button. The access point reboots with the factory default values including the IP address. Without a connected DHCP server, the AP defaults to 10.0.0.1/27. The standard Cisco IOS AP boot sequence output appears:

```
flashfs[0]: 141 files, 6 directories
flashfs[0]: 0 orphaned files, 0 orphaned directories
flashfs[0]: Total bytes: 7741440
flashfs[0]: Bytes used: 3331584
flashfs[0]: Bytes available: 4409856
flashfs[0]: flashfs fsck took 12 seconds.
Reading cookie from flash parameter block...done.
Base ethernet MAC Address: 00:0b:fd:4a:70:0c
Initializing ethernet port 0...
Reset ethernet port 0...
Reset done!
ethernet link up, 100 mbps, full-duplex
Ethernet port 0 initialized: link is up
button pressed for 5 seconds
process_config_recovery: set IP address and config to default 10.0.0.1
Loading "flash:/c1200-k9w7-mx.122-11.JA/c1200-k9w7-mx.122-11.JA"...############
################################
```

Step 2: Configuring PC1

Make sure the AP is connected to PC1 through a wired connection.

Configure the IP address, subnet mask, and gateway on PC1:

- IP address: 10.0.0.2

- Subnet Mask: 255.255.255.224

- Gateway: 10.0.0.1

Step 3: Connecting to AP Using the Web Browser

1. Open an Internet browser. The default IP address of an access point from the factory is 10.0.0.1.

2. Type the access point IP address in the browser address location field. Press **Enter**.

3. A login screen appears. Type in the password of **Cisco** (case sensitive), and click **OK**.

4. When the access point HOME page, shown in Figure 5-4, appears, click **Express Setup** if the Express Setup does not appear. The Express Setup page is shown in Figure 5-5.

5. Type a system name of Pod**P** (where **P** is the Pod or Team number) for the access point in the System Name field.

6. Select **Static IP** as a configuration server protocol from the Configuration Server Protocol selections.

Figure 5-4   Access Point HOME Page

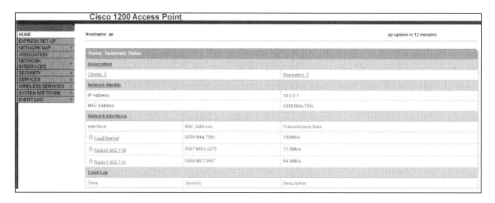

Figure 5-5   Express Setup Page

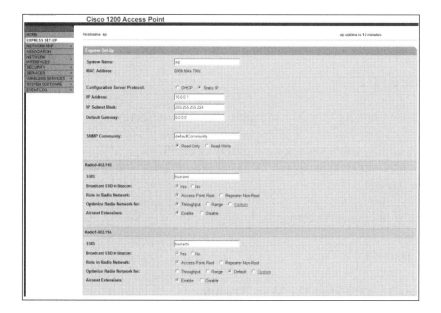

Note: If using the BR350 in AP mode, the VxWorks display will be slightly different than the IOS GUI display. These can allow two additional teams to complete the labs. All students should complete the labs with the new 1200 Cisco GUI. If students have available time, the same labs can be completed using the BR350 in AP mode, remembering the user interface is different. This allows students to be able to configure legacy Cisco Access Points, such as the AP 340, AP 350, and BR350, in AP mode.

Step 4: Assigning the IP Address and SSID

1.   Type the IP address shown in Table 5-2 in the IP Address field.

2.   What IP address will be assigned to this access point?

_____

Table 5-2   IP Addresses

Team	Access Point Name	SSID	AP Address	PC1 Address	PC2 Address
1	Pod1	AP1	10.0.1.1/24	10.0.1.10/24	10.0.1.12/24
2	Pod2	AP2	10.0.2.1/24	10.0.2.10/24	10.0.2.12/24

3.   Enter an IP subnet mask in the IP Subnet Mask field.

    a.   What subnet mask will be assigned to this access point? Write the answer in dotted decimal notation.

_____

    b. What is the subnet mask in binary?

_____

4.   Enter the IP address of the default Internet gateway in the Default Gateway field. Assume the router address is 10.0.P.254.

5.   Leave the SNMP Community field alone at this time.

6.   Type an SSID for the access point in the Radio Service Set ID (SSID) field.

    What SSID will be assigned to this access point?

_____

7.   Verify the **Access Point Root**: as the network role for the AP from the Role in Radio Network.

8.   Select **Throughput**: as the Optimize Radio Network.

9.   Click **OK**.

10.   The connection is lost.

11.   Reconfigure the IP address, subnet mask, and gateway on PC1.

- IP address: 10.0.P.10

- Subnet Mask: 255.255.255.0

- Gateway: 10.0.P.254

12.   Reconnect to the AP from PC1's web browser and verify the setting.

Step 5: Connect to the AP via Wireless PC

Using a laptop or desktop PC with a wireless adapter, connect to the correct access point. Make sure the wireless device is not connected through the wired network.

1. Configure and select a profile to connect to the AP. Make sure the SSID is configured in the profile to match the AP.

2. Configure a unique **Client Name** in the profile, such as a first initial and last name of one of the team members.

3. Make sure to check or configure the TCP/IP settings of the laptop or desktop PC to connect to the proper IP network. If a DHCP server is running, configure TCP/IP to receive the address automatically, or configure a static IP setting with 10.0.P.12/24.

Step 6: Verifying the Wireless Connection

1. Go to the Association page, shown in Figure 5-6, to check the wireless connection.

Figure 5-6   Association Page

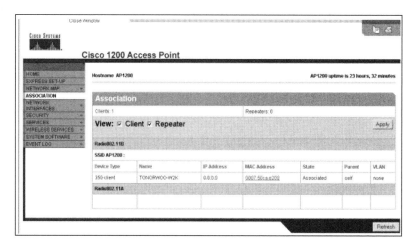

Does the Client Name that was previously configured appear?

_____

2. Record the MAC addresses of the devices associated with this access point. One of these should be the MAC address of the laptop or desktop PC configured in Step 4.

MAC Address

3. Check to see if the ACU icon in the system tray is green, as shown in Figure 5-7, which indicates a successful link to the AP. Double-click on the icon to verify the correct Access Point Name and Access Point IP Address.

Figure 5-7   Green ACU Icon in the System Tray

4. Record the values here.

_____

5. Check to see if a connection to the AP via a web browser can be achieved from the wireless device. Enter **http://10.0.P.1** for the URL within the browser. Did the AP GUI display?

6. Test connectivity to other devices via ping, Telnet, http, and ftp. This varies depending on the devices connected and configured on the wired network.

Step 7: Drawing a Current Topology

Using the space provided on the next page, use the existing topology, as shown in Figure 5-8, and draw an updated topology with the gateway router and updated IP addresses and subnet masks.

Figure 5-8   Existing Topology

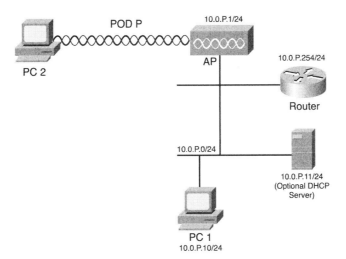

Step 8: Configuring the AP via IOS CLI

Open the HyperTerminal window on PC1. PC1 should still be connected via the console cable.

Enter privileged mode with the following command. *Cisco* is the default password:

```
PodP>enable
Password:
PodP#
```

Step 9: Erasing the Configuration via CLI

Enter global configuration mode with the following command:

```
PodP#erase start
Erasing the nvram filesystem will remove all files! Continue? [confirm]       (press Enter)
[OK]
Erase of nvram: complete
PodP# reload
System configuration has been modified. Save? [yes/no]:  N
Proceed with reload? [confirm]   (press Enter)
Radio system is preparing for reload...
Radio system is ready for reload.
*Mar  1 00:31:09.103: %SYS-5-RELOAD: Reload requested by console.
…..
```

Step 10: Configuring Host Name

The system name, while not an essential setting, helps identify the access point on your network. The system name appears in the titles of the management system pages.

1. Enter into configuration mode:

    ```
    Ap>enable
    Password:
    ap#
    ap#configure terminal
    ap(config)#
    ```

2. configure the host name with the following command:

    ```
    ap(config)#hostname PodP
    ! where P is the pod number
    PodP(config)#
    ```

Step 11: Configuring the Bridge Virtual Interface (BVI)

1. Enter bvi1 interface mode to configure the IP address subnet mask settings.

2. Assign an IP address and address mask to the BVI:

    ```
    PodP(config)#interface bvi1
    PodP(config-if)#ip address 10.0.P.1 255.255.255.0
    ```

Note: If you are connected to the access point using a Telnet session, you lose your connection to the access point when you assign a new IP address to the BVI. If you need to continue configuring the access point using Telnet, use the new IP address to open another Telnet session to the access point.

Step 12: Configuring Passwords

1. Configure the enable password to *cisco*. Also, configure the secret password to **class**. The password is not encrypted and provides access to Level 15 (traditional privileged EXEC mode access):

    ```
    PodP(config)#enable password cisco
    PodP(config)#enable secret class
    ```

2. Use the **level** keyword to define a password for a specific privilege level. After you specify the level and set a password, give the password only to users who need to have access at this level. Use the **privilege level** global configuration command to specify commands accessible at various levels.

    Set the **configure** command to privilege Level 15 and define *cisco* as the password users must enter to use Level 15 commands:

    ```
    PodP(config)#privilege exec level 15 configure
    PodP(config)#enable password level 15 cisco
    ```

Step 13: Configuring an SSID

Name an SSID and set the maximum number of client devices that can associate using this SSID to 15:

```
PodP(config)#interface dot11radio 0
PodP(config-if)#ssid APP
! where P is the pod number)
PodP(config-ssid)#max-associations 15
PodP(config-ssid)#exit  (or Ctrl-Z)
PodP#
```

Step 14: Checking the Running Configuration and Interface Status

1. Display the current configuration of the device:

```
PodP#show running-config
Pod1#show run
Building configuration...
Current configuration : 2660 bytes
!
version 12.2
no service pad
service timestamps debug datetime msec
service timestamps log datetime msec
service password-encryption
!
hostname PodP
! output omitted
```

2. Display the condition and information of the device interfaces:

```
PodP#show interface
```

Step 15: Saving and Verifying the Configuration Is Saved to Flash

1. Save the current configuration of the device into the configuration file:

```
PodP#copy running-config startup-config
```

2. Verify the startup configuration saved in Flash:

```
PodP#show startup-config
```

Step 16: Connecting to the AP via a Wireless PC

1. Using a laptop or desktop PC with a wireless adapter, connect to the correct access point. Make sure the wireless device is not connected via the wired network.

2. Configure and select a profile to connect to the AP. Make sure the SSID is configured in the profile to match the AP.

3. Configure a unique **Client Name** in the profile, such as a first initial and last name of one of the team members.

4. Make sure to check or configure the TCP/IP settings of the laptop or desktop PC to connect to the proper IP network. If a DHCP server is running, configure TCP/IP to receive the address automatically, or configure a static IP setting.

5. Now check to see if the ACU icon in the system tray is green, which indicates a successful link to the AP. Double-click on the ACU icon to verify the correct Access Point Name and Access Point IP Address.

6. Record the values here.

Step 17: Verifying the Associations

View the current device associations. The wireless device configured in Step 16 should appear in the association output:

```
PodP#show dot11 associations
802.11 Client Stations on Dot11Radio0:
SSID [tsunami] :
Others:  (not related to any ssid)
802.11 Client Stations on Dot11Radio1:
SSID [tsunami] :
Others:  (not related to any ssid)
PodP#
```

Step 18: Connecting to the AP Remotely via Telnet

Follow these steps to open the IOS CLI with Telnet. These steps are for a PC running Microsoft Windows with a Telnet terminal application. Check your PC operating instructions for detailed instructions for your operating system.

1. From PC2, Open a Telnet session to the AP located at 10.0.P.1.

2. If Telnet is not listed in your Accessories menu, select **Start > Run**, type **Telnet** in the entry field, and press **Enter**.

3. At the username and password prompts, enter your administrator username and password. The default username is **Cisco**, and the default password is **Cisco**. The default enable password is also **Cisco**. The enable secret password is **class**. Usernames and passwords are case sensitive.

    ```
    C:\>telnet 10.0.P.1
    User Access Verification
    Username:
    Password:
    PodP>
    ```

Lab 5.2.4: Using Features of the Internetworking Operating System (IOS) Command-Line Interface (CLI)

Estimated Time: 30 minutes

Number of Team Members: Students work in teams of two

Objective

In this lab, the student learns the following objectives:

- CLI help features

- Abbreviated commands

- Using the **no** command to remove configuration statements

- Command history

- Editing features

Scenario

Students learn the features of the access point internetworking operating system (IOS).

Topology

Figure 5-9 shows the topology used in this lab.

Figure 5-9   Lab Topology

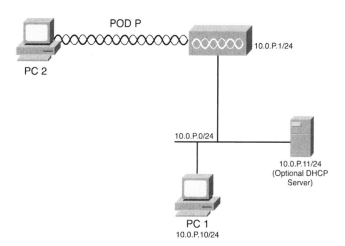

Preparation

Before beginning the steps in this lab activity, make sure the access points are configured according to the information shown in Table 5-3.

Table 5-3   Access Point Addressing Scheme

Team	Access Point Name	SSID	Address
1	Pod1	AP1	10.0.1.1/24
2	Pod2	AP2	10.0.2.1/24

Tools and Resources

Each team needs the following pieces of equipment:

- The access point

- A PC or laptop

- Console cable

Additional Materials

Consult the following URL for more information related to this lab:

> http://www.cisco.com/en/US/products/hw/wireless/ps430/products_installation_and_configuration_guide_book09186a0080147d69.html

Command List

This lab uses the commands listed and described in Table 5-4. Refer to this list if you need any assistance during the lab.

Table 5-4   Command List

Command	Description
help	Obtains a brief description of the help system in any command mode.
?	Lists all commands available for a particular command mode.
command?	Lists the associated keywords for a command.

Command	Description
command keyword ?	Lists the associated arguments for a keyword.
abbreviated-command-entry?	Obtains a list of commands that begin with a particular character string.
no	Use the no form to disable a feature or function or reverse the action of a command.
history	The number of commands that are displayed is determined by the setting of the terminal history global configuration command and history line configuration command.
terminal history	The number of commands that are displayed is determined by the setting of the terminal history global configuration command and history line configuration command.
show history	While in privileged EXEC mode, list the last several commands that you just entered.
Press **Ctrl-P** or the up arrow key	Recall commands in the history buffer, beginning with the most recent command. Repeat the key sequence to recall successively older commands.
Press **Ctrl-N** or the down arrow key	Return to more recent commands in the history buffer after recalling commands with Ctrl-P or the up arrow key. Repeat the key sequence to recall successively more recent commands.

Step 1: Connecting to the AP via the Console

1. Connect a Cisco rollover cable (console cable) between PC1 and the AP.

2. Open a terminal emulator. What settings are required?

    Bits per second (baud rate):

    _____

    Data bits:

    _____

    Parity:

    _____

Stop bits:

_____

Flow control:

_____

3.   Press **Enter** to get started:

```
ap>
```

Step 2: Entering Into Privileged Mode

Enter privileged mode. Cisco is the default password:

```
ap>enable
Password:
ap#
```

Step 3: Erasing the Existing Configuration

If there is an existing configuration on the AP, erase the configuration and reload:

```
ap#erase startup-config
Erasing the nvram filesystem will remove all files! Continue? [confirm] Y [OK]
Erase of nvram: complete
ap#
*Mar  1 00:42:37.099: %SYS-7-NV_BLOCK_INIT: Initialized the geometry of nvram
ap#reload
System configuration has been modified. Save? [yes/no]: no
Proceed with reload? [confirm]y
Radio system is preparing for reload...
Radio system is ready for reload.
*Mar  1 00:45:08.446: %SYS-5-RELOAD: Reload requested by console.
```

1.   What command checks the existing running configuration?

_____

2.   What command checks the existing startup configuration?

_____

Step 4: Configuring the AP

1.   Enter global configuration mode. Configure the host name, SSID, and passwords. Refer to Lab 5.2.2 for configuration help, if needed:

```
ap#configure terminal
ap(config)#
ap(config)#hostname PodP
PodP(config)#
...
```

2.   Configure the remaining steps.

3.   Configure a wireless PC or laptop to connect the AP.

4.   From PC2, Telnet to the AP to complete the remaining steps in this lab.

Step 5: Use the Access Point's Help Feature

The access point IOS includes help features. Typing the word **help** at the command prompt gives you a brief summary of the help usage features. Display the help usage summary by typing the command **help** at the prompt:

```
PodP#help
```

Help can be requested at any point in a command by entering a question mark '**?**'. If nothing matches, the help list will be empty, and you must back up until entering a '**?**' shows the available options.

Two styles of help are provided:

- Full help is available when you are ready to enter a command argument (for example, 'show ?'), and it describes each possible argument.

- Partial help is provided when an abbreviated argument is entered and you want to know what arguments match the input (for example, show pr?).

Step 6: Displaying the Available Commands of the Command Mode

To display a list of available commands of the command mode, type the **?** character at the command line prompt:

```
PodP#?
Exec commands:
  <1-99>            Session number to resume
  access-enable     Create a temporary Access-List entry
  access-template   Create a temporary Access-List entry
  archive           manage archive files
  cd                Change current directory
  clear             Reset functions
  clock             Manage the system clock
  configure         Enter configuration mode
  connect           Open a terminal connection
  copy              Copy from one file to another
  debug             Debugging functions (see also 'undebug')
  delete            Delete a file
  dir               List files on a filesystem
  disable           Turn off privileged commands
  disconnect        Disconnect an existing network connection
  dot11             IEEE 802.11 commands
  enable            Turn on privileged commands
  erase             Erase a filesystem
[output omitted]
```

To get help on a specific command, type the command name followed by the **?** at the command prompt.

Type **configure ?** at the command prompt to display the available options for **configure**:

```
PodP#configure ?
  memory            Configure from NV memory
  network           Configure from a TFTP network host
  overwrite-network Overwrite NV memory from TFTP network host
  terminal          Configure from the terminal
  <cr>
PodP#configure
```

Step 7: Using Abbreviated Commands

The IOS supports the use of abbreviated commands. Type a partial command at the command prompt, and press the tab button. Pressing Tab completes the partial command. Type in **show conf** rather than **show configuration**. Press the tab button, and it completes the partial command:

```
PodP#show conf  (press the tab button)
PodP#show configuration
Using 2660 out of 32768 bytes
!
version 12.2
no service pad
service timestamps debug datetime msec
service timestamps log datetime msec
service password-encryption
!
hostname AP1200
!
aaa new-model
!
!
aaa group server radius rad_eap
!
aaa group server radius rad_mac
[output omitted]
```

The navigation keystrokes listed in Table 5-5 help display the output, as needed.

Table 5-5   Abbreviated Command Keystroke Navigation

Key	Action
Return	Scroll down one line
Space	Scroll down one screen
Any other key	Exit the output

Step 8: Using Command History

The IOS provides a history or record of commands that you have entered. This feature is particularly useful for recalling long or complex commands or entries, including access lists. You can customize the command history feature to suit your needs, as described next.

By default, the access point records 10 command lines in its history buffer. Beginning in privileged EXEC mode, enter this command to set the number of command lines that the access point records during the current terminal session:

```
PodP# terminal history 10
```

(The range is from 0 to 256.)

Beginning in line configuration mode, enter this command to configure the number of command lines the access point records for all sessions on a particular line. The following example configures the number of lines to 10:

```
PodP(config)#line console 0
PodP(config-line)# history 10
```

(The range is from 0 to 256.)

Step 9: Using no Forms of Commands to Remove Configuration Statements

Most configuration commands also have a **no** form. In general, use the **no** form to disable a feature or function or reverse the action of a command. For example, the **no shutdown** interface configuration command reverses the **shutdown** of an interface. Use the command without the keyword **no** to re-enable a disabled feature, or to enable a feature that is disabled by default.

You perform a **no** command in Step 10.

Step 10: Enabling and Disabling Editing Features

This section describes the editing features that can help you manipulate the command line. Although enhanced editing mode is automatically enabled, you can disable it.

Re-enable the enhanced editing mode for the current terminal session by entering the following command in privileged EXEC mode:

```
PodP#terminal editing
PodP#
```

To reconfigure a specific line to have enhanced editing mode, enter the following command in line configuration mode:

```
PodP(config-line)# editing
```

To globally disable enhanced editing mode, enter the following command in line configuration mode:

```
PodP(config-line)# no editing
```

Step 11: Editing Commands Through Keystrokes

Use the keystrokes listed in Table 5-6 to practice editing command lines. Perform each keystroke starting at the top of the list.

Table 5-6   Keystrokes for Editing Command Lines

Keystroke	Purpose
Ctrl-B or the left arrow key	Move the cursor back one character.
Ctrl-F or the right arrow key	Move the cursor forward one character.

Keystroke	Purpose
Ctrl-A	Move the cursor to the beginning of the command line.
Ctrl-E	Move the cursor to the end of the command line.
Esc B	Move the cursor back one word.
Esc F	Move the cursor forward one word.
Ctrl-T	Transpose the character to the left of the cursor with the character located at the cursor.
Delete or Backspace	Erase the character to the left of the cursor.
Ctrl-P or the up arrow key	View the previous command in the command history buffer.
Ctrl-N or the down arrow key	View the next command in the command history buffer.

Lab 5.2.5: Manage AP Configuration and Image Files

Estimated Time: 30 minutes

Number of Team Members: Students work in teams of two

Objectives

In this lab, the student learns to manage configuration and image files.

Scenario

Students learn the file management features of the AP IOS and GUI.

Topology

Figure 5-10 shows the topology used in this lab.

Figure 5-10   Lab Topology

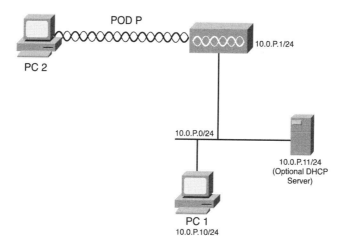

Preparation

Before beginning the steps in this lab activity, make sure the access points are configured according to the information shown in Table 5-7.

Table 5-7   Access Point Addressing Scheme

Team	Access Point Name	SSID	Address
1	Pod1	AP1	10.0.1.0/24
2	Pod2	AP2	10.0.2.1/24

Download and install TFTP server software on PC1.

Tools and Resources

Each team needs the following equipment:

- The access point

- A PC or laptop

- Console cable

Additional Materials

Consult the following URLs for more information related to this lab:

> http://www.cisco.com/en/US/products/hw/wireless/ps430/products_installation_and_
> configuration_guide_book09186a0080147d69.html

> SolarWinds TFTP: http://www.solarwinds.net/Download-Tools.htm

Command List

This lab uses the commands listed and described in Table 5-8. Refer to this list if you need any assistance during the lab.

Table 5-8   Command List

Command	Description
show file systems	Display the available file systems on the AP.
dir	View directory information.
ping	Ping an IP address to test connectivity.
copy	Move files between the AP and a backup server.

Step 1: Erasing the Existing Configuration

1.   Enter privileged mode. Cisco is the default password:

```
Ap>enable
Password:
ap#
```

2.   If there is an existing configuration on the AP, erase the configuration and reload:

```
ap#erase startup-config
ap#reload
```

    a.   What command checks the existing running configuration?

_____

    b.   What command checks the existing startup configuration?

_____

3.   Configure the AP according to the preparation table. Also, make sure the equipment is cabled and configured as shown in the topology.

Step 2: Displaying the AP File System

Display the available file systems on the AP:

```
PodP#show file systems
File Systems:
     Size(b)       Free(b)        Type   Flags   Prefixes
*    7741440       4412416       flash     rw    flash:
        -             -          opaque    rw    bs:
     7741440       4412416      unknown    rw    zflash:
       32768         32716        nvram    rw    nvram:
        -             -          network    rw    tftp:
        -             -          opaque    rw    null:
        -             -          opaque    rw    system:
        -             -          opaque    ro    xmodem:
        -             -          opaque    ro    ymodem:
        -             -          network    rw    rcp:
        -             -          network    rw    ftp:
        -             -          network    rw    scp:
```

What do the Flags values represent?

_____

Step 3: Displaying Information on the File System

1.   View the available options for the **dir** command:

```
PodP#dir ?
  /all            List all files
  /recursive      List files recursively
  all-filesystems List files on all filesystems
  bs:             Directory or file name
  flash:          Directory or file name
  null:           Directory or file name
  nvram:          Directory or file name
  system:         Directory or file name
  xmodem:         Directory or file name
  ymodem:         Directory or file name
  <cr>
```

2.   List all files for the current directory:

```
PodP#dir /all
Directory of flash:/
    2  -rwx         167    Mar 01 1993 00:12:51  env_vars
    4  -rwx           5    Mar 01 1993 00:08:45  private-config
    6  drwx         320    Jan 01 1970 00:07:15  c1200-k9w7-mx.122-11.JA
7741440 bytes total (4412416 bytes free)
```

3.   View the NVRAM files:

```
PodP#dir /nvram:
Directory of nvram:/
   30  -rw-           0                <no date>  startup-config
```

```
    31 ----          0              <no date>  private-config
32768 bytes total (32716 bytes free)
```

4.   View the System files:

```
PodP#dir /system:
Directory of system:/
    2  dr-x            0            <no date>  memory
    1  -rw-         1748            <no date>  running-config
No space information available
```

5.   View all files in all directories:

```
PodP#dir /all- filesystems:
```

Step 4: Backing Up Configurations Using TFTP

Backup configurations can save an administrator much when restoring, deploying, or modifying configurations.

1.   First, view the available **copy** command options:

```
PodP#copy ?
    /erase           Erase destination file system.
    Bs:              Copy from bs: file system
    flash:           Copy from flash: file system
    ftp:             Copy from ftp: file system
    null:            Copy from null: file system
    nvram:           Copy from nvram: file system
    rcp:             Copy from rcp: file system
    running-config   Copy from current system configuration
    scp:             Copy from scp: file system
    startup-config   Copy from startup configuration
    system:          Copy from system: file system
    tftp:            Copy from tftp: file system
    xmodem:          Copy from xmodem: file system
    ymodem:          Copy from ymodem: file system
    zflash:          Copy from zflash: file system
```

2.   Ping the TFTP server to check connectivity. Make sure the TFTP server is enabled and configured properly:

```
PodP#ping 10.0.1.10
Type escape sequence to abort.
Sending 5, 100-byte ICMP Echoes to 10.0.1.10, timeout is 2 seconds:
!!!!!
Success rate is 100 percent (5/5), round-trip min/avg/max = 1/1/1 ms
```

3.   Save the current configuration to Flash:

```
PodP#copy run start
```

4.   Upload a configuration file from the AP running configuration to a TFTP server:

```
PodP#copy running-config tftp://10.0.P.10
or
PodP#copy run tftp
Address or name of remote host []? 10.0.P.10
Destination filename [PodP-confg]?
```

5.   On PC1, verify the file is saved. Open the file with a text editor, such as WordPad, to verify the configuration.

6.   Upload a configuration file from an AP startup configuration to a TFTP server for storage:

```
PodP#copy startup-config tftp://10.0.P.10
```

or

```
PodP#copy start tftp
Address or name of remote host []? 10.0.P.10
Destination filename [Podp-confg]?
```

7.   Modify the saved AP configuration on PC1. Change the host name to **PodPrestore**.

8.   Upload a configuration file TFTP server to the AP startup-config:

```
PodP#copy tftp start
Address or name of remote host []? 10.0.P.10
Destination filename [Podp-confg]?
```

9.   Verify the uploaded configuration file in NVRAM:

```
PodP#show start
```

Step 5: Managing System Image Files

Maintaining a record of the AP System Software version is important for security and operation.

1.   Open a browser on PC1. Enter the IP address of the AP in the URL locator. Press **Enter**.

2.   Log in to the AP.

3.   From the Home page, go to the System Software Page, as shown in Figure 5-11.

Figure 5-11   System Software Page

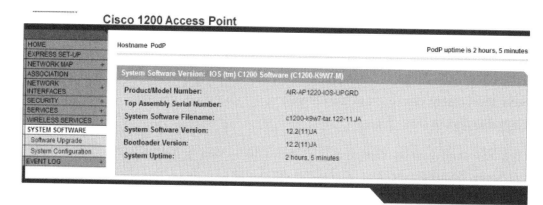

a.   What is the Product/Model Number?

_____

b.   What is the System Software Filename?

_____

The **System Software** > **Software Upgrade** page, as shown in Figure 5-12, provides the easiest method to upgrade a system image.

Figure 5-12   Software Upgrade Page

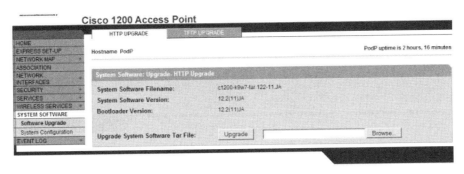

4.   Click the **Browse** button to locate the desired Tar file located on PC1, as shown in Figure 5-13.

Figure 5-13   Browse to the File

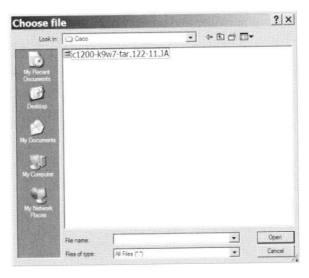

Note: AP image files are available at http://www.cisco.com/public/sw-center/sw-wireless3.shtml.

5.   Select the image file and click **Open**.

6.   The image now appears in the File box, as shown in Figure 5-14.

Note: Before proceeding with Upgrade, get the instructor's approval.

7.   Click the **Upgrade** button.

8.   It is best to maintain a console connection to monitor the upgrade progress.

Figure 5-14   The Image Appears in the File Box

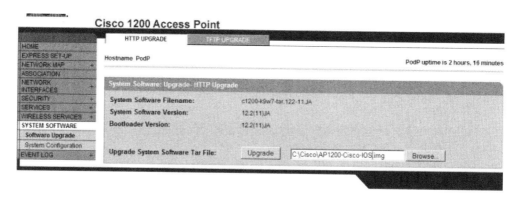

Caution: **Never** reboot once the upgrade process begins! It is a good practice to connect the AP to a UPS.

Step 6: Backup Configurations Using FTP (Optional Challenge)

Download, install, and configure an FTP server on PC1. Configure a user of **netadmin1** with a password of **mypass**.

1. From a console or Telnet connection to the AP, copy the running-config to an FTP server without configuring the username and password:

```
PodP# copy run ftp://netadmin1:mypass@10.0.P.10/ap1-confg
Write file ap1-confg on host 10.0.P.10?[confirm]
Building configuration...[OK]
Connected to 10.0.P.10
PodP#
```

2. Now, copy the startup-config to an FTP server:

```
PodP(config)#ip ftp username netadmin1
PodP(config)#ip ftp password mypass
PodP(config)#end
PodP#copy start ftp
Remote host[]? 10.0.P.10
Name of configuration file to write [ap1-confg]?
Write file ap1-confg on host 10.0.P.10?[confirm]
![OK]
```

3. Finally, copy a backup configuration to the startup-config:

```
PodP#configure terminal
PodP(config)# ip ftp username netadmin1
PodP(config)# ip ftp password mypass
PodP(config)# end
PodP# copy ftp start
Address of remote host []? 10.0.P.10
Name of configuration file[rtr1-confg]? host1-confg
Configure using host1-confg from 10.0.P.10?[confirm]
Connected to 10.0.P.10
Loading 1112 byte file host1-confg:![OK]
[OK]
```

Lab 5.3.5: Configure a Ethernet/FastEthernet Interface

Estimated Time: 15 minutes

Number of Team Members: Students work in teams of two

Objectives

In this lab, students use the access point setting pages to enter speed and duplex information for the access point.

Scenario

This section describes how to configure the access point radio Ethernet and FastEthernet interfaces to lock in speed and duplex settings.

Topology

Figure 5-15 shows the topology used in this lab.

Figure 5-15   Lab Topology

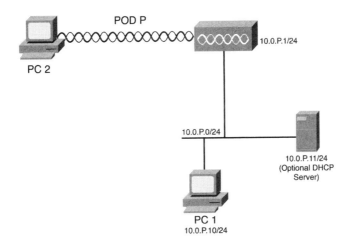

Preparation

Table 5-9 documents the basic settings to be applied to the AP.

Table 5-9   AP Settings for Lab

Team	Access Point Name	SSID	Address
1	Pod1	AP1	10.0.1.1/24
2	Pod2	AP2	10.0.2.1/24

Tools and Resources

Each team needs the following equipment:

- One AP

- PCs with properly installed Cisco wireless client adapters and utility

- Several PCs on the wired network that can maintain connectivity to the configuration management pages on the access point

Step 1: Obtaining and Assigning an IP Address

1. If needed, console into the AP and configure the BVI IP address to 10.0.P.1/24. Set the host name, as well, according to Table 5-9. Make sure the wired PC TCP/IP settings are configured according to the Topology. A wireless connection to the AP can also be used.

    Record the configuration commands needed for Step 2.

    _____

    _____

    _____

    _____

    _____

2. Open up a browser on PC1 and browse to the access point's **Home** page, as shown in Figure 5-16.

Figure 5-16   Access Point Home Page

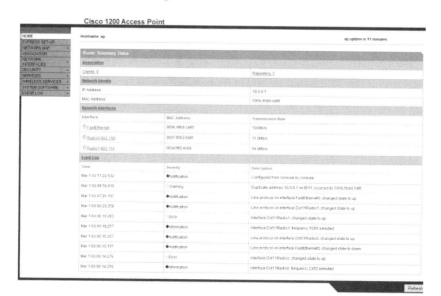

Step 2: Express Set-Up Page

Browse to the **Express Set-Up** Page, as shown in Figure 5-17, and verify the settings configured in Step 1 via GUI.

Figure 5-17   Express Set-Up Page

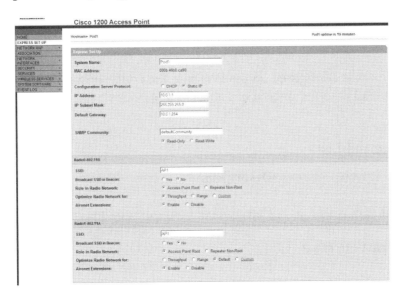

Step 3: Verifying the Data Rate Speed and Duplex of the FastEthernet Interface

1.   Go to the **NETWORK INTERFACES > FastEthernet** page, as shown in Figure 5-18, and click the Settings tab of the AP.

Figure 5-18   NETWORK INTERFACES > FastEthernet Page

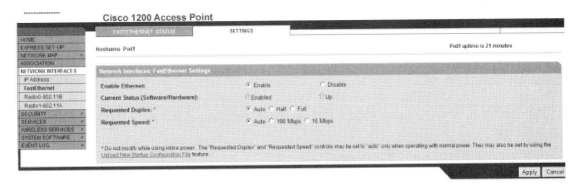

2.   The **Enable Ethernet** setting should be set to **Enable**.

Note: If the FastEthernet settings are modified while connected via the wired network, the connection may be lost. These are actually modified in Step 4 via the console.

3. The Requested Duplex setting should be set to **Auto**, by default. In a production environment, the duplex should be locked into the optimum setting of the connected switch.

4. The Requested Speed setting should be set to **Auto**, by default. In a production environment, the speed should be locked into the optimum setting of the connected switch.

Step 4: Configuring Ethernet/FastEthernet Interfaces via IOS CLI

Typically, an IP address is configured on the BVI interface only; however, some other settings should be set on the FastEthernet interface. Table 5-10 provides a list of commands used in this step.

Table 5-10   Command List

Command	Description
configure terminal	Enter global configuration mode.
interface fastEthernet *interface number*	Enter the device Ethernet/FastEthernet interface.
duplex auto | full | half	Set the role of the access point device.
show interfaces *<cr>|interface number*	View the interface(s) detailed status.
show ip interface brief	View a brief status of IP interfaces.
show running-config	View the running configuration.
speed 10 | 100 | auto	Set the data rate of the access point.

1. Console into the AP.

2. Beginning in configuration mode, follow these steps to set the AP Ethernet/ FastEthernet settings:

    ```
    PodP(config)#interface fastEthernet 0
    ```

3. Now see what duplex settings are possible:

    ```
    PodP(config-if)#duplex ?
      auto  Enable AUTO duplex configuration
      full  Force full duplex operation
      half  Force half-duplex operation
    ```

4. Set the duplex to **full**:

    ```
    PodP(config-if)#duplex full
    ```

5. Now see what speed settings are possible:

```
PodP(config-if)# speed ?
   10    Force 10 Mbps operation
   100   Force 100 Mbps operation
   auto  Enable AUTO speed configuration
```

6. Set the speed to 100 Mbps:

```
PodP(config-if)#speed 100
```

7. Check the running configuration:

```
PodP#show running-config
```

8. Display the FastEthernet interface status:

```
PodP#show interfaces fastEthernet 0
FastEthernet0 is up, line protocol is up
  Hardware is PowerPC405GP Ethernet, address is 000b.46b8.ca90 (bia 000b.46b8.ca90)
  MTU 1500 bytes, BW 100000 Kbit, DLY 100 usec,
     reliability 255/255, txload 1/255, rxload 1/255
  Encapsulation ARPA, loopback not set
  Keepalive set (10 sec)
  Full-duplex, 100Mb/s, MII
  ARP type: ARPA, ARP Timeout 04:00:00
  Last input 00:23:18, output 00:01:54, output hang never
  Last clearing of "show interface" counters never
  Input queue: 0/75/0/0 (size/max/drops/flushes); Total output drops: 0
  Queueing strategy: fifo
  Output queue :0/40 (size/max)
  5 minute input rate 0 bits/sec, 0 packets/sec
  5 minute output rate 0 bits/sec, 0 packets/sec
     1783 packets input, 164809 bytes
     Received 29 broadcasts, 0 runts, 0 giants, 0 throttles
     0 input errors, 0 CRC, 0 frame, 0 overrun, 0 ignored
     0 watchdog
     0 input packets with dribble condition detected
     1141 packets output, 449852 bytes, 0 underruns
     0 output errors, 0 collisions, 4 interface resets
     0 babbles, 0 late collision, 0 deferred
     0 lost carrier, 0 no carrier
     0 output buffer failures, 0 output buffers swapped out
```

9. Quickly verify all the interfaces are up:

```
PodP#show ip interface brief
Interface              IP-Address      OK? Method Status      Protocol
BVI1                   10.0.P.1        YES other  up          up
Dot11Radio0            unassigned      YES TFTP   up          up
Dot11Radio1            unassigned      YES TFTP   up          up
FastEthernet0          unassigned      YES other  up          up
Virtual-Dot11Radio0    unassigned      YES TFTP   down        down
Virtual-Dot11Radio1    unassigned      YES TFTP   down        down
PodP#
```

10. Check the detailed status of all the interfaces:

```
PodP#show interfaces
```

Lab 5.4.4: Configure Radio Interfaces Through the GUI

Estimated Time: 20 minutes

Number of Team Members: Students work in teams of two

Objectives

In this lab, students use the Radio 802.11b-setting page to enter basic channel and data rate information for the access point radio. The Radio 802.11b page is also accessed to enter basic settings for the transmit power, antennas, and operating thresholds on the access point.

Scenario

This section describes how to configure the access point radio. Use the AP Radio interface pages in the management system to set the radio configuration.

Topology

Figure 5-19 shows the topology used in this lab.

Figure 5-19   Lab Topology

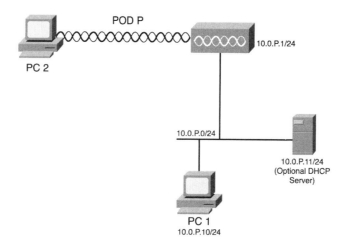

Preparation

The student PC should be connected to the AP via an isolated wired network or crossover cable. The access point should be set to factory defaults. A DHCP service can be used to assign an address to the AP.

Table 5-11 documents the basic settings to be applied to the AP for each team.

Table 5-11   AP Settings for Lab

Team	Access Point Name	SSID	Address
1	Pod1	AP1	10.0.1.1/24
2	Pod2	AP2	10.0.2.1/24

Tools and Resources

This lab requires the following equipment:

- Cisco access points

- PCs with properly installed Cisco wireless client adapters and utility

- Several PCs on the wired network that can maintain connectivity to the configuration management pages on the access point

Step 1: Displaying Radio Interface Information

1. Type in the IP address of the access point in the address field located on the browser, log in using the appropriate username and password to bring up the access point Home page, as shown in Figure 5-20.

Figure 5-20   Access Point Home Page

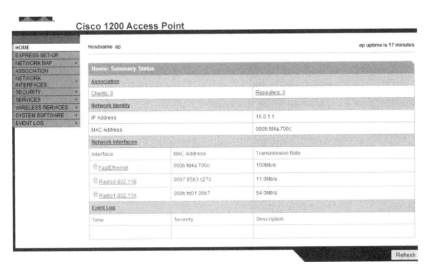

2. Obtain the access point information from this page. It is important for the network administrator to be familiar with the settings on the network equipment.

   a. Are there any **Clients** or **Repeaters** connected to the access point? What is the number for each?

b. What is the **IP Address** of the access point?

_____

c. What network interfaces are available?

_____
_____
_____

d. What is the **Ethernet/FastEthernet** MAC address?

_____

e. If available, what is the Radio 802.11b MAC address?

_____

f. If available, what is the Radio 802.11b Transmission rate?

_____

g. If available, what is the Radio 802.11a MAC address?

_____

h. If available, what is the Radio 802.11a Transmission rate?

_____

Step 2: Verifying Radio Interface Settings

1. If available, click the **Network Interfaces>Radio0-802.11B,** as shown in Figure 5-21. Next, click the **Settings** tab. Record the following settings from the Radio Interface page:

Figure 5-21   Interface Page

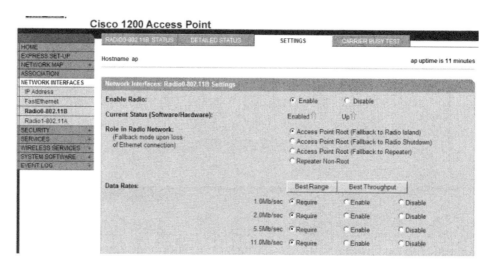

a. What is the Enable Radio setting and Current Status?

_____

b.   What is the role of this access point?

_____

c.   What speeds are configured for the data rates?

_____

2.   If available, click the **Network Interfaces** > **Radio0-802.11B**. Next, click the **Settings** tab. Record the following settings from the Radio Interface page:

a.   What is the Enable Radio setting and Current Status?

_____

b.   What is the role of this access point?

_____

c.   What speeds are configured for the data rates?

_____

Step 3: Verifying Radio Settings (Continued)

Figure 5-22 shows the radio settings.

Figure 5-22   Radio Settings

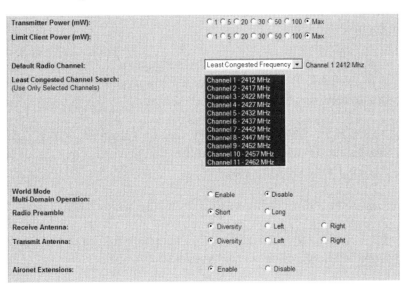

a.   What is the Transmitter Power setting?

_____

b.   What is the Default Radio Channel?

_____

c. What are the other settings on this page? Record your answers in the space provided.

_____

_____

_____

_____

_____

_____

_____

_____

_____

_____

_____

_____

_____

Step 4: Connecting to the AP via Wireless PC

Using a laptop or desktop with a wireless adapter, connect to the correct access point. Make sure the wireless device is not connected via the wired network.

1. Configure and select a profile to connect to the AP. Make sure the SSID is configured in the profile to match the AP.

2. Configure a unique **Client Name** in the profile, such as a first initial and last name of one of the team members.

3. Make sure to check or configure the TCP/IP settings of the laptop or desktop to connect to the proper IP network. If a DHCP server is running, configure TCP/IP to receive the address automatically, or configure static IP setting.

4. Now check to see if the ACU icon in the system tray is green, which indicates a successful link to the AP. Double-click on the icon to verify the correct **Access Point Name** and **Access Point IP Address.**

Step 5: Displaying and Recording Information from the Association Page

1. To check which clients are associated to this access point, go to the **Association** page, as shown in Figure 5-23, and click on the **Association** button.

2. Record the MAC addresses of the devices associated to this access point in the space provided.

_____

_____

_____

_____

_____

Figure 5-23   Association Page

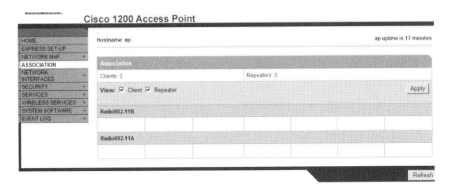

3.   Check the wireless connection to the AP via a web browser. Enter **http://10.0.P.1** for the URL within the browser. Did the AP GUI display?

4.   Test connectivity to other devices via ping, telnet, HTTP, and FTP. This varies depending on the devices connected and configured on the wired network.

Step 6: Displaying and Recording Advanced Radio Settings

Figure 5-24 shows the advanced radio settings.

Figure 5-24   Advanced Radio Settings

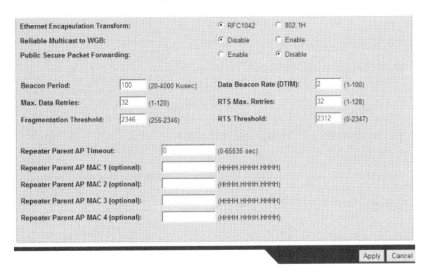

1.   What is the Reliable Multicast to WGB setting? To what wireless device does this setting pertain?

2.   What is the Public Secure Packet Forwarding setting? Why would this be enabled?

3.　What is the Beacon Period? What are the advantages and disadvantages of lowering or raising the value?

_____

4.　What is the Data Beacon Rate (DTIM)? What are the advantages and disadvantages of lowering or raising the value?

_____

5.　What is the Max Data Retries setting? What are the advantages and disadvantages of lowering or raising the value?

_____

6.　What is RTS Max Retries setting? What are the advantages and disadvantages of lowering or raising the value?

_____

7.　What is the Fragmentation Threshold? What are the units for this value?

_____

8.　What is the RTS Threshold setting?

_____

9.　What is Repeater Parent AP timeout?

_____

10.　What is Repeater Parent AP MAC 1 (optional)?

_____

11.　What is Repeater Parent AP MAC 2 (optional)?

_____

12.　What is Repeater Parent AP MAC 3 (optional)?

_____

13.　What is Repeater Parent AP MAC 4 (optional)?

_____

Step 7: Making Changes to the Access Point's Radio Interface (Optional)

Make changes to the radio interface. Perform the setting changes through the web browser interface. As changes are made, use several of the Cisco Aironet client utility tools to test various settings on the radio interface. Take care to make one change at a time, and monitor the performance change in either of the site survey or link status meter tools.

1. Make a change to the access point's receive and transmit antenna settings. By default, they are set to diversity. Change the setting to left or right. Have your lab partner move about the site with the laptop and see if any degradation or improvement occurs in the radio signal.

    a. Which antenna setting had the best performance?

    _____

    b. Which antenna setting had the worst performance?

    _____

Note: If congestion causes a delay, change the channel settings and see if performance improves. Remember, on the 802.11b, there are only three nonoverlapping channels (1, 6, and 11) that can be used in the BSS/ESS topology that this lab is creating. Coordinate channel settings with other team members, or set the access point to seek a less congested channel.

    c. Which channel setting had the best performance?

    _____

    d. Which channel setting had the worst performance?

    _____

2. Change the Transmitter Power settings and make note of any data rate performance or range. Was there any enhancement or degradation in the performance of the access point? With the instructor's permission, see how far the wireless client can roam with the lowest/highest setting.

    _____

    a. If there was, which Transmitter Power setting gave the furthest range or strongest signal?

    _____

    b. Which Transmitter Power setting gave the fastest data rate?

    _____

Lab 5.4.5: Configure Radio Interfaces Through the IOS CLI

Estimated Time: 30 minutes

Number of Team Members: Students work in teams of two

Objective

In this lab, students enter basic channel and data rate information for the access point radio.

Scenario

This section describes how to configure the access point radio. Use the AP Radio interface pages in the management system to set the radio configuration.

Topology

Figure 5-25 shows the topology used in this lab.

Figure 5-25   Lab Topology

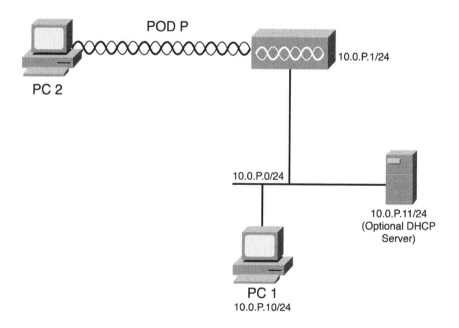

Preparation

Configure a PC and AP according to the topology.

Tools and Resources

This lab requires the following equipment:

- One AP

- PCs with properly installed Cisco wireless client adapters and utility

- Several PCs on the wired network that can maintain connectivity to the configuration management pages on the access point

Command List

Table 5-12 lists the commands used in this lab. Refer to this list if you need assistance during the lab.

Table 5-12   Command List

Command	Description
configure terminal	Enters global configuration mode
interface dot11radio *number*	Enters the device radio interface. The *number* is 0 for 11b and 1 for 11a. Depending on the installed radio(s), one or both will be available.
station-role	Sets the role of the access point device
speed basic	Sets the data rate of the access point
power client	Sets the power level output of the access point
channel	Sets the channel of the access point
world-mode	Sets world-mode on the access point
preamble	Sets the preamble
antenna	Sets the receive or transmit antenna

Step 1: Connecting to the AP

Connect to the AP via console or Telnet by entering global configuration mode with the following command:

```
PodP#configure terminal
Enter configuration commands, one per line.  End with CNTL/Z.
PodP(config)#
```

Step 2: Viewing the Available 802.11b Radio Settings

The AP radio has many available settings. Use the following commands to view the available commands for the 802.11b radio:

```
PodP(config)#interface dot11radio 0
PodP(config-if)#?
  antenna                dot11 radio antenna setting
  beacon                 dot11 radio beacon
  channel                Set the radio frequency
  description            Interface specific description
  dot11                  IEEE 802.11 config interface commands
  dot1x                  IEEE 802.1X subsystem
  exit                   Exit from interface configuration mode
  fair-queue             Enable Fair Queuing on an Interface
  mac-address            Manually set interface MAC address
  power                  Set radio transmitter power levels
  preamble-short         Use 802.11 short radio preamble
  rts                    dot11 Request To Send
  shutdown               Shutdown the selected interface
  speed                  Set allowed radio bit rates
  ssid                   Configure radio service set parameters
  station-role           role of the radio
  world-mode             Dot11 radio world mode
```

Notice that many more configuration settings are available.

Step 3: Configuring the Role in Radio Network

In this step, you configure the access point station role. First, view the available station roles. Then configure the access point as a root access point:

```
PodP(config-if)#station-role ?
  repeater  Repeater access point
  root      Root access point
PodP(config-if)#station-role root
```

Step 4: Configuring Radio Data Rates

Use the data rate settings to choose the data rates the access point uses for data transmission. The rates are expressed in megabits per second.

1. View the available speeds by entering the following command:

    ```
    PodP(config-if)#speed ?
      1.0          Allow 1 Mb/s rate
      11.0         Allow 11 Mb/s rate
      2.0          Allow 2 Mb/s rate
      5.5          Allow 5.5 Mb/s rate
      basic-1.0    Require 1 Mb/s rate
      basic-11.0   Require 11 Mb/s rate
      basic-2.0    Require 2 Mb/s rate
      basic-5.5    Require 5.5 Mb/s rate
      range        Set rates for best range
      throughput   Set rates for best throughput
      <cr>
    PodP(config-if)#
    ```

2. Use the following command to set up the access point for 11-Mbps service only:

    ```
    PodP(config-if)#speed basic-11.0 1.0 2.0 5.5
    PodP(config-if)#
    ```

Step 5: Configuring Radio Transmit Power

You can manually set the power level on client devices that associate to the access point and the AP radio power.

1. Use the help feature to view the power settings that can be configured:

```
PodP(config-if)#power ?
  client  Client radio transmitter power level
  local   Local radio transmitter power level
PodP(config-if)#
```

2. To see which power levels are configurable on the AP, use the following commands:

```
PodP(config-if)#power local ?
  <1-100>  One of: 1 5 20 30 50 100
  maximum  Set local power to allowed maximum
PodP(config-if)#
```

3. Configure the access point radio power to 5mW:

```
PodP(config-if)#power local 5
*Mar  1 02:07:19.457: %LINK-5-CHANGED: Interface Dot11Radio0, changed state to reset
*Mar  1 02:07:19.475: %LINK-3-UPDOWN: Interface Dot11Radio0, changed state to up
PodP(config-if)#
```

4. When a client device associates to the access point, the access point sends the maximum power level setting to the client. Enter the **power client** command to specify a maximum allowed power setting on all client devices that associate to the access point. The example below sets the radio transmit power to 100mW:

```
PodP(config-if)#power client 100
PodP(config-if)#
```

    Now lower the setting to 5mW:

```
PodP(config-if)#power client 5
*Mar  1 02:01:42.123: %LINK-5-CHANGED: Interface Dot11Radio0, changed state to reset
*Mar  1 02:01:42.141: %LINK-3-UPDOWN: Interface Dot11Radio0, changed state to up
PodP(config-if)#
```

Step 6: Configuring Radio Channel Settings

The default channel setting for the access point radios is least congested; at startup, the access point scans for and selects the least-congested channel. For most consistent performance after a site survey, however, we recommend that you assign a static channel setting for each access point. The channel settings on your access point correspond to the frequencies available in your regulatory domain.

1. See what channels are available:

```
PodP(config-if)#channel ?
<1-2462>         One of: 1 2 3 4 5 6 7 8 9 10 11 2412 2417 2422 2427 2432 2437 2442 2447
2452 2457 2462
  least-congested  Scan for best frequency
PodP(config-if)#
```

2. To assign a static channel setting for the access point, enter the **channel** command. The example that follows sets the radio to channel 1:

```
PodP(config-if)#channel 1   (or the channel frequency)
*Mar  1 02:10:46.872: %LINK-5-CHANGED: Interface Dot11Radio0, changed state to reset
```

```
*Mar  1 02:10:46.890: %LINK-3-UPDOWN: Interface Dot11Radio0, changed state to up
PodP(config-if)#
```

3.   Now assign a least-congested channel setting for the access point. The example that follows sets the radio to the least-congested channel setting:

```
PodP(config-if)#channel least-congested
*Mar  1 02:12:38.761: %LINK-5-CHANGED: Interface Dot11Radio0, changed state to reset
*Mar  1 02:12:39.760: %LINEPROTO-5-UPDOWN: Line protocol on Interface Dot11Radio 0,
changed state to down
*Mar  1 02:12:43.265: %DOT11-6-FREQ_USED: Interface Dot11Radio0, frequency 2412 selected
*Mar  1 02:12:43.285: %LINK-3-UPDOWN: Interface Dot11Radio0, changed state to up
*Mar  1 02:12:44.267: %LINEPROTO-5-UPDOWN: Line protocol on Interface Dot11Radio 0,
changed state to up
PodP(config-if)#
```

Notice the output on the console displays the AP selecting the frequency that is least congested at that point and time.

Step 7: Enabling and Disabling World-Mode

When world-mode is enabled, the access point adds channel carrier set information to its beacon. Client devices with world-mode enabled receive the carrier set information and adjust their settings automatically. For example, a client device used primarily in Japan could rely on world-mode to adjust its channel and power settings automatically when it travels to Italy and joins a network there. World-mode is disabled by default.

To enable world mode on the access point, enter the **world-mode** command, as follows:

```
PodP(config-if)#world-mode
*Mar  1 02:14:32.793: %LINK-5-CHANGED: Interface Dot11Radio0, changed state to reset
*Mar  1 02:14:32.811: %LINK-3-UPDOWN: Interface Dot11Radio0, changed state to up
PodP(config-if)#
```

To disable world-mode on the access point, enter the **no world-mode** command, as follows:

```
PodP(config-if)#no world-mode
*Mar  1 02:15:00.730: %LINK-3-UPDOWN: Interface Dot11Radio0, changed state to down
*Mar  1 02:15:00.732: %LINK-5-CHANGED: Interface Dot11Radio0, changed state to reset
*Mar  1 02:15:00.750: %LINK-3-UPDOWN: Interface Dot11Radio0, changed state to up
PodP(config-if)#
```

Step 8: Disabling and Enabling Short Radio Preambles

The radio preamble (sometimes called a *header*) is a section of data at the head of a packet that contains information that the access point and client devices need when sending and receiving packets. The radio preamble can be set to long or short:

- **Short**—A short preamble improves throughput performance. Cisco Aironet Wireless LAN Client Adapters support short preambles. Early models of Cisco Aironet's Wireless LAN Adapter (PC4800 and PC4800A) require long preambles.

- **Long**—A long preamble ensures compatibility between the access point and all early models of Cisco Aironet Wireless LAN Adapters (PC4800 and PC4800A). If these client devices do not associate to your access points, you should use short preambles.

1. To disable short radio preambles, enter the following command:

```
PodP(config-if)#no preamble-short
*Mar  1 02:16:03.156: %LINK-5-CHANGED: Interface Dot11Radio0, changed state to reset
*Mar  1 02:16:03.174: %LINK-3-UPDOWN: Interface Dot11Radio0, changed state to up
PodP(config-if)#
```

2. Follow these steps to enable short radio preambles:

```
PodP(config-if)#preamble-short
*Mar  1 02:16:24.843: %LINK-5-CHANGED: Interface Dot11Radio0, changed state to reset
*Mar  1 02:16:24.861: %LINK-3-UPDOWN: Interface Dot11Radio0, changed state to up
PodP(config-if)#
```

Step 9: Configuring Transmit and Receive Antennas

You can set the access point to select the antenna the access point uses to receive and transmit data. There are three options for both the receive and the transmit antenna:

- **Diversity**—This default setting tells the access point to use the antenna that receives the best signal. If your access point has two fixed (nonremovable) antennas, you should use this setting for both receive and transmit.

- **Right**—If your access point has removable antennas and you install a high-gain antenna on the access point's right connector, you should use this setting for both receive and transmit. When you look at the access point's back panel, the right antenna is on the right.

- **Left**—If your access point has removable antennas and you install a high-gain antenna on the access point's left connector, you should use this setting for both receive and transmit. When you look at the access point's back panel, the left antenna is on the left.

1. To view the available antenna settings, enter the following command:

```
PodP(config-if)#antenna ?
  receive   receive antenna setting
  transmit  transmit antenna setting
```

2. To set the access point receive and transmit to right, enter the following command (the interfaces resets after each change):

```
PodP(config-if)#antenna receive right
PodP(config-if)#antenna transmit right
PodP(config-if)#
```

3. To set the access point receive and transmit to left, enter the following command:

```
PodP(config-if)#antenna receive left
PodP(config-if)#antenna transmit left
PodP(config-if)#
```

4. To set the access point back to receive and transmit to diversity, enter the following command:

```
PodP(config-if)#antenna receive diversity
PodP(config-if)#antenna transmit diversity
PodP(config-if)#
```

Step 10: Disabling the Radio

If the PC is connected via wireless, it is important to switch to a console connection.

Use the **shutdown** command to turn off the radio. Afterwards, re-enable the interface:

```
PodP(config-if)#shutdown
*Mar  1 02:27:18.082: %LINK-5-CHANGED: Interface Dot11Radio0, changed state to administratively
  down
*Mar  1 02:27:18.082: %LINK-5-CHANGED: Interface Virtual-Dot11Radio0, changed state to
  administratively down
*Mar  1 02:27:19.083: %LINEPROTO-5-UPDOWN: Line protocol on Interface Dot11Radio0, changed state
  to down
PodP(config-if)#
PodP(config-if)#no shutdown
*Mar  1 02:28:00.414: %LINK-5-CHANGED: Interface Dot11Radio0, changed state to reset
*Mar  1 02:28:00.414: %LINK-3-UPDOWN: Interface Virtual-Dot11Radio0, changed state to down
*Mar  1 02:28:00.433: %LINK-3-UPDOWN: Interface Dot11Radio0, changed state to up
*Mar  1 02:28:01.432: %LINEPROTO-5-UPDOWN: Line protocol on Interface Dot11Radio 0, changed state
  to up
```

The sections that follow document the optional steps for 802.11a radio, if available.

Step 11: Viewing the Available 802.11a Radio Settings

The AP radio has many available settings.

Use the following commands to view the available commands for the 802.11a radio:

```
PodP(config)#interface dot11radio 1
PodP(config-if)#
```

What command is needed to see the available commands in the interface mode?

_____

Step 12: Configuring the Role in Radio Network

Configure the AP as a root access point.

What command is needed?

_____

Step 13: Configuring Radio Data Rates

View the available data rates for the 11a radio.

       a. What command is needed?

_____

       b. What speeds are available?

_____

_____

_____

Step 14: Configuring Radio Transmit Power

1. View the available power settings that can be configured.

   What command is needed? What power settings are configurable?

   _____

2. See which power levels are configurable on the AP radio.

   What command is needed? What are the available power levels for the local radio transmitter?

   _____

3. Configure the access point radio power to 10 mW.

   What command is needed?

   _____

4. Configure the client radio transmit power to 40 mW.

   What command is needed?

   _____

5. Now lower the setting to 5mw.

   What command is needed?

   _____

Step 15: Configuring Radio Channel Settings

1. See what 11a channels are available.

   What command is needed? What channels are available?

   _____
   _____
   _____

2. Assign static channel 36 to the access point.

   What command is needed?

   _____

3.   Now assign a least-congested channel setting for the access point.

What command is needed?

_____

Step 16: Configuring Transmit and Receive Antennas

1.   View the available antenna settings.

What command is needed? What settings are available?

_____
_____
_____

2.   Configure the access point to receive and transmit to right. (The interfaces reset after each change.)

What commands are needed?

_____
_____

3.   Set the access point to receive and transmit to left.

What commands are needed?

_____
_____

4.   Set the access point back to receive and transmit to diversity.

What commands are needed?

_____
_____

Step 17: Disabling the Radio

If the PC is connected via wireless, it is important to switch to a console connection.

Use the **shutdown** command to turn off the radio. Afterwards, re-enable the interface.

What commands are needed?

_____
_____

Lab 5.4.8: Configure an AP as a Repeater Through the IOS CLI

Estimated Time: 30 minutes

Number of Team Members: Students work in teams of two

Objective

The student extends the coverage of a basic service set topology by implementing an access point as a repeater.

Scenario

An access point can be configured as a repeater to extend the wireless infrastructure range or to overcome an obstacle that blocks radio communication. The repeater forwards traffic between wireless users and the wired LAN by sending packets to either another repeater or to an access point connected to the wired LAN. The data is sent through the route that provides the best performance for the client. In this lab, the Root AP is Pod*P*. The repeater AP is Pod*Q*.

A chain of several repeater access points can be setup, but throughput for client devices at the end of the repeater chain is quite low. Because each repeater must receive and then re-transmit each packet on the same channel, throughput is cut in half for each repeater you add to the chain.

Topology

Figure 5-26 shows the topology used in this lab.

Figure 5-26   Lab Topology

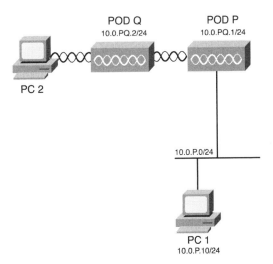

Preparation

Table 5-13 documents the basic settings each team should apply to the AP.

Table 5-13   AP Settings for Lab

Team	Access Point Name	SSID	Address
1	Pod1 (root) P	AP12	10.0.12.1/24
2	Pod2 (repeater) Q	AP12	10.0.12.2/24
3	Pod3 (root)	AP34	10.0.34.3/24
4	Pod4 (repeater)	AP34	10.0.34.4/24

PC1 should be connected to the wired network.

Tools and Resources

Each team needs the following equipment:

- Two access points

- A wired PC (PC1)

- A wireless PC or laptop (PC2)

- Console cable

Additional Materials

Consult the following URL related to the tasks in this lab:

> http://www.cisco.com/en/US/products/hw/wireless/ps430/products_installation_and_
> configuration_guide_book09186a0080147d69.html

Step 1: Basic AP Configuration to Both Access Points

Console into the AP. Clear the configuration on both of the access points. Then, put a basic configuration in the access points.

A sample configuration using Pod 1 (root AP) follows:

```
ap(config)#hostname Pod1
Pod1(config)#enable secret cisco
Pod1(config)#int bvi 1
Pod1(config-if)#ip address 10.0.12.1 255.255.255.0
Pod1(config-if)#no ssid tsunami
Pod1(config-if)#ssid AP12
Pod1(config-if-ssid)#authentication open
```

```
Pod1(config-if-ssid)#infrastructure-ssid
Pod1(config-if-ssid)#end
Pod1#copy run start
```

A sample configuration using Pod 2 (repeater AP) follows:

```
ap(config)#hostname Pod2
Pod2(config)#enable secret cisco
Pod2(config)#int bvi 1
Pod2(config-if)#ip address 10.0.12.2 255.255.255.0
Pod2(config-if)#no ssid tsunami
Pod2(config-if)#ssid AP12
Pod2(config-if-ssid)#authentication open
Pod2(config-if-ssid)#infrastructure-ssid
Pod2(config-if-ssid)#end
Pod2#copy run start
```

Configure a client and make sure it can associate with the first AP and then the second AP. You will probably have to power off the AP that you are not testing. This confirms that the Access Points are configured and operational and clients can connect to the AP*P*.

Step 2: Configuring the Repeater AP

The examples that follow use Pod 1 as root and Pod 2 as repeater.

1. Pod*P* is the root AP and should have a SSID of "AP*PQ*". Pod*Q* becomes the repeater AP. The repeater AP does not require any Ethernet cables when configured in repeater mode. Also, if Aironet extensions are disabled, enable Aironet extensions.

2. Set the AP role in the wireless LAN to repeater:

    ```
    Pod2#config t
    Pod2(config)#int Dot11Radio 0
    Pod2(config-if)#station-role repeater
    Pod2(config-if)#dot11 extension aironet
    Pod2(config-if)#end
    Pod2# copy run start
    ```

3. MAC addresses can be entered for up to four parent access points. The repeater attempts to associate to MAC address 1 first; if that access point does not respond, the repeater tries the next access point in its parent list. (Optional) Enter the MAC address for the access point's radio interface to which the repeater should associate:

    ```
    Pod2(config-if)#parent 1 RRRR.RRRR.RRRR
    ```

    (where RRRR.RRRR.RRRR = the MAC address of Pod1 11.b radio [not the FastEthernet interface])

4. Verify the configuration:

    ```
    Pod2#show run
    interface Dot11Radio0
     no ip address
     no ip route-cache
     !
     ssid AP12
        authentication open
        infrastructure-ssid
     !
     parent 1 0987.1234.e345 <MAC address will vary>
     speed basic-1.0 basic-2.0 basic-5.5 basic-11.0
     rts threshold 2312
     station-role repeater
    ```

Step 3: Verifying Client Associates with Root

After the repeater is set up, force the client to associate with the repeater and not the root. Make sure the TCP/IP settings and SSID are configured on the laptop. The client can be associated with the repeater or the root. To ensure that the client is associated to the repeater AP, do the following:

1. Make sure the configuration on the root AP is saved by using the **copy run start** command.

2. Remove the power from the root AP.

3. Verify that the client is associated to the repeater using the Aironet Client Utility.

4. When the client is associated with the repeater, repower the root AP.

5. After the root AP has booted, ping the root bridge from the client.

Step 4: Verifying Connections on Repeater

After the client is associated with the repeater AP, check the LEDs on top of the repeater AP. If the repeater is functioning correctly, the LEDs on the repeater and the root AP to which it is associated behave like this:

- The status LED on the root AP is steady green, indicating that at least one client device is associated with it (in this case, the repeater).

- The status LED on the repeater AP is steady green when it is associated with the root AP and the repeater has client devices associated to it. The repeater's status LED flashes (steady green for 7/8 of a second and off for 1/8 of a second) when it is associated with the root AP but the repeater has no client devices associated to it.

The repeater AP should also appear as associated with the root AP in the root access point's association table. On Pod*P*, verify that Pod*Q* is connected. Other wireless clients can also be associated.

1. In privilege mode of the repeater, enter the following command to view what information can be displayed.

   ```
   Pod2#show dot11 associations ?
   ```

   What information is available?

   _____

   _____

   _____

   _____

   _____

2. Check the detailed status of all clients:

```
Pod2#show dot11 associations all-clients
Pod2#show dot11 associations all-client
Address            : 0007.85b3.8850    Name              : Pod2
IP Address         : 10.0.12.2         Interface         : Dot11Radio 0
Device             : ap1200-Parent     Software Version :
State              : Assoc             Parent            : Our Parent
SSID               : AP12              VLAN              : 0
Hops to Infra      : 0                 Association Id    : 1
Current Rate       : 11.0             Encryption        : Off
Key Mgmt type      : NONE
Supported Rates    : 1.0 2.0 5.5 11.0
Signal Strength    : -27  dBm          Connected for     : 2541 seconds
Signal Quality     : 80 %             Activity Timeout  : 66 seconds
Power-save         : Off               Last Activity     : 0 seconds ago
Packets Input      : 444               Packets Output    : 145
Bytes Input        : 63984             Bytes Output      : 25975
Duplicates Rcvd    : 0                 Data Retries      : 2
Decrypt Failed     : 0                 RTS Retries       : 0
MIC Failed         : 0
MIC Missing        : 0
```

3. In privilege mode of the repeater, verify that the laptop is associated. Other wireless clients can also be associated.

4. Check the detailed status of all clients:

```
Pod2#show dot11 associations all-clients
Address            : 0007.eb30.a37d    Name              : VIAO
IP Address         : 10.0.12.20        Interface         : Dot11Radio 0
Device             : 350-client        Software Version : 5.20
State              : Assoc             Parent            : self
SSID               : AP12              VLAN              : 0
Hops to Infra      : 1                 Association Id    : 3
Clients Associated: 0                 Repeaters associated: 0
Current Rate       : 11.0             Encryption        : Off
Key Mgmt type      : NONE
Supported Rates    : 1.0 2.0 5.5 11.0
Signal Strength    : -32  dBm          Connected for     : 2866 seconds
Signal Quality     : 88 %             Activity Timeout  : 22 seconds
Power-save         : Off               Last Activity     : 3 seconds ago
Packets Input      : 333               Packets Output    : 1
Bytes Input        : 20624             Bytes Output      : 80
Duplicates Rcvd    : 0                 Data Retries      : 0
Decrypt Failed     : 0                 RTS Retries       : 0
MIC Failed         : 0
MIC Missing        : 0
Address            : 000b.be0e.27e5    Name              : AP2
IP Address         : 10.0.12.8         Interface         : Dot11Radio 0
Device             : ap1200-Rptr       Software Version : 12.2
State              : Assoc             Parent            : self
SSID               : AP12              VLAN              : 0
Hops to Infra      : 1                 Association Id    : 2
Clients Associated: 0                 Repeaters associated: 0
Current Rate       : 11.0             Encryption        : Off
Key Mgmt type      : NONE
Supported Rates    : 1.0 2.0 5.5 11.0
Signal Strength    : -25  dBm          Connected for     : 2870 seconds
Signal Quality     : 85 %             Activity Timeout  : 43 seconds
Power-save         : Off               Last Activity     : 20 seconds ago
Packets Input      : 155               Packets Output    : 480
Bytes Input        : 29388             Bytes Output      : 69571
Duplicates Rcvd    : 0                 Data Retries      : 4
Decrypt Failed     : 0                 RTS Retries       : 0
MIC Failed         : 0
MIC Missing        : 0
```

Is the laptop associated? What information can be used to verify the connection?

_____

_____

_____

Step 5: Configuring the 802.11a Radio as a Repeater (Optional)

Erase the configuration on both APs. Return to Step 1 and configure the repeater topology using the 801.11a radio instead. In this case, disable the 11b radios.

Chapter 6

Bridges

Lab 6.3.6: Configure Site-to-Site Wireless Link

Estimated Time: 60 minutes

Number of Team Members: Students work in teams of two

Objective

Configure a site-to-site bridged network.

Scenario

A remote location several miles away requires connectivity to the existing wired network. The connection can be bridged wirelessly with the use of two Cisco Aironet Bridges (BR350s).

Topology

Figure 6-1 shows the topology used in this lab.

Figure 6-1   Lab Topology

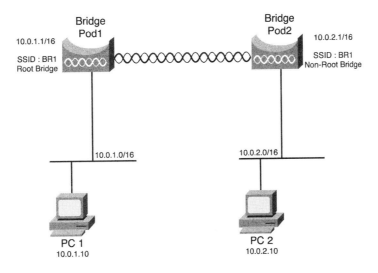

Preparation

Table 6-1 shows the device configuration for this lab.

Table 6-1   Lab Device Configuration

Device Name	Label	SSID	Address
BPod1	BR1	BR1	10.0.1.1/16
BPod2	BR2	BR1	10.0.2.1/16

Tools and Resources

Each team requires the following equipment to complete this lab:

- Two wired LAN segments that will be bridged together

- Two Cisco BR350s

- PC with FTP server loaded and a file to transfer in the root directory of the FTP server

Step 1: Cable and Power the Bridge

1.   First, attach two rubber duck antennas to the RP-TNC connectors.

2.   Plug the RJ-45 Ethernet cable into the Ethernet port on the back of the bridge. Plug the other end of the Ethernet cable into the Cisco Aironet power injector, as shown in Figure 6-2 (to AP/BRIDGE end).

3.   Connect the power cable to the inline power injector and to the receptacle.

Figure 6-2   Cisco Aironet Power Injector

Step 2: Connecting to the Bridge

Connect a nine-pin, male-to-female, straight-through serial cable to the COM port on a computer and to the RS-232 serial port on the bridge, as shown in Figure 6-3. (This cable ships with the bridge.)

Figure 6-3   Serial Cable Attachment

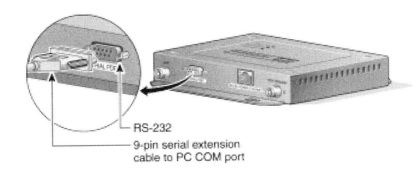

1.   Open a terminal emulator.

2.   Enter the following settings for the connection:

   • Bits per second (baud rate): 9600

   • Data bits: 8

   • Parity: none

   • Stop bits: 1

   • Flow control: Xon/Xoff

3.   Press = to display the bridge's home page. If the bridge has not been configured before, the Express Setup page appears as the home page (go to Step 3).

4.   If the bridge is already configured, the Summary Status page appears as the home page. When the Summary Status screen appears, type :**resetall**, and press **Enter**.

   Enter **YES** to confirm Resetting All parameters to factory defaults:

   ```
   YES
   00:02:12 (FATAL): Rebooting System due to Resetting Factory Defaults
   *** Restarting System in 5 seconds...
   ```

5.   Type **yes**, and press **Enter** to confirm the command.

6.   Power cycle the bridge by removing the power.

Step 3: Connecting to the BR350 via Express Setup

1.   Plug a second RJ-45 Ethernet cable into the power injector end labeled TO NETWORK. Plug the other end of the Ethernet cable into the Ethernet port on a switch or hub. Then, connect PC1 to the switch. A crossover cable can be used to connect directly from the inline power injector to PC1/PC2.

2. Configure PC1 to 10.0.0.2/24.

3. Open a web browser, enter the default bridge address, http://10.0.0.1, and press **Enter**.

4. Either of the following pages will appear:

    - The **Summary Status** page, also known as the **Home** page, as shown in Figure 6-4

    - The **Express Setup** page, as shown in Figure 6-5.

Figure 6-4   Summary Status Page

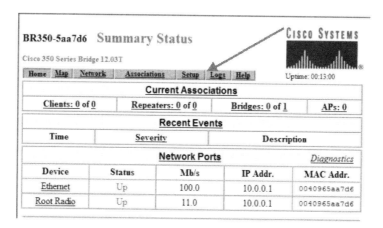

Figure 6-5   Express Setup Page

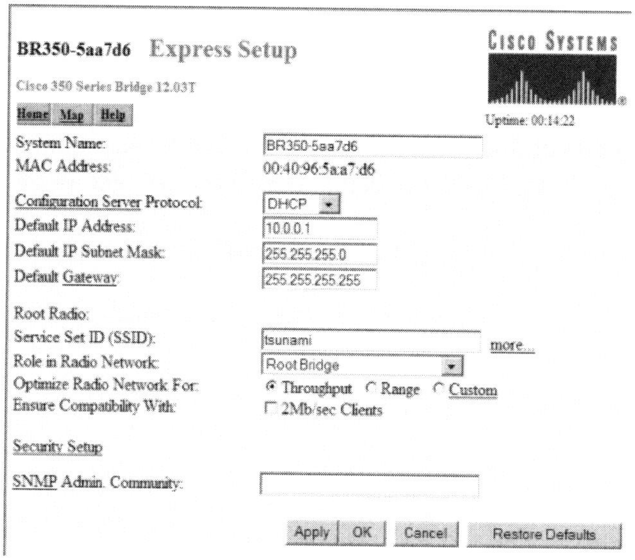

5. If the Express Setup page does not appear, from the Summary Status page, click the **Setup** hyperlink, as shown in Figure 6-6. This brings up the Setup page.

Figure 6-6   Setup Hyperlink

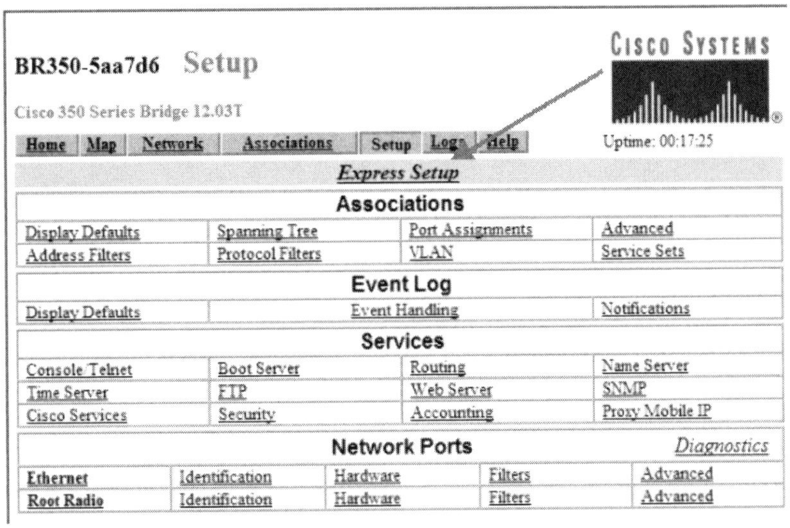

6.   Click the **Express Setup** link. This brings up the Express Setup page.

Step 4: Configuring the Bridge Settings

1.   Configure the settings in Table 6-2, as shown in Figure 6-7.

Table 6-2   Bridge Settings

Parameter	BPod1	BPod2
System Name	BPod1	BPod2
Configuration Server Protocol	None	None
Default IP address	10.0.1.1	10.0.2.1
Default Gateway	10.0.1.254	10.0.1.254
Service Set ID	BR1	BR1
Role in Radio Network	Root bridge	Non-Root Bridge w/o clients

Figure 6-7   Bridge Settings

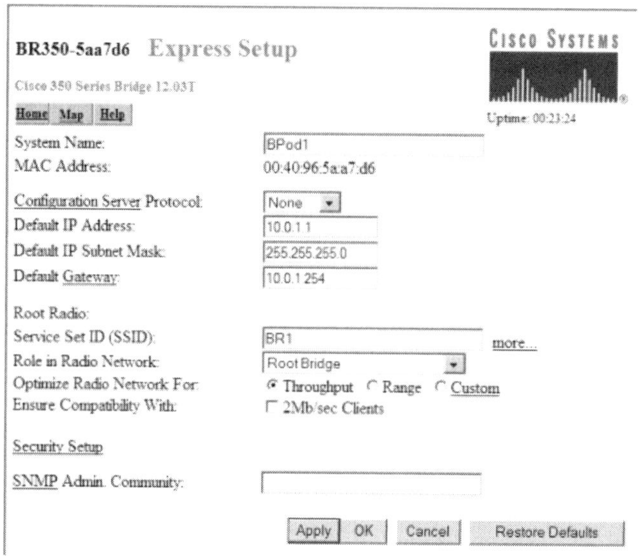

2.   Click **Apply**. The connection drops.

3.   Configure the PCs:

  •   PC1 with an IP address of 10.0.1.10/24

  •   PC2 with an IP address of 10.0.2.10/24

4.   Reconnect using the browser. Enter **10.0.P.1** and connect.

Note: The topology figures and lab examples contains **P** values. The **P** value in the addressing and naming scheme refers to *your* assigned Pod number.

Examples of determining **P** values follow:

  •   Pod2 is looking at a topology figure and is trying to determine the **P** values in the figure. In this scenario, the **P** values equal **2**. 10.0.**P**.12 becomes 10.0.**2**.12, 172.30.**P**.2 becomes 172.30.**2**.2, and so on.

  •   Pod1 is looking at a topology figure and is trying to determine the **P** values in the figure. In this scenario, the **P** values equal **1**. 10.0.**P**.12 becomes 10.0.**1**.12, 172.30.**P**.2 becomes 172.30.**1**.2, and so on.

In both examples, the **P** values are directly related to the Pod number of the team.

5.   Verify the settings.

What roles can the bridge serve in the network?

_____

_____

_____

Step 5: Establishing Advanced Radio Settings for the Non-Root Bridge

1. From the **Setup** Page, click on the **Root Radio > Advanced** link, shown in Figure 6-8, to go to the **Radio Advanced** page of the Non-Root Bridge.

Figure 6-8   Root Radio > Advanced Link

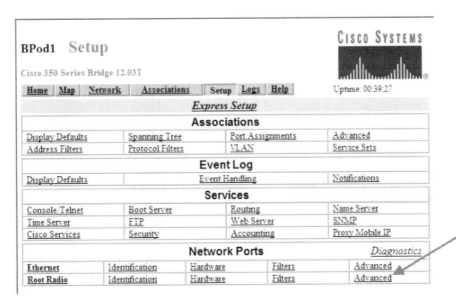

2. Enter the MAC address of the Root Bridge into the **Preferred Access Point 1:** field, as shown in Figure 6-9.

    This can be found on the bottom of the Root Bridge or from the Root Bridge **Home** page, as shown in Figure 6-10.

3. Click the **Apply** button, shown in Figure 6-11, to apply the settings.

Figure 6-9   Preferred Access Point 1: Field

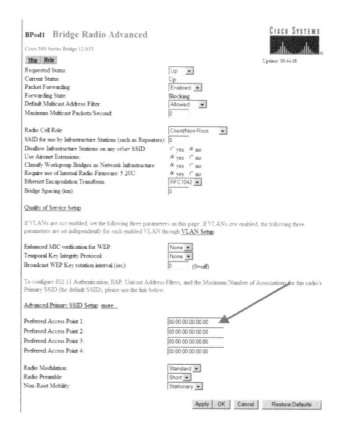

Figure 6-10   Finding the MAC Address

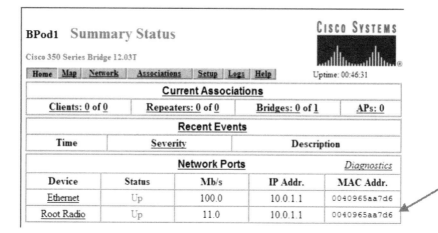

Figure 6-11   Apply Button

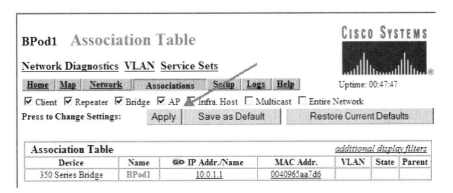

4.   Go to the **Associations** page of the Root Bridge. Is the Non-Root Bridge in the Association table?

Step 7: Testing the Connection

Verify that client PCs are configured with the appropriate IP address. The only wireless devices on this topology are the two wireless multifunction bridges used for the point-to-point connection.

1.   After the wireless bridge link is configured properly, ping from PC1 to BPod2. Then ping from PC1 to PC2. Were these successful?

---

2.   Test Layer 7 connectivity by browsing to BPod2 from PC1.

3.   Configure FTP or web services on PC1 and PC2. Transfer a files from PC1 to PC2 and vice versa. Calculate the download performance across the wireless link.

    a.   What was the download speed in Mbps?

    ---

    b.   How was this calculated?

    ---

    c.   What is the speed limitation?

Lab 6.4.4: Configure Bridge Services

Estimated Time: 30 minutes

Number of Team Members: Students work in teams of two

Objectives

In this lab, students configure the identity services, IP routing table, console parameters, and the time server parameters of the bridge unit.

Scenario

Configuring services includes the following:

- The Boot Server page determines how the bridge obtains its IP address and assigns required identifiers.

- Configuring the Routing Services page controls how IP packets originating from the bridge are forwarded.

- The Console/Telnet page can set up essential system parameters.

- The Time Server menu page sets time parameters.

Topology

Figure 6-12 shows the topology used in this lab.

Figure 6-12   Lab Topology

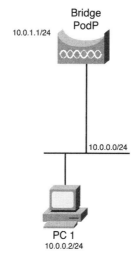

Preparation

The students should read and familiarize themselves with the concepts and procedures of Chapter 6 from the *Cisco Networking Academy Program Fundamentals of Wireless LANs Companion Guide* prior to the lab.

Tools and Resources

Each team requires the following equipment to complete this lab:

- One multifunction wireless bridge properly set up for web browser access

- One PC to configure each bridge

Step 1: Configuring the Identity Process of the Bridge Unit

1. After connecting to the bridge through a web browser, select the **Setup** tab to go to the Setup screen. From the Services section, select the **Boot Server**, as shown in Figure 6-13.

Figure 6-13   Boot Server Page

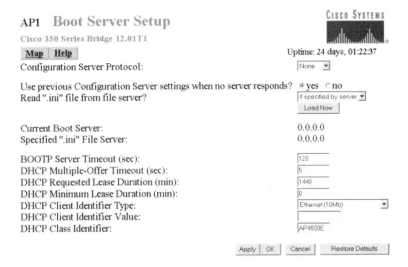

2. Select the identity process, that the Configuration Server Protocol will use with the bridge.

   There are three options:

   - **None**—Disable BOOTP and DHCP, which is the default setting

   - **BOOTP**—Configures BOOTP only

   - **DHCP**—Configures DHCP

For Root Units, select **DHCP**.

For nonroot units, select **None**.

What is the BOOTP selection for?

_____

_____

Step 2: Configuring the IP Routing Table Parameters of the Bridge Unit

1. From the Setup page in the Services section, select the **Routing** option, as shown in Figure 6-14.

Figure 6-14   Routing Setup Page

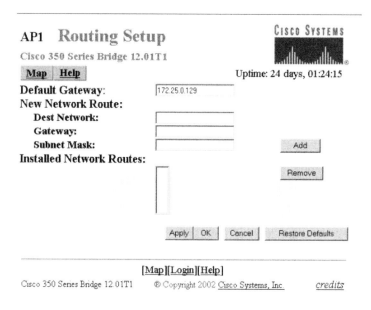

If the destination IP address exactly matches a host entry in the routing table, the packet is forwarded to the MAC address corresponding to the next-hop IP address from the table entry.

If the destination address is on another subnet and matches the infrastructure portion of a net entry in the table (using the associated subnet mask), the packet is forwarded to the MAC address corresponding to the next-hop IP address from the table entry.

2. To configure the IP Routing Table parameters, complete the following steps:

    a.   If DHCP has been used for the identity process, the default gateway router IP Address will be in the default gateway field.

b.   If a static route is to be added for handling destination addresses, fill in the following fields:

Destination Network:

_____

Gateway:

_____

Subnet Mask:

                                            .

_____

Step 3: Configuring the Console/Telnet Parameters of the Bridge Unit

1.   From the Setup page in the Services section, select the **Console/Telnet** option.

2.   Use the Console/Telnet setup page, shown in Figure 6-15, to configure the parameters for HyperTerminal and/or Telnet sessions to the bridge unit.

Figure 6-15   Console/Telnet Setup Page

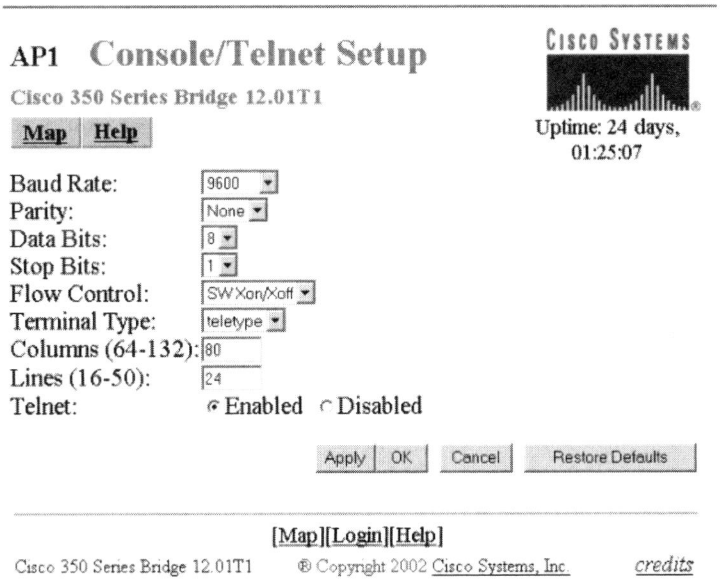

Document the following settings:

   a.   Baud rate

_____

   b.   Parity

_____

c.   Data bits

_____

d.   Stop bits

_____

e.   Flow Control

_____

3.   If remote access to the bridge is a concern, you can disable the bridge unit's Telnet feature by checking the **Disabled** button on this page.

Step 4: Configuring the Time Server Parameters of the Bridge Unit to Set the Time

1.   From the Setup page in the Services section, select the **Time Server** option, as shown in Figure 6-16.

Figure 6-16   Time Server Setup Page

Simple Network Time Protocol (SNTP) is a lightweight version of Network Time Protocol (NTP). NTP is designed for extreme accuracy, while SNTP is designed for easy synchronization. SNTP clients can obtain time from an NTP server. Even though SNTP is simple, it can easily provide accuracy within a few milliseconds.

2.   Configure the bridge unit's Time Server parameters to set the time. Use the Time Server Setup page to change the time settings.

a.   Change the time to one hour ahead. When would this step be necessary?

_____

b.   Change the time back to the current time.

Lab 6.5.3: Manage Bridge Configuration and Image Files

Estimated Time: 20 minutes

Number of Team Members: Students work in teams of two

Objectives

In this lab, the student learns the features of the wireless bridge configuration dump and the process used for wireless bridge configuration and image load processes. Additionally, in this lab, the student learns the process for distributing firmware and configurations.

Scenario

As a network administrator, it is important to maintain backup configuration and image files for all WLAN devices. This helps when deploying new WLAN devices, managing change, and in disaster recovery.

Topology

Figure 6-17 shows the topology used in this lab.

Figure 6-17   Lab Topology

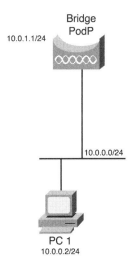

Preparation

The students should read and familiarize themselves with the concepts in Chapter 6 of the *Fundamentals of Wireless LANs Companion Guide* prior to attempting this lab.

Tools and Resources

Each team requires the following equipment to complete this lab:

- One BR350

- One PC on the wired LAN for bridge configuration

Step 1: Backing Up the Current Configuration File

To back up the current configuration files, complete the following steps:

1.   On PC1, open a web browser and access the bridge. From the Home page, click the
        Setup tab, as shown in Figure 6-18.

Figure 6-18   Click the Setup Tab

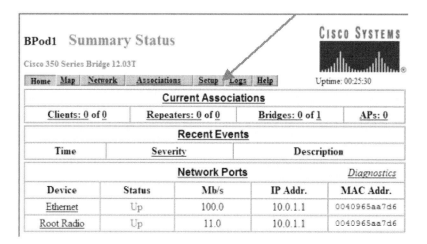

2.   From the Services section, select **Cisco Services**, as shown in Figure 6-19.

Figure 6-19   Select Cisco Services

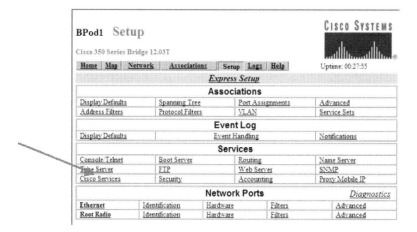

3.   Click the **Manage System Configuration** link, as shown in Figure 6-20.

Figure 6-20   Manage System Configuration Link

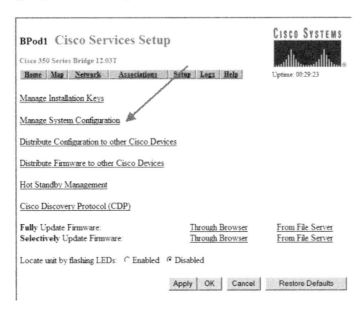

4.   Click the **Download All System Configuration** link from the screen shown in Figure 6-21.

Figure 6-21   Download All System Configuration

5.   When the File Download screen appears, click the **Save** button, shown in Figure 6-22.

Figure 6-22   File Download Screen

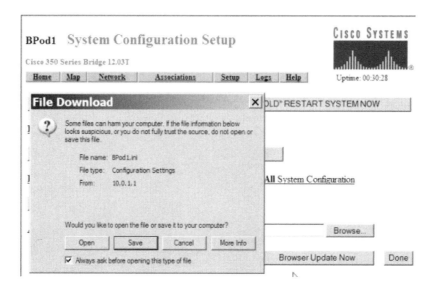

6.   Choose a filename and location, as shown in Figure 6-23, or click **Save** to accept the defaults.

Figure 6-23   Save As

In this example, Bpod1.ini was selected as the file name, and C:\Cisco directory was selected as the location to save the configuration file.

7.   Verify that the configuration file is saved on PC1, as shown in Figure 6-24.

Figure 6-24   Verify That the Configuration File Has Been Saved

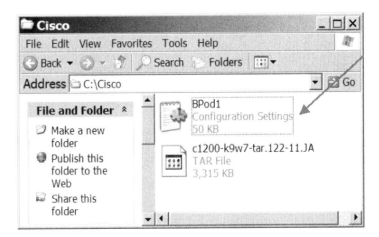

8.   On PC1, open the configuration file with Notepad. Edit the "sysName=" value to BPod1backup, as shown in Figure 6-25.

Figure 6-25   Edit the "sysName=" Value

9.   Save the changes and exit Notepad.

Step 2: Loading a Configuration File

If the configuration is ever lost or corrupted, you can restore it by using the Additional System Configuration File. This is an option from the **Cisco Services** Setup menu or page to move the configuration file into the bridge. The system automatically restores the configuration based on these commands.

To load a configuration file, complete the following steps:

1.   On the Cisco Services Setup page, click the **Manage System Configuration** button.

2.   From the System Configuration Setup Page, click the **Browse...** button to the right of the Additional System Configuration File: field, as shown in Figure 6-26.

Figure 6-26   The Browse... Button

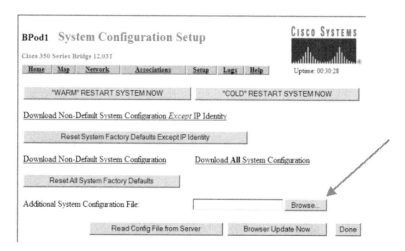

3.   Choose the configuration file BPod1, as shown in Figure 6-27, that is to be loaded, and click the **Open** button.

Figure 6-27   Choose the Configuration File

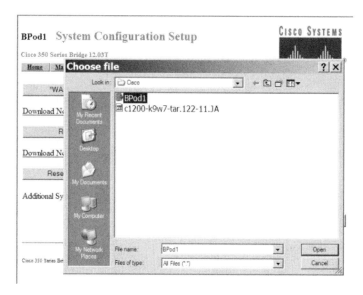

4.   Click the **Browser Update Now** button, as shown in Figure 6-28, to load the file. After about 10 seconds, the page will update. Notice the System name changes in the upper-left corner.

Figure 6-28   Browse Update Now Button

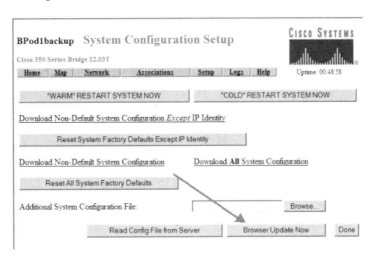

Was it possible to load the saved configuration file into the current configuration of the bridge? How is this confirmed?

_____

_____

Step 3: Update Bridge Firmware Through a Browser

Bridges might need to be updated to provide new services or greater security features.

To update firmware through a web browser, complete the following steps:

1.   Download the latest BR350 image from Cisco.com, as shown in Figure 6-29. Save the image file on PC1.

2.   From the Cisco Services Setup Page, click on the **Fully Update Firmware: Through Browser** link, as shown in Figure 6-30.

3.   From the Update All Firmware Through Browser Page, click on the **Browse...** button across from the New File for All Firmware, as shown in Figure 6-31.

Figure 6-29   Download Firmware Image

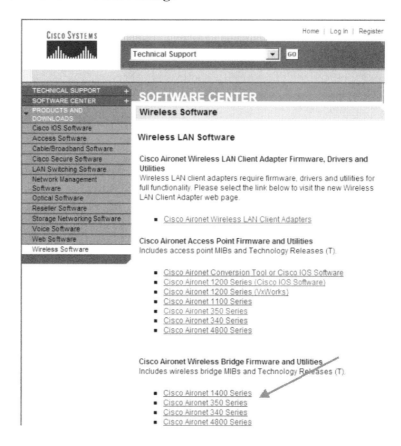

Figure 6-30   Update Firmware Through a Browser Link

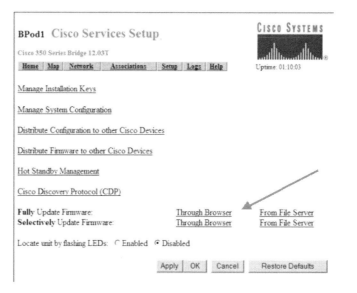

Figure 6-31   Browse... Button

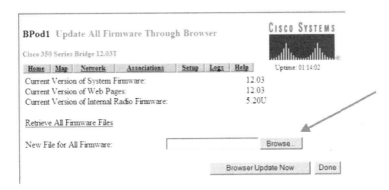

4.   Select the downloaded BR350 image file, as shown in Figure 6-32, and click the **Open** button.

Figure 6-32   The Downloaded BR350 Image File

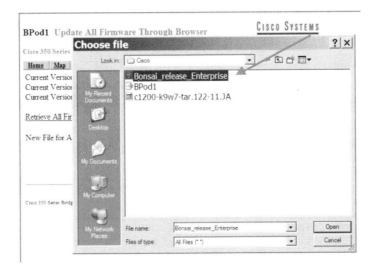

5.   The image file location now appears in the field, as shown in Figure 6-33.

Figure 6-33   File Location in the Browse... Field

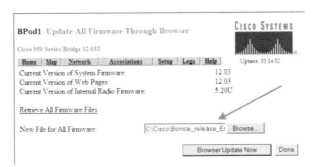

Note: If the bridge has the latest image installed, skip the next step. If the bridge requires updating, ask for instructor permission before upgrading.

6.   Click the **Browser Update Now** button.

Caution: Do not interrupt the update process once the update begins. This corrupts the bridge operating system, rendering the bridge inoperable.

Step 4: Distributing Bridge Firmware

The Cisco Services Setup menu provides an option for distributing firmware or configuration from one bridge to all other bridges on the infrastructure. These options reduce the time needed to perform firmware upgrades or make global changes to the configuration.

To distribute firmware, complete the following steps:

1.   Click **Distribute Firmware to other Cisco Devices** from the Cisco Services Setup page, as shown in Figure 6-34.

Figure 6-34   Distribute Firmware to Other Cisco Devices

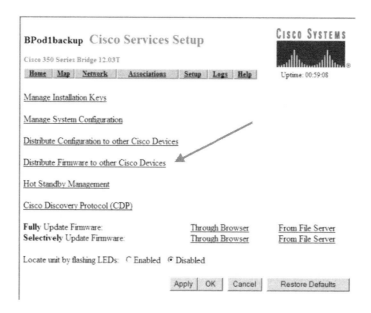

2.   From the Distribute Firmware Page, choose the **yes** radio button for the Distribute all firmware option, as shown in Figure 6-35.

3.   Click the **Start** button.

The bridge searches for other bridges to distribute its firmware to, which is indicated by the SEARCHING status in the lower left-hand corner of the page, as shown in Figure 6-36. If it locates a bridge, the distribution occurs automatically. If no other bridges are available, the status displays INACTIVE.

Figure 6-35   The yes Radio Button for the Distribute All Firmware Option

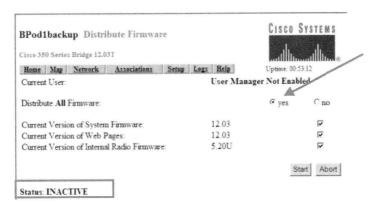

Figure 6-36   Searching for Other Bridges

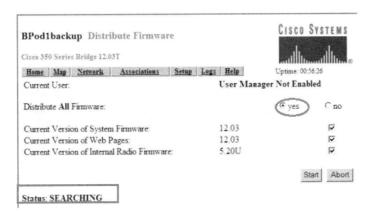

Step 5: Resetting the Bridge Configuration

The bridge provides an option to restore the bridge configuration back to factory defaults through a web browser. To reset the bridge, complete the following steps:

1.   From the Cisco Services Setup page, click the **Manage System Configuration** link, as shown in Figure 6-37.

2.   From the System Configuration Setup Page, click the **Reset All System Factory Defaults** button, as shown in Figure 6-38.

Figure 6-37   Manage System Configuration Link

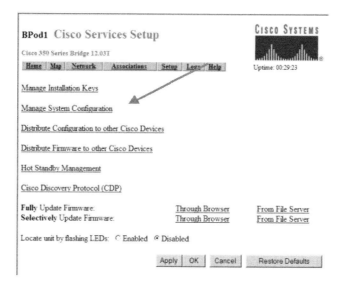

Figure 6-38   Reset All System Factory Defaults Button

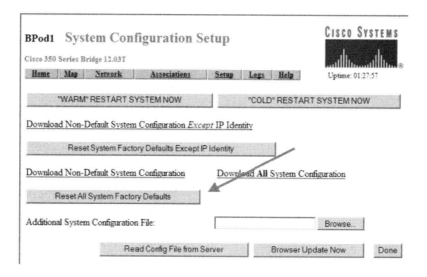

Lab 6.5.5: Configure Layer 3 Site-to-Site Wireless Link (Optional Challenge Lab)

Estimated Time: 45 minutes

Number of Team Members: Students work in teams of two

Objectives

Configure a site-to-site bridge network separated by a Layer 3 device. Test the speed of the wireless bridge link.

Scenario

A remote location, which is several miles away, requires connectivity to the existing wired network. The connection can be bridged wirelessly with two BR350s. In large networks, it is necessary to provide Layer 2 broadcast control using routers.

Topology

Figure 6-39 shows the topology used in this lab.

Figure 6-39   Lab Topology

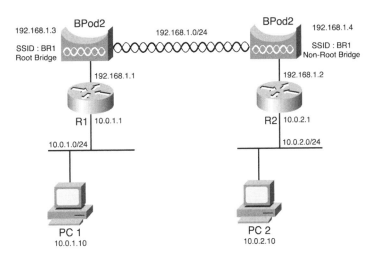

Preparation

The instructor or students must cable and configure the perimeter routers in addition to the wired LAN. The routers' Ethernet interfaces must be configured and enabled. Static routing should be configured on the routers. Ensure that the devices are configured according to the topology. Table 6-3 shows how the bridge devices should be configured.

Table 6-3   Lab Bridge Configurations

Device Name	Label	SSID	Address
BPod1	BR1	BR1	192.168.1.3/24
BPod2	BR2	BR1	192.168.1.4/24

Tools and Resources

Each team requires the following equipment to complete this lab:

- Two wired LAN segments that will be bridged together

- Two Cisco BR350s with 2.4dBi dipole antenna(s)

- Two dual Ethernet routers

- Two switches or hubs(optional)

Step 1: Connecting and Resetting Both Bridges

Connect a nine-pin, male-to-female, straight-through serial cable to the COM port on a computer and to the RS-232 serial port on the bridge. (This cable ships with the bridge.)

1.   Open a terminal emulator.

2.   Enter the following settings for the connection:

- Bits per second (baud rate): 9600

- Data bits: 8

- Parity: none

- Stop bits: 1

- Flow control: Xon/Xoff

3.   Press = to display the bridge's home page. If the bridge has not been configured before, the Express Setup page appears as the home page. (Go To Step 3.)

4.   If the bridge is already configured, the Summary Status page appears as the home page. When the Summary Status screen appears, type :**resetall**, and press **Enter**.

Enter YES to confirm Resetting All parameters to factory defaults:

```
YES
00:02:12 (FATAL): Rebooting System due to Resetting Factory Defaults
*** Restarting System in 5 seconds...
```

5. Type **yes**, and press **Enter** to confirm the command.

6. Power cycle the bridge by removing the power.

Step 2: Connect to the BR350s Through Express Setup

1. Plug a second RJ-45 Ethernet cable into the power injector end labeled TO NETWORK. Plug the other end of the Ethernet cable into the Ethernet port on a switch or hub. Then connect PC1 to the switch. A crossover cable can be used to connect directly from the inline power injector to PC1/PC2.

2. Configure PC1 to 10.0.0.2/24.

3. Open a web browser, enter the default bridge address, http://10.0.0.1, and press **Enter**.

4. Either of the following pages appears:

   • The **Summary Status** page, also known as the **Home** page, shown in Figure 6-40

   • The **Express Setup** page, shown in Figure 6-41

Figure 6-40   Summary Status Page

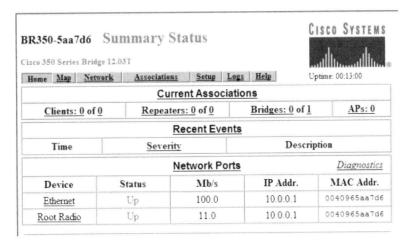

5. If the Express Setup page does not appear, from the Summary Status page, click the **Setup** hyperlink. This brings up the Setup page.

6. Click the **Express Setup** link, as shown in Figure 6-42. This now brings up the Express Setup page.

Figure 6-41   Express Setup Page

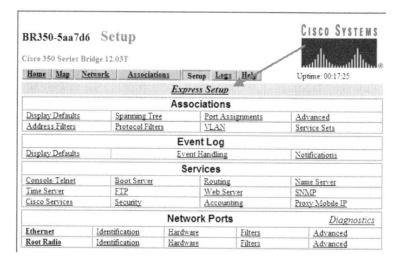

Figure 6-42   Express Setup Link

Step 3: Configuring the Bridge Settings

1.   Configure the settings in Table 6-4 in the screen displayed in Figure 6-43.

Table 6-4   Bridge Settings

Parameter	Bpod1	BPod2
System Name	Bpod1	BPod2
Configuration Server Protocol	None	None

Parameter	Bpod1	BPod2
Default IP address	192.168.1.3	192.168.1.4
Default Gateway	192.168.1.1	192.168.1.2
Service Set ID	BR1	BR1
Role in Radio Network	Root Bridge	Non-Root Bridge w/o Clients

Figure 6-43   Bridge Settings

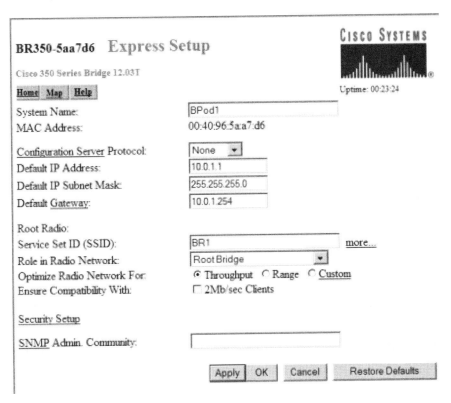

2.   Click **Apply**. The connection drops.

What roles can the bridge serve in the network?

Step 4: Cable and Configure the Routers and PCs

1. Using dual Ethernet routers, such as an 806, 2514, or equivalent, configure both routers as shown in Table 6-5.

Table 6-5   Router Configurations

```
hostname Router1                      hostname Router2
int fa0/0                             int fa0/0
 ip address 192.168.1.1                ip address 192.168.1.2 255.255.255.0
255.255.255.0                          description outside
 description outside                   no shut
 no shut                              !
!                                     int fa0/1
int fa0/1                              ip address 10.0.2.1 255.255.255.0
 ip address 10.0.1.1 255.255.255.0     description inside
 description inside                    no shut
 no shut                              !
!                                     router eigrp 1
router eigrp 1                         network 10.0.0.0
 network 10.0.0.0                      network 192.168.1.0
 network 192.168.1.0                   no auto-summary
 no auto-summary                      !
!                                     line vty 0 4
line vty 0 4                           password cisco
 password cisco                        login
 login
```

2. Configure the PCs:

   - PC1 with an IP address of 10.0.1.10/24

   - PC2 with an IP address of 10.0.2.10/24

3. Reconnect using the browser. Enter **10.0.P.1** and connect.

4. Verify the settings.

   a. What other routing method can be used instead of EIGRP?

   _____

   _____

   b. Can static routes be used? If so, what is the advantage/disadvantage?

   _____

   _____

Step 5: Entering Advanced Radio Settings for the Non-Root Bridge

1. From the Setup Page, click on the **Root Radio > Advanced** link to go to the Radio Advanced page of the Non-Root Bridge, as shown in Figure 6-44.

2. Enter the MAC address of the Root Bridge into the **Preferred Access Point 1:** field, as shown in Figure 6-45.

165

Figure 6-44   Root Radio > Advanced Link

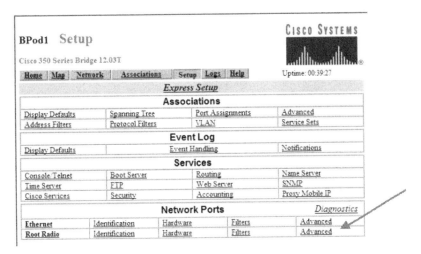

Figure 6-45   Preferred Access Point 1: Field

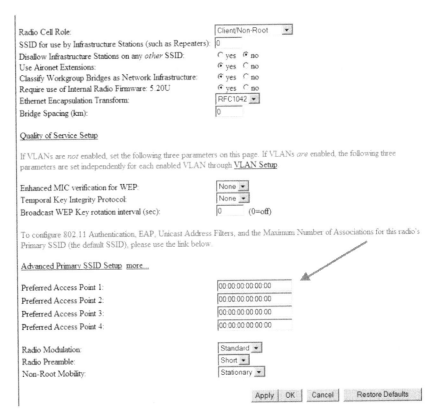

This can be found on the bottom of the Root Bridge or from the Root Bridge Home page, as shown in Figure 6-46.

Figure 6-46   MAC Address

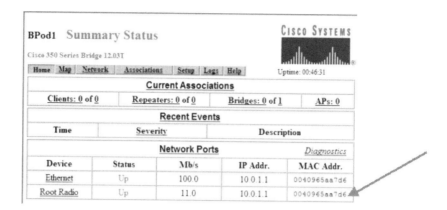

3.   Click the **Apply** button to apply the settings.

4.   Go to the Associations page of the Root Bridge, as shown in Figure 6-47.

Figure 6-47   Associations Page

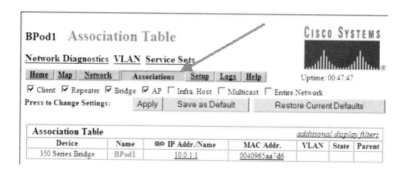

Is the Non-Root Bridge in the Association table?

Step 6: Testing the Connection

Verify that client PCs are configured with the appropriate IP address. The only wireless devices on this topology are the two wireless multifunction bridges used for the point-to-point connection.

1.   After the wireless bridge link is configured properly, ping from PC1 to Router 1 inside Ethernet port. Then ping to Router1 outside port. If successful, ping from PC1 to BPod2. Ping from PC1 to Router2 outside port, followed by a ping to Router2 inside port. Finally, Ping from PC1 to PC2.

Were these successful?

---

2. Test Layer 7 connectivity by browsing to BPod2 from PC1.

3. Configure FTP or web services on PC1 and PC2. Transfer a file from PC1 to PC2 and vice versa. Calculate the download performance across the wireless link.

    A. What was the download speed in Mbps?

    _____

    B. How was this calculated?

    _____

    C. What is the speed limitation?

    _____

Chapter 7

Antennas

Lab 7.1.4: Antenna Setup

Estimated Time: 15 minutes

Number of Team Members: Students work in teams of two

Objectives

This lab orientates the user to the Cisco Aironet Access Point antenna configuration.

Scenario

An antenna is used to radiate transmitted signals and/or capture received signals. Different antenna components have different ranges and capabilities in the area of signal they radiate. Placement of the antenna can have different effects on the range or the ability of the access point to transmit and receive the radio wave signals.

Cisco antennas use a Reverse Polarity Threaded Navy Connector (RP-TNC). This connector looks like a TNC, but the center contacts have been reversed. This prohibits a standard off-the-shelf antenna from being attached to a Cisco RF product. The U.S. Federal Communication Commission (FCC) requires vendors to use nonstandard connectors to prevent accidental connections to wireless equipment.

Preparation

Prior to the lab, the student should have a Cisco Aironet Access Point configured as a root unit and performing properly. The student also needs a laptop computer with a Cisco Aironet client adapter and the utilities installed and performing properly.

The students perform some online Internet research and need a computer with Internet access.

Tools and Resources

Each team requires the following equipment to complete this lab:

- Cisco Aironet Access Point with two standard antennas

- Laptop PC with a client adapter and client utility properly installed

- Cisco Aironet Antenna components to be tested

Step 1: Antenna Orientation of the Access Point

To familiarize yourself with the Cisco Aironet Antenna, complete the following steps:

1. Note the image of the Aironet AP1200 series Access Point in Figure 7-1.

Figure 7-1   Aironet AP1200 Series Access Point

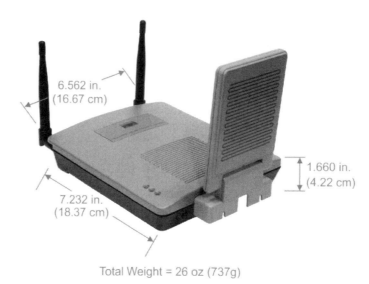

Total Weight = 26 oz (737g)

2. Note the dual RP-TNC connectors on the access point. The right antenna coupling is the coupling on the right when looking at the access point back panel.

    a. What does RP-TNC stand for?

    _____

    b. What is Vertical Polarization?

    _____
    _____

    c. Define antenna beam width.

    _____
    _____

    d. Define antenna bandwidth.

    _____
    _____

Step 2: Aironet AP1200 Access Point with Dipole Antennas Orientation

1. Note the image of the Aironet AP1200 Access Point with the standard dipole antennas.

The orientation of the antenna is important if the standard dipole antennas are not used. When in diversity mode, the access point uses either the left or right antenna, but not both. Which access point it uses depends on the signal strength. When an optional antenna is used, the antenna receive and transmit setting must be changed to one side, either the left or right.

2.   The Cisco part number for the pictured antenna in Figure 7-2 is CISCO AIR-ANT4941. Do some online research (http://www.cisco.com/en/US/products/hw/wireless/ps469/ products_data_sheet09186a0080092285.html) and obtain the following information on this part.

Figure 7-2   CISCO AIR-ANT4941 Antenna

a.   Gain (in dBi)

_____

b.   Frequency range

_____

c.   What is the part number for the Cisco lightning arrestor?

_____

d.   What does the Cisco lightning arrestor do?

_____

e.   What is the gain of Cisco part number CISCO AIR-ANT1949?

_____

Lab 7.1.8.1: Configure AP Diversity Settings

Estimated Time: 15 minutes

Number of Team Members: Students work in teams of two

Objectives

The student tests the effects of various antenna diversity settings on the Cisco Aironet Access Point. The student configures the access point radio antennas via GUI and IOS command line.

Scenario

APs have two RP-TNC connectors. These two antenna connectors are used for diversity in signal reception, and their purpose is not to increase coverage. They help eliminate the null path and RF being received out of phase. Only one antenna at a time is active.

Which antenna is active is selected on a per-client basis for optimal signal and only applies to that specific client. The access point can hop back and forth between antennas when talking to different clients. PCMCIA cards also have antenna diversity built into the card.

Topology

Figure 7-3 shows the topology used in this lab.

Figure 7-3   Lab Topology

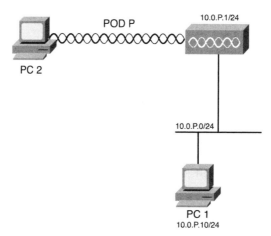

Note: The topology figures and lab examples contain **P** values. The **P** value in the addressing and naming scheme refers to *your* assigned Pod number.

Examples of determining **P** values follow:

- Pod2 is looking at a topology figure and is trying to determine the **P** values in the figure. In this scenario, the **P** values equal **2**. 10.0.**P**.12 becomes 10.0.**2**.12, 172.30.**P**.2 becomes 172.30.**2**.2, and so on.

- Pod1 is looking at a topology figure and is trying to determine the **P** values in the figure. In this scenario, the **P** values equal **1**. 10.0.**P**.12 becomes 10.0.**1**.12, 172.30.**P**.2 becomes 172.30.**1**.2, and so on.

In both examples, the **P** values are directly related to the Pod number of the team.

Preparation

Prior to the lab, the student should have a Cisco Aironet Access Point configured as a root unit and performing properly. The student also needs a laptop computer with a Cisco Aironet client adapter and the utilities installed and performing properly.

Tools and Resources

Each team requires the following equipment to complete this lab:

- One AP

- One wired PC or laptop

- One wireless laptop or PC with a client adapter properly installed

Command List

Table 7-1 lists and describes the commands used in this lab exercise. Refer to this list if assistance or help is needed during the lab exercise.

Table 7-1   Command List

Command	Description
configure terminal	Enters global configuration mode
interface dot11radio 0	Enters the device radio interface
antenna	Sets the receive or transmit antenna

Step 1: Configuring the Cisco Aironet Antenna Settings

1.   Open a web browser and type the access point's IP address in the browser address box.

2.   Go to the **Radio0-802.11B** Settings page of the access point, as shown in Figure 7-4.

Figure 7-4 **Settings Page**

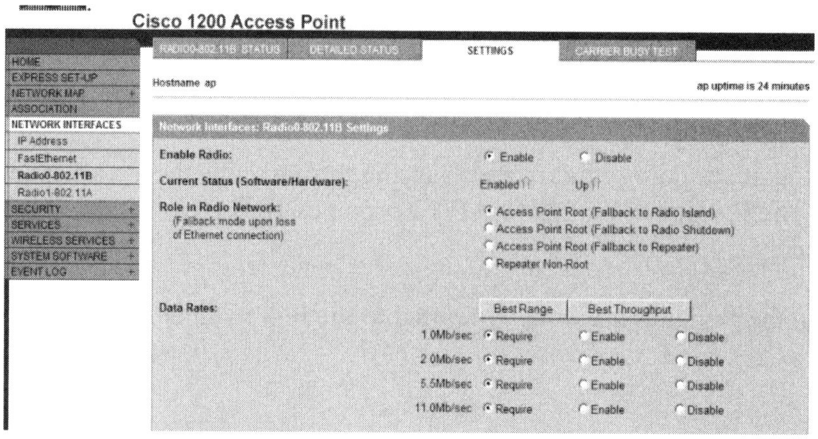

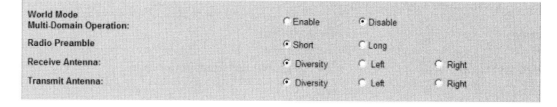

3.   Record the following information:

  a.   Enable Radio Setting

  _____

  b.   Role in Radio Network

  _____

  c.   Default Radio Channel

  _____

Step 2: Entering Antenna Settings

1.   On the middle of the **AP Radio Hardware** page are selections for the **Receive Antenna** and one for the **Transmit Antenna,** as shown in Figure 7-5.

Figure 7-5 **Receive Antenna and Transmit Antenna Settings**

2.   Record the Receive Antenna Setting.

  _____

3.   Record the Transmit Antenna Setting.

  _____

Step 3: Changing Antenna Settings

1.   Before you make any changes to the antenna settings, open the Site Survey utility on the PC, shown in Figure 7-6. Note the signal quality and signal strength before any changes are made.

Figure 7-6   Site Survey Utility

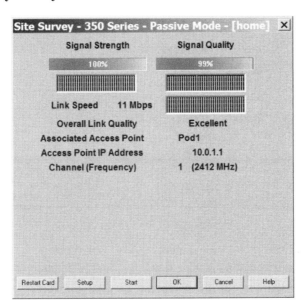

2.   Record the current signal strength.

_____

3.   Record the current signal quality.

_____

Step 4: Changing Antenna Settings (Continued)

1.   Is it actually necessary for you to physically remove the antennas?

_____

2.   Change the Receive and Transmit antenna settings to Left, Right, Diversity, or various combinations, and note any changes on the Site Survey Meter after the changes are applied.

     If using only one antenna, the Receive and Transmit antenna settings must correspond to the proper access point antenna setting for RF reception.

3.   If you are using two standard dipole antennas, very little change is effected on the Site Survey Meter. If you remove one of the antennas, you observe a more dramatic effect in

the setting changes, as shown in Figure 7-7. Make numerous changes with the antenna settings and check the results with the PC Aironet Client Site Survey utility. Remember to only make one change at a time so that you have a good idea which setting change caused the effect.

Figure 7-7   Change in the Site Survey Meter

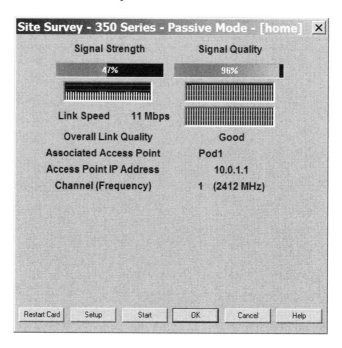

a.   Which antenna setting gave the strongest signal quality (Left, Right, or Diversity)?

_____

b.   Which antenna setting gave the strongest signal strength (Left, Right, or Diversity)?

_____

c.   Which setting gave the weakest signal strength (Left, Right, or Diversity)?

_____

d.   Which setting gave the weakest signal quality (Left, Right, or Diversity)?

_____

Step 5: Configuring the 802.11b Antenna via IOS CLI

This section describes how to configure the access point radio antennas via IOS command line.

1.   To set the access point Receive and Transmit to Right, enter the following commands:

```
PodP(config)#interface dot11radio 0
PodP(config-if)#antenna receive right
PodP(config-if)#antenna transmit right
PodP(config-if)#
```

2. To set the access point Receive and Transmit to Left, enter the following commands:

```
PodP(config)#interface dot11radio 0
PodP(config-if)#antenna receive left
PodP(config-if)#antenna transmit left
PodP(config-if)#
```

3. To set the access point Receive and Transmit to Diversity, enter the following commands:

```
PodP(config)#interface dot11radio 0
PodP(config-if)#antenna receive diversity
PodP(config-if)#antenna transmit diversity
PodP(config-if)#
```

Step 6: Configuring 802.11a Antenna via IOS CLI (Optional)

Repeat Step 5 for the 802.11a radio.

Lab 7.1.8.2: Configure Bridge Diversity Settings

Estimated Time: 15 minutes

Number of Team Members: Students work in teams of two

Objectives

The student tests the effects of various antenna diversity settings on the Cisco BR350.

Scenario

Bridges have two RP-TNC connectors attached to them. These two antennas connectors are for diversity in signal reception, and their purpose is not to increase coverage or distance. They help eliminate the null path and RF being received out of phase. Only one antenna at a time is active.

Which antenna is active is selected on a per-client basis for optimal signal and only applies to that specific client. The bridge can hop back and forth between antennas when talking to different clients. This can be useful in a point-to-multipoint installation.

Topology

Figure 7-8 shows the topology used in this lab.

Figure 7-8   Lab Topology

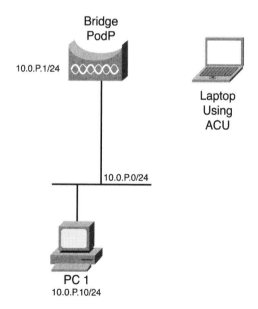

Preparation

Prior to the lab, the student should have a Cisco BR350 configured as a root unit and performing properly. The student also needs a laptop computer with a Cisco Aironet client adapter and the utilities installed and performing properly.

Tools and Resources

Each team requires the following equipment to complete this lab:

- Cisco BR350

- Laptop or PC with a client adapter properly installed

Step 1: Configuring the Cisco Aironet Antenna Settings

1.   Open a web browser and type the bridge's IP address in the browser address box.

2.   Go to the bridge's Root Radio Hardware page, as shown in Figure 7-9.

Figure 7-9   Root Radio Hardware Page

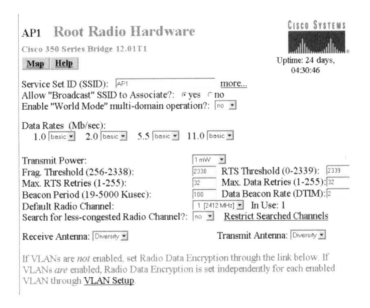

3.   Record the following information:

    a.   Service Set ID

    _____

    b.   Transmit power

    _____

    c.   Default radio channel

    _____

    d.   Search for a less congested channel (for this lab, keep this setting on **no**).

    _____

The Receive and Transmit antenna settings should both be set to Diversity at this time.

4. Located near the bottom of the **Radio Hardware** page, you can see two pull down selection menu boxes, one for the **Receive Antenna** and one for the **Transmit Antenna**, as shown in Figure 7-10.

Figure 7-10   Receive Antenna Pull Down Menu

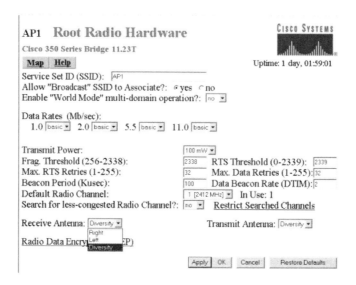

5. Before making any changes to the antenna settings, open the Site Survey utility on the PC. Note the signal quality and signal strength, as shown in Figure 7-11, before any changes are made.

Figure 7-11   Signal Quality and Strength

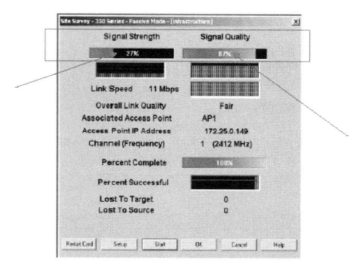

6. Change the Receive and Transmit antenna settings to Left, Right, Diversity, or various combinations, as shown in Figure 7-12, and note any changes on the Site Survey Meter after you have applied the changes.

Figure 7-12   Change the Receive and Transmit Antenna Settings

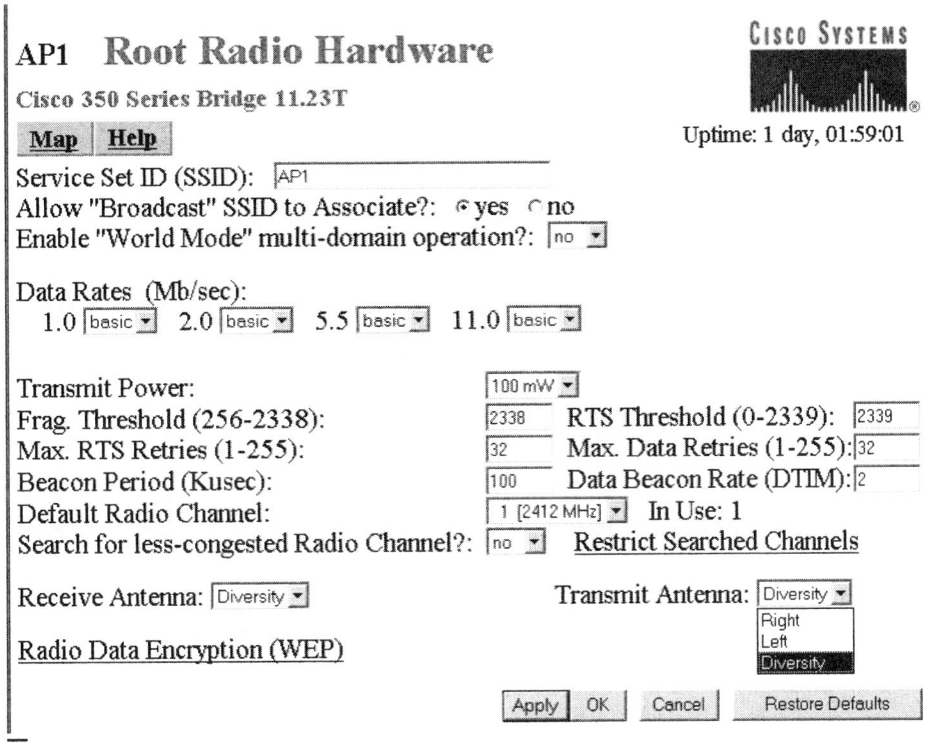

Is it actually necessary for you to physically remove the antennas?

_____

7.   If using only one antenna, the Receive and Transmit antenna settings must correspond to the proper bridge antenna setting for RF reception.

8.   If using two standard dipole antennas, very little change is effected on the Site Survey Meter. If you remove one of the antennas, you observe a more dramatic effect in the setting changes, as shown in Figure 7-13. Make numerous changes with the antenna settings, and check the results with the PC Aironet Client Site Survey utility. Remember to only make one change at a time so that you have a good idea which setting change caused the effect.

　　a.   Which antenna setting gave the strongest signal quality (Left, Right, or Diversity)?

_____

　　b.   Which antenna setting gave the strongest signal strength (Left, Right, or Diversity)?

_____

c. Which setting gave the weakest signal strength (Left, Right, or Diversity)?

d. Which setting gave the weakest signal quality (Left, Right, or Diversity)?

Figure 7-13   Changes in the Site Survey Meter

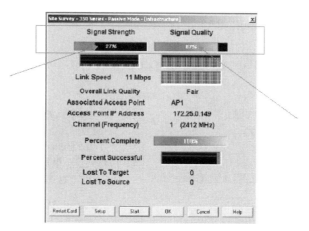

Lab 7.2.6: Omnidirectional Antennas

Estimated Time: 15 minutes

Number of Team Members: Students work in teams of two

Objectives

Test the range capabilities of the Cisco Aironet AP with an omnidirectional antenna configuration.

Scenario

Omnidirectional antennas create more coverage area away from the antenna in all directions, but the energy level directly below the antenna becomes lower. Omnidirectional antennas are generally used for point-to-multipoint implementations.

Topology

Figure 7-14 shows the topology used in this lab.

Figure 7-14   Lab Topology

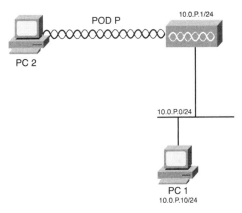

Note: The topology figures and lab examples contain **P** values. The **P** value in the addressing and naming scheme refers to *your* assigned Pod number.

Examples of determining **P** values follow:

- Pod2 is looking at a topology figure and is trying to determine the **P** values in the figure. In this scenario, the **P** values equals **2**. 10.0.**P**.12 becomes 10.0.**2**.12, 172.30.**P**.2 becomes 172.30.**2**.2, and so on.

- Pod1 is looking at a topology figure and is trying to determine the **P** values in the figure. In this scenario, the **P** values equal **1**. 10.0.**P**.12 becomes 10.0.**1**.12, 172.30.**P**.2 becomes 172.30.**1**.2, and so on.

In both examples, the **P** values are directly related to the Pod number of the team.

Preparation

Prior to the lab, configure a Cisco Aironet Access Point as a root unit and ensure it is performing properly. Obtain a laptop computer with a Cisco Aironet client adapter and the utilities installed.

Tools and Resources

Each team requires the following equipment to complete this lab:

- Cisco Aironet Access Point installed with Cisco Aironet AIR-ANT4941 2.2 dBi dipole antenna

- PC with a client adapter properly installed

Step 1: Setting Up the Omnidirectional Antenna

To set up the Cisco Aironet omnidirectional antenna, shown in Figure 7-15, complete the following steps (the access point should be turned on and configured).

Figure 7-15   Cisco Aironet Omnidirectional Antenna

1. Open a web browser and type in the access point IP address in the browser address box. This should bring up the access point Summary Status or Home page.

2. Check the Receive and Transmit mode of the antennas. Because two standard dipole antennas are being used on the access point, the Receive and Transmit antenna modes should be set to Diversity, as shown in Figure 7-16. This allows the access point to use the left or right antenna, depending on which is receiving the stronger signal.

3. Double-click the Link Status Meter (LSM) icon on the laptop, and note the signal quality and signal strength meter, as shown in Figure 7-17.

Figure 7-16　Antenna Modes Set to Diversity

Figure 7-17　Link Status Meter

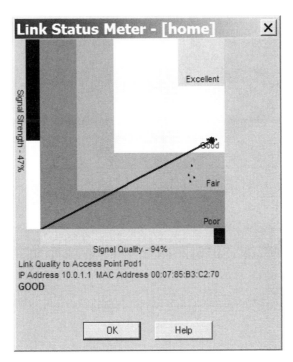

4.　Move the laptop computer around the room (and around the building, if possible) to note any changes in the Link Status Meter. This gives an indication of the coverage area afforded this particular antenna configuration.

This lab is using an omnidirectional antenna and should generate a radio signal uniformly in all directions.

　　a.　Approximately how far is the indoor range of the access point (meters or feet)?

_____

　　b.　Experiment with changing the data rate on the access point. Were you able to extend your coverage range?

_____

Step 2: Omnidirectional 5GHz Patch (If Available)

To set up the Cisco Aironet 5GHz Omnidirectional antenna, flip up the patch antenna perpendicular to the Aironet AP1200, as shown in Figure 7-18.

Figure 7-18   Patch Antenna

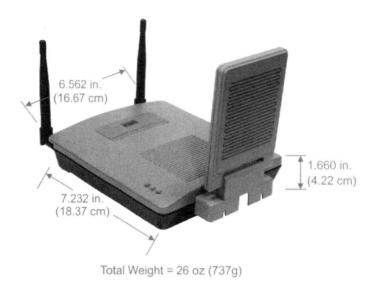

Total Weight = 26 oz (737g)

The patch now operates in Omnidirectional mode. The antenna is also dual diversity.

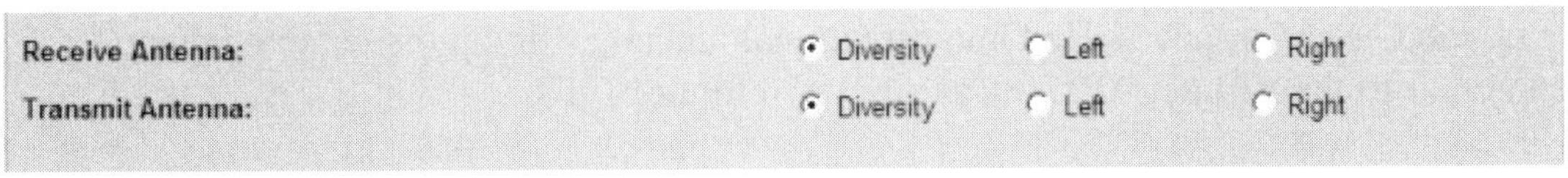

Receive Antenna: ⊙ Diversity   ○ Left   ○ Right
Transmit Antenna: ⊙ Diversity   ○ Left   ○ Right

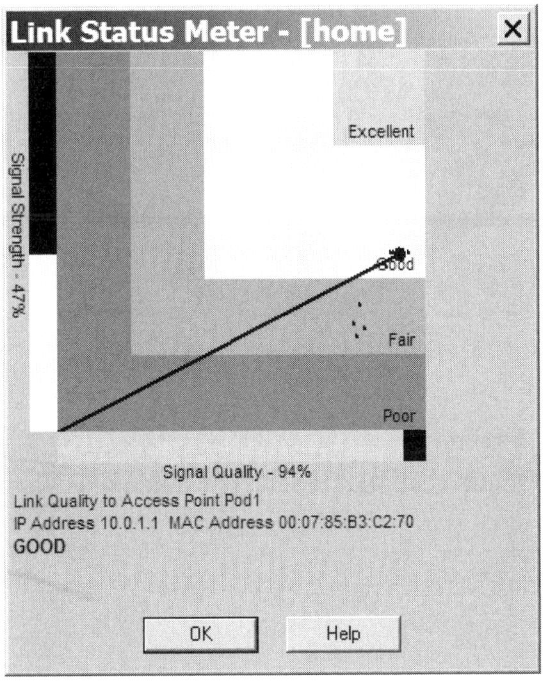

Lab 7.3.4: Directional Antennas

Estimated Time: 15 minutes

Number of Team Members: Students work in groups of two

Objectives

In this lab, students test the range capabilities of the Cisco Aironet Access Point with a directional antenna configuration.

Scenario

Directional antennas create a coverage area in a particular area caused by the condensed energy of the signal being pushed in a certain direction. Very little energy is in the backside of a directional antenna.

Topology

Figure 7-19 shows the topology for this lab.

Figure 7-19   Lab Topology

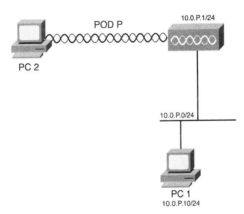

Note: The topology figures and lab examples contain **P** values. The **P** value in the addressing and naming scheme refers to *your* assigned Pod number.

Examples of determining **P** values follow:

- Pod2 is looking at a topology figure and is trying to determine the **P** values in the figure. In this scenario, the **P** values equal **2**. 10.0.**P**.12 becomes 10.0.**2**.12, 172.30.**P**.2 becomes 172.30.**2**.2, and so on.

- Pod1 is looking at a topology figure and is trying to determine the **P** values in the figure. In this scenario, the **P** values equal **1**. 10.0.**P**.12 becomes 10.0.**1**.12, 172.30.**P**.2 becomes 172.30.**1**.2, and so on.

In both examples, the **P** values are directly related to the Pod number of the team.

Preparation

Prior to the lab, the student should have a Cisco Aironet 1200 Access Point configured as a root unit and performing properly. A laptop computer is also needed with a Cisco Aironet 802.11a and a 802.11b client adapter and the utilities installed and performing properly.

Tools and Resources

Each team requires the following equipment to complete this lab:

- Cisco Aironet Access Point with a Cisco Integrated 802.11a patch antenna for AP1200

- Laptop PC with an 802.11b client adapter properly installed

- Cisco Aironet AIR-ANT1949 13.5 dBi Yagi Mast Mount antenna to be tested (optional)

Step 1: Setting Up the Directional Antenna (11a Patch)

To set up the Cisco Aironet directional antenna, shown in Figure 7-20, complete the following steps.

Figure 7-20   Cisco Aironet Directional Antenna

1. For lab purposes, orient the Patch antenna by placing the antenna in the closed position, which is its directional polarization. The antenna should be pointing toward the area of coverage.

2. The access point can be turned on and configured.

3. Open a web browser and type in the access point IP address in the browser address box.

4. Check the Receive and Transmit mode of the antenna on the AP **Radio0-802.11A** page.

5.   When using the built-in Patch antenna on the access point, the Receive and Transmit antenna modes should be set to **Diversity**. This allows the access point to use both antennas for transmitting and receiving. Apply these settings.

6.   On the PC, double-click the Link Status Meter (LSM) icon on the laptop, and note the signal quality and signal strength meter, as shown in Figure 7-21.

Figure 7-21   Link Status Meter

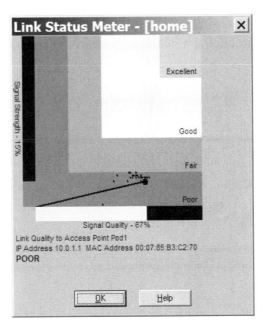

7.   Move the laptop computer around the room (and around the building, if possible) to note any changes in the Link Status Meter. This gives an indication of the coverage area given to this particular antenna configuration.

8.   Sketch the shape of the coverage of the antenna used. Show the access point and the PC client at their farthest distance.

a. What is the signal quality at the farthest distance that still maintains a fair connection? What is the approximate distance?

_____

b. What is the signal strength at the farthest distance that still maintains a fair connection? What is the approximate distance?

_____

Step 2: Setting Up the Yagi Directional Antenna (Optional)

To set up the Cisco Aironet directional antenna, shown in Figure 7-22, complete the following steps.

Figure 7-22   Cisco Aironet Directional Antenna

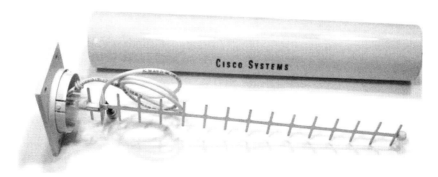

1. Turn the power off on the access point and unscrew both standard dipole antennas from the rear of the access point, as shown in Figure 7-23. Then install the Yagi Mast Mount antenna to the access point by screwing the antenna TNC connector to the AP right TNC connector.

Figure 7-23   Rear View of the Access Point

2. For lab purposes, orient the Yagi Mast Mount antenna by placing the antenna in a horizontal position, which is its polarization. The antenna should be pointing toward the area of coverage. Positioning of the Yagi Mast Mount is very important and affects the coverage area.

3. The access point can be turned on and configured.

4. Open a web browser and type in the access point IP address in the browser address box.

5. Check the Receive and Transmit mode of the antenna on the AP **Radio0-802.11** page, shown in Figure 7-24.

Figure 7-24   Receive and Transmit Modes

6. When using a single Yagi Mast Mount antenna on the access point, the Receive and Transmit antenna modes should be set to **Right**. This allows the access point to use the right antenna for transmitting and receiving. Apply these settings.

7. Double-click the Link Status Meter (LSM) icon on the laptop, and note the signal quality and signal strength meter, as shown in Figure 7-25.

Figure 7-25   Link Status Meter

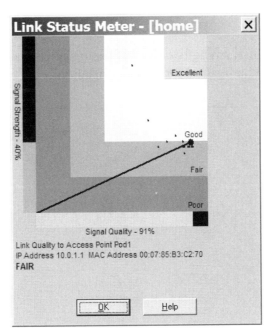

8. Move the laptop computer around the room (and around the building, if possible) to note any changes in the Link Status Meter. This gives an indication of the coverage area given to this particular antenna configuration.

9. Sketch the shape of the coverage of the antenna used. Show the access point and the PC client at their farthest distance.

   a. What is the signal quality at the farthest distance that still maintains a fair connection? What is the approximate distance?

   _____

   b. What is the signal strength at the farthest distance that still maintains a fair connection? What is the approximate distance?

   _____

Chapter 8

Security

Lab 8.2.4: Wireless Attacks and Countermeasures

Estimated Time: 25 minutes

Number of Team Members: Students work in teams of two

Objectives

In this lab, students gain an understanding of the primary attack methods used to bypass conventional security measures on WLANs. Additionally, students learn the countermeasures that can be implemented for security on a WLAN.

Scenario

Network security is the process by which digital information assets are protected. The goals of security are to maintain integrity, protect confidentiality, and assure availability.

This lab focuses on understanding wireless security concepts.

Preparation

The students require access to the Internet for online research.

Tools and Resources

Each student team needs one PC with Internet access to complete this lab.

Step 1: Understanding Network Security Goals

Answer the following questions:

1. List the three primary goals of network security covered in Chapter 8, "Security," from the *Fundamentals of Wireless LANs Companion Guide*.

    _____

    _____

    _____

2. Which of the goals refers to the assurance that data is not altered or destroyed?

    _____

3. Which of the goals refers to the protection of data from unauthorized disclosure?

    _____

4. Which of the goals refers to the continuous operation of the computing system?

    _____

Step 2: Understanding Network Security Weaknesses

Answer the following questions:

1. List the three primary network security weaknesses covered in Chapter 8 from the *Fundamentals of Wireless LANs Companion Guide*.

    _____
    _____
    _____

2. Which of the weaknesses refers to a lack of a written security policy?

    _____

3. Which of the weaknesses refers to unsecured default settings?

    _____

4. Which of the weaknesses refers to weak initialization vector, poor encryption and authentication schemes, and firewall holes?

    _____

Step 3: Understanding Network Security Threats

Answer the following question:

List the four basic network security threats covered in Chapter 8 from the *Fundamentals of Wireless LANs Companion Guide*.

_____
_____
_____
_____

Step 4: Understanding Attack Methods

Answer the following questions:

1.   List the three primary attack methods covered in Chapter 8 from the *Fundamentals of Wireless LANs Companion Guide*.

       _____

       _____

       _____

2.   Which of the attacks is occurring when the attacker now controls one system and can either deface the public web presence or continue hacking for more interesting information?

       _____

3.   How is this attack performed? What tools are available?

       _____

       _____

       _____

4.   Which of the attacks is occurring when the attack results in obtaining address ranges, hosts, and services? In this case, the known servers and the firewall may or may not be detected.

       _____

5.   How is this attack performed? What tools are available?

       _____

6.   Which of the attacks is occurring when the attacker has disabled valid users from accessing the target network, causing lost revenue, lost communications, and damaged software and hardware?

       _____

7.   How is this attack performed? What tools are available?

       _____

Step 5: Understanding the Security Wheel

Answer the following questions:

1. List the four processes involved in building a secure network.

    _____

    _____

    _____

    _____

2. Which of the processes involves collecting and analyzing information from the monitoring and testing phases to make security improvements?

    _____

3. Which of the processes involves monitoring the network for violations and attacks against the corporate security policy?

    _____

4. Which of the processes involves testing the effectiveness of the security safeguards in place?

    _____

5. Which of the processes involves implementing security devices, which include firewalls, identification authentication systems, and virtual private networks?

    _____

6. What is at the center of the Wireless Security Wheel?

    _____

Step 6: Understanding WLAN Security Technologies

Answer the following questions:

1. List the two first-generation security technologies covered in Chapter 8 from the *Fundamentals of Wireless LANs Companion Guide*.

    _____

    _____

2. Name the one that serves to logically segment the users and access points that form part of a wireless subsystem.

    _____

3. Name the other that replaces the original data payload with the output of the encryption algorithm.

_____

4. What are the two types of authentication methods defined in IEEE 802.11?

_____

_____

5. What are the three states of authentication covered in Chapter 8 from the *Fundamentals of Wireless LANs Companion Guide*?

_____

_____

_____

Lab 8.3.1.1: Configure Basic AP Security via GUI

Estimated Time: 30 minutes

Number of Team Members: Students work in teams of two

Objectives

In this lab, students learn the following objectives:

- Password protect the console.

- Define administrator accounts.

- Configure accurate time and check firmware.

- Configure Secure Shell (SSH).

- Disable Telnet and web (optional).

Scenario

Students learn to secure the AP via GUI. The company's security policy mandates all devices should be locked down according to minimum standards. Also, SSH must be used for remote management.

SSH is a program, similar to Telnet, which allows a network administrator to log into another computer over a network. SSH allows an administrator to execute commands in a remote machine, and to move files from one machine to another. SSH provides strong authentication and secure communications over insecure networks. Two versions of SSH are currently available: SSH version 1 and SSH version 2. Only SSH version 1 is implemented in Cisco IOS Software.

Topology

Figure 8-1 shows the topology used in this lab.

Note: The topology figures and lab examples contain **P** values. The **P** value in the addressing and naming scheme refers to *your* assigned Pod number.

The following are examples of determining **P** values:

- Pod2 is looking at a topology figure and is trying to determine the **P** values in the figure. In this scenario, the **P** values equals **2**. 10.0.**P**.12 becomes 10.0.**2**.12, 172.30.**P**.2 becomes 172.30.**2**.2, and so on.

- Pod1 is looking at a topology figure and is trying to determine the **P** values in the figure. In this scenario, the **P** values equals **1**. 10.0.**P**.12 becomes 10.0.**1**.12, 172.30.**P**.2 becomes 172.30.**1**.2, and so on.

In both examples, the **P** values are directly related to the Pod number of the team.

Figure 8-1   Lab Topology

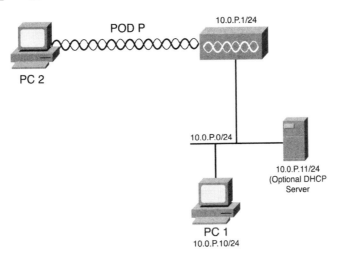

Preparation

The instructor should have a working wired network. PC1 should be connected to the wired network. Prior to starting the lab, ensure that each host PC is loaded with an SSH client. Numerous SSH clients are available for free on the Internet. The lab was developed using the PuTTY SSH client. Table 8-1 shows the settings for the access points in this lab.

Table 8-1   AP Settings

Team	Access Point Name	SSID	Address
1	Pod1	AP1	10.0.1.1/24
2	Pod2	AP2	10.0.2.1/24

Tools and Resources

Each team needs the following equipment and software to complete this lab:

- An access point

- A PC or laptop

- Console cable

- SSH client software

Additional Materials

Consult the following URLs for more information concerning the topics covered in this lab:

http://www.cisco.com/en/US/products/hw/wireless/ps430/products_installation_and_configuration_guide_book09186a0080147d69.html

http://www.chiark.greenend.org.uk/~sgtatham/putty/

Step 1: Configuring Basic AP Settings

1. If there is an existing configuration on the AP, erase the configuration and reload either via GUI or IOS CLI (see Figure 8-2).

2. Configure the host name, SSID, and BVI interface according to the settings listed in Table 8-1.

Figure 8-2   System Configuration

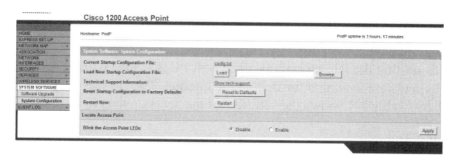

Step 2: Configuring a New Administrator Account

One of the easiest ways for hackers to gain access to network devices is by using default usernames and passwords. One easy preventative measure to guard against this attack is to change the administrator account from the defaults by completing the following steps:

1. Configure a new administrator account from the **Security: Admin Access** page, shown in Figure 8-3. Give this user Read-Write privileges.

    Username: cIsCo123

    Password: cIsCo123

2. In a production environment, it is necessary to delete the old account. However, in the lab, do not remove the existing account. Also, it is important to encrypt the passwords in the configurations if there are multiple administrator accounts with various privilege levels. By default, encryption is enabled on the AP 1200. Notice the password is bulleted out.

Figure 8-3 Admin Access Page

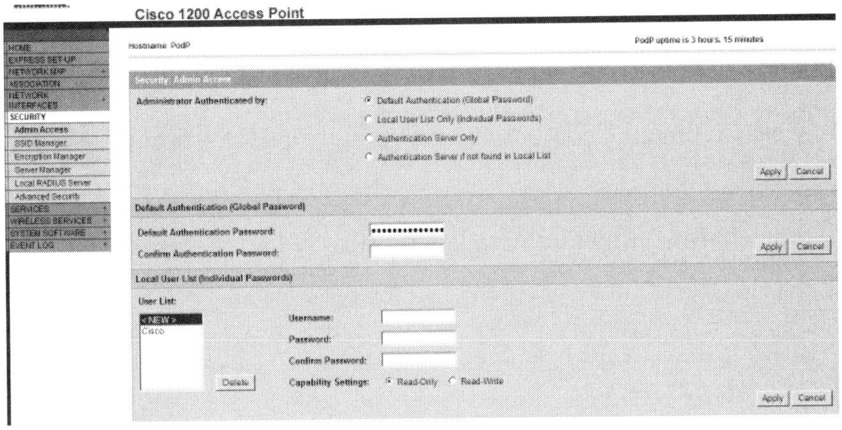

3. Now, enable only **Local User List Only** and click **Apply**. At this point, the AP requires authentication with the new Username, as shown in Figure 8-4.

Figure 8-4 Authentication

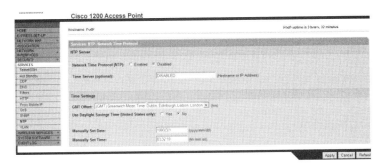

Step 3: Configuring Accurate Time

To keep track on any potential attacks, it is important to maintain proper time. To do this, manually set the correct time and date, as shown in Figure 8-5. Click **Apply** to save the changes.

Figure 8-5 Manually Set the Correct Date and Time

Step 4: Verifying the AP Image File

You can prevent many attacks by maintaining the most up-to-date image.

1.   To keep up with any vulnerabilities in Cisco products, go to the following:

http://www.cisco.com/en/US/products/hw/vpndevc/ps2284/products_tech_note09186a00
80132a8a.shtml

Are there any wireless vulnerabilities listed? If so, what are they?

_____

_____

_____

2.   From the **System Software** main page, shown in Figure 8-6, check the current image.

Figure 8-6   System Software Page

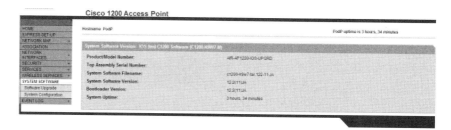

a.   What version is running?

_____

b.   Does this access point have any known vulnerabilities?

_____

Step 5: Configuring SSH

In some circumstances, attackers might be able to use a packet analyzer to intercept Telnet passwords, which may enable them to gain access to the AP or other networking devices. The SSH protocol is a secure form of Telnet, providing both authentication and encryption. Figure 8-7 shows the Telnet/SSH Page.

1.   Enable Secure Shell.

2.   Enter the System name of **PodP**. (Where P is the pod number?)

3.   Enter a domain name of **fwl.com**.

4.   Enter a key size (optional).

Figure 8-7   Telnet/SSH Page

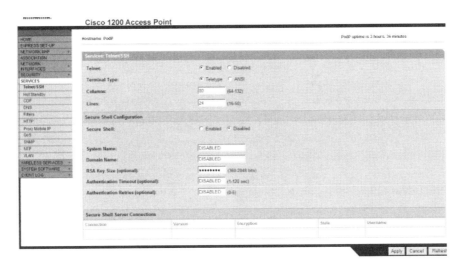

5.   Keep the default Timeout and Retries values.

6.   Click **Apply**.

What is the default size, in bits, of the key modulus?

_____

7.   Press **OK** to accept the default key size and continue.

Note: In a production environment, after enabling SSH, Telnet and HTTP should be disabled.

Step 8: Establishing Communication Between an SSH PC (Client) to AP (Server)

The basic settings to allow a PC and an AP to establish an SSH session are now configured. To establish an SSH session, launch the SSH client from the student PC.

1.   The configurations vary amongst the different SSH clients. If PuTTY is being used as the SSH client, following these instructions. Launch the PuTTY.exe file and a pane with various configuration options opens.

2.   In the **Host Name (or IP address)** input box, enter the IP address of the pod AP, as shown in Figure 8-8. Next, change the protocol to **SSH**. These two values must be sent to establish the SSH. To test the connection, press the **Open** command button at the bottom of the window.

Figure 8-8   Host Name (or IP Address) Input Box

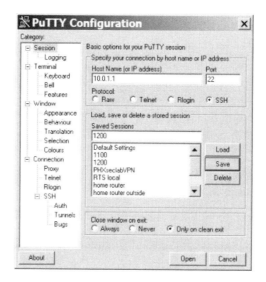

3.   The SSH Client pops up a Security Alert window, as shown in Figure 8-9. Click **Yes** to trust the host.

Figure 8-9   Security Alert Window

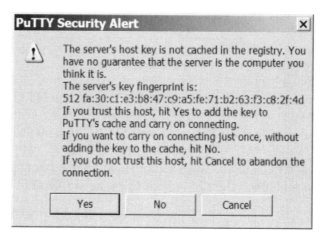

4.   The SSH client prompts for the local username and password that was previously set on the Pod AP. Enter **cisco** for the username and **student** for the password, as shown in Figure 8-10.

Figure 8-10   Enter Username and Password

Was the SSH connection successful? If so, how is the prompt displayed?

Step 9: Verifying SSH Connections

1.   From the **Services > Telnet/SSH** page, shown in Figure 8-11, view the active SSH sessions.

Figure 8-11   Telnet/SSH Page

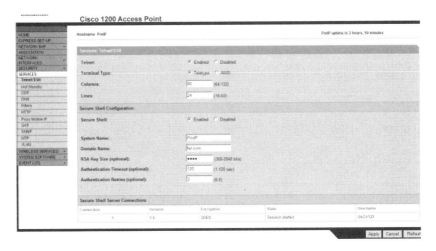

2.   Fill in the appropriate values in Table 8-2, based on the active Secure Shell Server Connections.

Table 8-2   SSH Connection Information

Connection	Version	Encryption	State	Username

3.   Reset the AP back to the factory default configuration.

Lab 8.3.1.2: Configure Basic AP Security via IOS CLI

Estimated Time: 30 minutes

Number of Team Members: Students work in teams of two

Objectives

In this lab, students learn the following objectives:

- Password protect the console.

- Define administrator accounts.

- Configure accurate time and check firmware.

- Configure SSH.

- Limit vty to SSH.

- Use access-list to secure SSH.

- Disable Telnet and Web.

Scenario

Students learn to secure the AP via Cisco Internetworking Operating System (IOS) software. The company's security policy mandates all devices should be locked down according to minimum standards. Also, SSH must be used for remote management.

SSH is a program, similar to Telnet, which allows a network administrator to log into another computer over a network. SSH allows an administrator to execute commands in a remote machine, and to move files from one machine to another. SSH provides strong authentication and secure communications over insecure networks. Two versions of SSH are currently available: SSH version 1 and SSH version 2. Only SSH version 1 is implemented in the Cisco IOS Software.

Topology

Figure 8-12 shows the topology used in this lab.

Note: The topology figures and lab examples contain **P** values. The **P** value in the addressing and naming scheme refers to *your* assigned Pod number.

Figure 8-12   Lab Topology

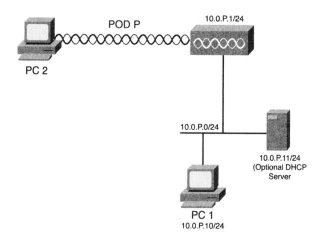

The following are examples of determining P values:

- Pod2 is looking at a topology figure and is trying to determine the **P** values in the figure. In this scenario, the **P** values equal **2**. 10.0.**P**.12 becomes 10.0.**2**.12, 172.30.**P**.2 becomes 172.30.**2**.2, and so on.

- Pod1 is looking at a topology figure and is trying to determine the **P** values in the figure. In this scenario, the **P** values equal **1**. 10.0.**P**.12 becomes 10.0.**1**.12, 172.30.**P**.2 becomes 172.30.**1**.2, and so on.

In both examples, the **P** values are directly related to the Pod number of the team.

Preparation

The instructor should have a working wired network. PC1 should be connected to the wired network. Prior to starting the lab, ensure that each host PC is loaded with an SSH client. Numerous SSH clients are available for free on the Internet. The lab was developed using the PuTTY SSH client. Table 8-3 shows the settings for the access points in this lab.

Table 8-3   AP Settings

Team	Access Point Name	SSID	Address
1	Pod1	AP1	10.0.1.1/24
2	Pod2	AP2	10.0.2.1/24

Tools and Resources

Each team needs the following equipment and software to complete this lab:

- The access point

- A PC or laptop

- Console cable

- SSH client software

Additional Materials

Consult the following URLs for more information concerning the topics covered in this lab:

http://www.cisco.com/en/US/products/hw/wireless/ps430/products_installation_and_configuration_guide_book09186a0080147d69.html

http://www.chiark.greenend.org.uk/~sgtatham/putty/

Command List

Table 8-4 lists and describes the commands used in this lab. Refer to this list if you need assistance during the lab.

Table 8-4   Lab Command List

Command	Description
crypto key generate rsa	Generates Rivest, Shamir, and Adleman (RSA) key pairs
hostname	Changes the AP's host name
ip domain-name	Defines a default domain name that the Cisco IOS software uses to complete unqualified host names
ip ssh	Configures SSH control parameters on the AP
transport input	Defines which protocols to use to connect to a specific line of the AP

Step 1: Configuring Basic AP Settings

1. Connect a Cisco rollover cable (console cable) between PC1 and the AP.

2. Open a terminal emulator.

3. Press **return** to get started.

4. If there is an existing configuration on the AP, erase the configuration and reload:

```
ap>
```

5. Configure the host name, SSID, and domain name according to the Preparation table:

```
PodP(config)#
PodP(config)#ip domain-name fwl.com
```

6. Configure a wireless PC or laptop to connect the AP. This will be used later in the lab to test the security configuration.

7. Remain on PC1 to configure the next steps.

8. While in configuration mode, check the configuration:

```
PodP(config)#do show run
```

Step 2: Configuring a New Administrator Account

One of the easiest ways for hackers to gain access to network devices is by using default usernames and passwords. One easy preventative measure to guard against this attack is to change the administrator account from the defaults by completing the following steps:

1. Configure a new administrator account:

```
PodP(config)#username cIsCo123 password cIsCo123
```

2. In a production environment, it is necessary to delete the old account:

```
PodP(config)#no username Cisco password Cisco
```

3. Also, it is important to encrypt the passwords in the configurations if there are multiple administrator accounts with various privilege levels. By default, this is enabled on the AP 1200:

```
PodP(config)#service password-encryption
```

4. While in configuration mode, verify the user accounts and password encryption:

```
PodP(config)#do show run
```

5. Secure the console connection by requiring a password:

```
PodP(config)#line con 0
PodP(config)#login
PodP(config)#password cIsCo123
```

6. Exit out of the AP and log back in:

```
User Access Verification
Password:
PodP>
```

7. A more secure method is to require a username and password combination. Return to configuration mode and configure local authentication on the console:

```
PodP(config)#line con 0
PodP(config)#login local
```

8. Exit out of the AP and log back in using the username password combination configured in Step 1:

```
User Access Verification
Username:
Password:
ap>
```

Step 3: Configuring Accurate Time

To keep track of any potential attacks, it is important to maintain proper time.

1. Configure the correct time. Use the help feature if you need to.

```
PodP#clock set
```

2. Set the correct time zone.

```
PodP(config)#clock timezone [name of time zone] [offset in hours]
```

Example:

```
PodP(config)#clock timezone PhoenixAZ -7
```

3. (Optional) Configure Daylight Savings time. Use the help feature or command reference, if needed.

```
PodP(config)#clock summer-time
```

4. Check the clock settings while in configuration mode.

```
PodP(config)#do show clock
```

Step 4: Configuring MOTD and Login Banner

1. Configure a message-of-the-day (MOTD). The MOTD banner appears on all connected terminals at login, and is useful for sending messages that affect all network users (such as impending system shutdowns).

```
PodP(config)#banner motd #
This is a secure site. Only authorized users are allowed.
For access, contact technical support.
#
PodP(config)#
```

2. Exit out of the console or Telnet session to check the MOTD.

```
con0 is now available
Press RETURN to get started.
This is a secure site. Only authorized users are allowed.
For access, contact technical support.
```

3. Configure a login banner. This banner appears after the MOTD banner and before the login prompt.

```
PodP(config)#banner login $
Access for authorized users only. Please enter your username and password.
$
PodP(config)#
```

4. Exit out of the console to check the banner.

```
con0 is now available
Press RETURN to get started.
This is a secure site. Only authorized users are allowed.
For access, contact technical support.
Access for authorized users only. Please enter your username and password.
User Access Verification
Username:
```

Step 5: Verifying the Image File

You can prevent many attacks by maintaining the most up-to-date image. To keep up with any vulnerabilities in Cisco products, go to the following site:

http://www.cisco.com/en/US/products/hw/vpndevc/ps2284/products_tech_note 09186a0080132a8a.shtml

1. Are there any wireless vulnerabilities listed? If so, what are they?

_____

_____

_____

2. Check the current image.

```
PodP#show version
```

3. What version is running?

_____

4. Does this access point have any known vulnerabilities?

_____

Step 6: Configuring SSH

In some circumstances, attackers might be able to use a packet analyzer to intercept Telnet passwords, which might enable them to gain access to the AP or other networking devices. The SSH protocol is a secure form of Telnet, providing both authentication and encryption.

1. Generate the asymmetric keys used in the SSH authentication process.

   a. Generate RSA keys.

Enter the following command in the configuration mode:

```
PodP(config)#crypto key generate rsa ?
```

What are the available help options for this command?

---

b.   Generate RSA keys (continued).

To enable SSH for local and remote authentication on the AP, enter the command **crypto key generate rsa** and press **Enter**. The AP responds with a message showing the naming convention for the keys.

What is the default size, in bits, of the key modulus?

---

2.   Press **Enter** to accept the default key size and continue.

Step 7: Configuring SSH Timeouts

Configuring SSH timeouts and authentication retries is a way of providing additional security for the connection. Use the command ip ssh {[time-out *seconds*]} {authentication-retries *integer*} to enable timeouts and authentication retries. Set the SSH timeout to 15 seconds and the amount of retries to 3 by entering the following commands:

```
PodP(config)#ip ssh time-out 15
PodP(config)#ip ssh authentication-retries 3
```

What is the maximum timeout value allowed? What is the maximum amount of authentication retries allowed?

Step 8: Configuring Local Authentication and VTY

Use the following commands to define a local user and assign SSH communication to the vty lines:

```
PodP(config)# username cisco password student
PodP(config)# line vty 0 4
PodP(config-line)# transport input ssh
PodP(config-line)# login local
```

What are the available parameters for the transport input command?

Step 9: Establishing Communication Between an SSH PC (Client) to AP (Server)

The basic settings to allow a PC and an AP to establish an SSH session are now configured. To establish an SSH session, launch the SSH client from the student PC.

1. The configurations vary amongst the different SSH clients. If PuTTY is being used as the SSH client, following these instructions. Launch the PuTTY.exe file, and a pane with various configuration options opens, as shown in Figure 8-13.

Figure 8-13   PuTTY Configuration

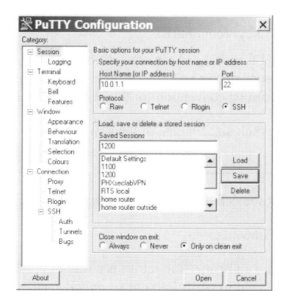

2. In the **Host Name (or IP address)** input box, enter the IP address of the pod AP. Next, change the protocol to **SSH**. These two values must be sent to establish the SSH. To test the connection, press the **Open** command button at the bottom of the window.

3. The SSH client prompts for the local username and password that was previously set on the Pod AP. Enter **cisco** for the username and **student** for the password, as shown in Figure 8-14.

Figure 8-14   Enter Username and Password

Was the SSH connection successful? If so, how is the prompt displayed?

Step 10: Debugging and Verifying SSH

1.   Enable debugging of SSH by entering the following commands:

```
PodP(config)#logging on
PodP(config)#logging console
PodP#debug ip ssh
```

2.   View SSH debug output.

     a.   Open another instance of the SSH client and connect to the AP. Use the correct username and password to log in to the AP. The debug output should be similar to the following output:

```
03:45:37: SSH1: starting SSH control process
03:45:37: SSH1: sent protocol version id SSH-1.5-Cisco-1.25
03:45:37: SSH1: protocol version id is - SSH-1.5-PuTTY-Release-0.53b
03:45:37: SSH1: SSH_SMSG_PUBLIC_KEY msg
03:45:38: SSH1: SSH_CMSG_SESSION_KEY msg - length 112, type 0x03
03:45:38: SSH: RSA decrypt started
03:45:39: SSH: RSA decrypt finished
03:45:39: SSH: RSA decrypt started
03:45:39: SSH: RSA decrypt finished
03:45:39: SSH1: sending encryption confirmation
03:45:39: SSH1: keys exchanged and encryption on
03:45:41: SSH1: SSH_CMSG_USER message received
03:45:41: SSH1: authentication request for userid cisco
03:45:41: SSH1: SSH_SMSG_FAILURE message sent
03:45:44: SSH1: SSH_CMSG_AUTH_PASSWORD message received
03:45:44: SSH1: authentication successful for cisco
03:45:44: SSH1: requesting TTY
03:45:44: SSH1: setting TTY - requested: length 24, width 80; set: length 24, width 80
03:45:44: SSH1: SSH_CMSG_EXEC_SHELL message received
03:45:44: SSH1: starting shell for vty03:45:37: SSH1: starting SSH control process
```

     b.   To get an idea of the debugging process and the debugging message, open another instance of the SSH client and intentionally enter the wrong username or password. View the debugging output for failed authentication.

     c.   Disable debugging.

```
PodP#undebug all
All possible debugging has been turned off
```

3.   View SSH session.

     a.   Use the **show ssh** command to view the active SSH sessions.

     b.   Fill in the appropriate values in Table 8-5, based on the output of the **show ssh** command.

Table 8-5   SSH Session Values as Determined by *show ssh* **Command Output**

Connection	Version	Encryption	State	Username

4.   View SSH parameters.

To display the version information and SSH parameters, use the **show ip ssh** command.

Is the output displayed exactly as the output below? If not, what are the differences?

```
PodP>show ip ssh
SSH Enabled - version 1.5
Authentication timeout: 15 secs; Authentication retries: 3
```

_____

_____

_____

Step 11: AP to AP SSH Connection (Optional)

1.   Confirm peer SSH configurations.

    a.   Verbally communicate with the peer team to ensure the peer AP has been configured to accept an SSH connection. Instead of using an SSH client running on a host computer, the AP is the SSH client and establishes a connection to the peer AP. By default, Cisco IOS software acts as both an SSH server and SSH client.

    b.   To communicate between the two APs across the wired LAN, the BVI interfaces has to be on the same subnet. This can be accomplished by changing the masks to 255.255.0.0 on both AP BVI interfaces. One other option is to use a router between the two APs, which routes between the two subnets.

2.   Test Telnet.

When the peer group is ready, enter the **telnet** command and establish connectivity with the peer AP:

```
PodP#telnet 10.0.Q.1   (where Q is the peer team AP)
```

Was the Telnet connection successful? Why or why not?

_____

3.   View SSH parameters.

Enter the following command to establish an SSH connection to the peer AP:

```
PodP(config)#ssh ?
```

    a.   What are the additional arguments of the **ssh** command?

_____

    b.   What encryption algorithms are available?

_____

4.   Establish an AP-to-AP SSH connection.

Enter the following command to establish an SSH connection to the peer AP:

```
PodP>ssh -c des -l cisco 10.0.Q.1    (where Q is the peer team AP)
```

This command makes an SSH connection to a peer AP with an address of 10.0.Q.2, DES as the encryption, and **cisco** as the login username.

Was the SSH connection successful?

_____

5.   Verify SSH.

Enter the following command to verify the SSH connection:

```
PodP#show ip ssh
PodP#show ssh
```

What other commands could be useful to verify and troubleshoot SSH connections?

_____

_____

Step 12: Disabling Web (Optional)

Many security policies might mandate that HTTP access to devices be disabled. If HTTPS is not available, SSH is the second best option for secure communication to remote LAN devices.

1.   Now that SSH is configured, disable web access to the AP:

```
PodP(config)#
PodP(config)#no ip http server
```

2.   Open a web browser and try to connect to the AP. Is this possible?

_____

3.   If the configuration was saved to Flash memory, erase the startup configuration and reload the AP.

```
PodP#erase startup-config
PodP#reload
```

Lab 8.3.2: Configure Filters on AP

Estimated Time: 25 minutes

Number of Team Members: Students work in teams of two

Objectives

In this lab, the students learn how to set and enable a protocol filter on the access point, and how to set and enable filters on AP.

Scenario

Protocol filters prevent or allow the use of specific protocols through the AP. Individual protocol filters or sets of filters can be set up for either the Radio or Ethernet ports. Protocols can be filtered for wireless client devices, users on the wired LAN, or both.

MAC address filters allow or disallow the forwarding of unicast and multicast packets either sent from, or addressed to, specific MAC addresses. A filter can be created that passes traffic to all MAC addresses except those that are specified. A filter can also be created that blocks traffic to all MAC addresses except those that are specified.

Topology

Figure 8-15 shows the topology used in this lab.

Figure 8-15   Lab Topology

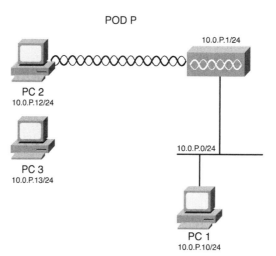

Note: The topology figures and lab examples contain **P** values. The **P** value in the addressing and naming scheme refers to *your* assigned Pod number.

The following are examples of determining **P** values:

- Pod2 is looking at a topology figure and is trying to determine the **P** values in the figure. In this scenario, the **P** values equal **2**. 10.0.**P**.12 becomes 10.0.**2**.12, 172.30.**P**.2 becomes 172.30.**2**.2, and so on.

- Pod1 is looking at a topology figure and is trying to determine the **P** values in the figure. In this scenario, the **P** values equal **1**. 10.0.**P**.12 becomes 10.0.**1**.12, 172.30.**P**.2 becomes 172.30.**1**.2, and so on.

In both examples, the **P** values are directly related to the Pod number of the team.

Preparation

The student should read and understand the concepts presented in Chapter 8 from the *Fundamentals of Wireless LANs Companion Guide* prior to the lab.

The access points and PC client adapter and utility should be installed and properly configured prior to the lab. The students should also familiarize themselves with the various EtherType, IP, and port filters available on the access point.

Tools and Resources

Each team of students requires the following equipment to complete this lab:

- Cisco Aironet access point

- 1 wired PC or laptop

- 2 wireless PCs with ACU

Step 1: Verifying the Network Setup and Connectivity

1. Make sure the topology is cabled and configured according to Figure 8-15.

2. Verify the SSID is configured.

3. Verify both PC2 and PC3 are associated and TCP/IP is configured.

4. Verify both PC2 and PC3 can ping the AP at 10.0.P.1.

Step 2: Creating a MAC Address Filter

Follow this path to reach the Address Filters page:

1. Click **Services** in the page navigation bar.

2. In the Services page list, click **Filters**.

3.   On the Apply Filters page, click the **MAC Address Filters** tab at the top of the page.

4.   Make sure **<NEW>** (the default) is selected in the Create/Edit Filter Index menu, as shown in Figure 8-16.

Figure 8-16   MAC Address Filters Page

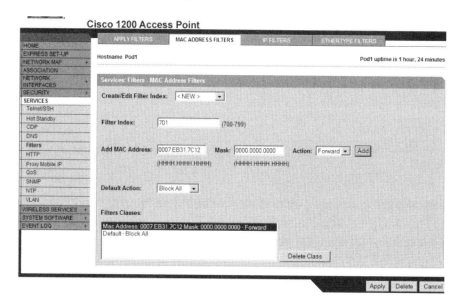

5.   In the Filter Index field, name the filter with a number from 700-799. 701 is used in this example.

6.   Enter a MAC address wireless PC2 in the Add MAC Address field. Enter the address with periods separating the three groups of four characters (0007.50CA.E208, for example).

7.   Select **Permit All** from the Action menu.

8.   Click **Add**. The MAC address appears in the Filters Classes field.

9.   Repeat Steps 1 through 8 to add addresses to the filter.

10. Click **Apply**. The filter is saved on the AP, but it is not enabled until it is applied on the Apply Filters page.

Step 3: Applying the MAC Address Filter

1.   From the **Services > Filters** Page, go to the Apply Filters tab, as shown in Figure 8-17.

2.   Select the filter number 701 from the Radio0-802.11B MAC drop-down menu. Apply the filter to incoming and outgoing packets.

3.   Click **Apply**. The filter is enabled on the selected ports.

Figure 8-17   Apply Filters Tab

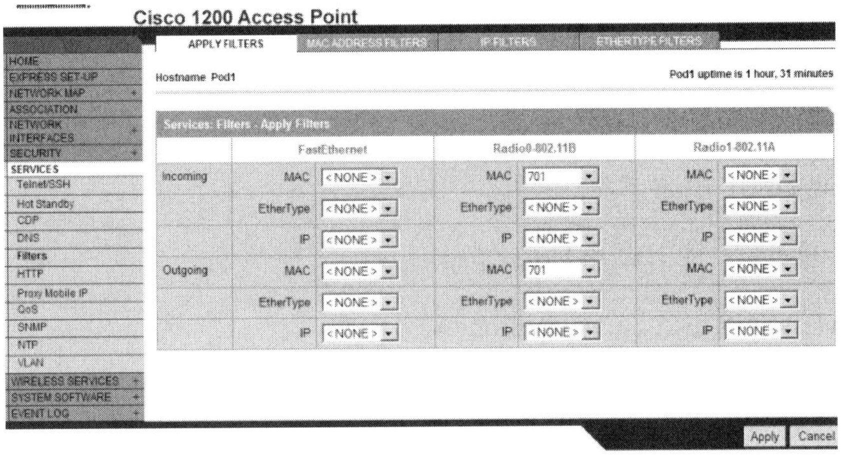

Note: Client devices with blocked MAC addresses cannot send or receive data through the access point, but they might remain in the Association Table as unauthenticated client devices. Client devices with blocked MAC addresses disappear from the Association Table when the access point stops monitoring them, when the access point reboots, or when the clients associate with another access point.

Step 4: Testing the MAC Address Filter

When applying any security, it is important to test the configuration.

1.   From PC 3, located at 10.0.P.13, ping the AP at 10.0.P.1.

   Was this successful? Should it be successful?

   _____

   _____

2.   From PC 2, located at 10.0.P.12, ping the AP at 10.0.P.1

   Was this successful? Should it be successful?

   _____

   _____

Step 5: Removing the MAC Address Filter

Before configuring any IP Filters, delete the existing MAC filter.

1.   From the **Services>Filters** page, shown previously in Figure 8-17, change the 701 to **<NONE>** on both Incoming and Outgoing.

2.   Click **Apply**.

3.   From PC 2 and PC 3, ping the AP at 10.0.P.1.

      Was this successful? Should it be successful?

_____

_____

Step 6: Creating an IP Filter

Follow this link path to reach the IP Filters page:

1.   Click **Services** in the page navigation bar.

2.   In the Services page list, click **Filters**.

3.   On the **Apply Filters** page, click the **IP Filters** tab at the top of the page, as shown in Figure 8-18.

Figure 8-18   IP Filters Tab

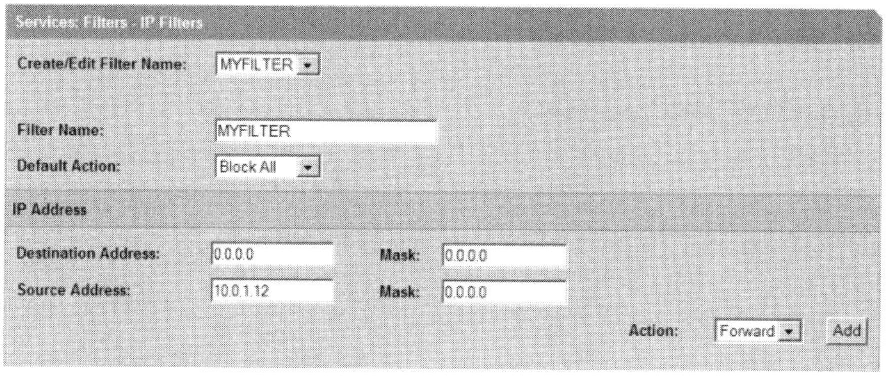

4.   Make sure **<NEW>** (the default) is selected in the Create/Edit Filter Index menu.

5.   Enter a descriptive name of **MYFILTER** for the new filter in the Filter Name field.

6.   Select **Block All** as the filter's default action from the Default Action menu.

7.   Add 10.0.P.12 (where P is the Pod number) as the IP address to the Source address field with a 0.0.0.0 mask to permit PC2 traffic.

8.   Verify the configuration in the Filters Classes box, as shown in Figure 8-19.

9.   If the configuration is correct, click **Apply**.

Figure 8-19   Filters Classes Box

Step 7: Applying the IP Filter

1.   Select the **MYFILTER** from the radio ports incoming and outgoing packets, as shown in Figure 8-20.

Figure 8-20   Select MYFILTER

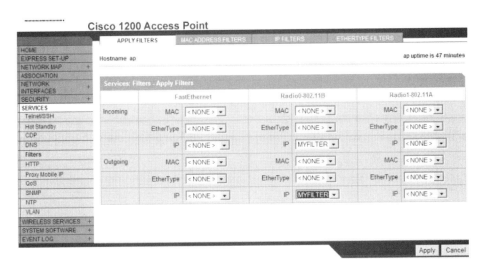

2.   Click **Apply**. The filter is enabled on the selected ports.

Step 8: Testing the IP Filter

When applying any security, it is important to test the configuration.

1.   From PC 3, located at 10.0.P.13, ping the AP at 10.0.P.1 (where P is the Pod number).

Was this successful? Should it be successful?

_____

_____

2.   From PC 2, located at 10.0.P.12, ping the AP at 10.0.P.1 (where P is the Pod number)

Was this successful? Should it be successful?

_____

_____

3.   List three of the EtherType filters that can be used.

_____

_____

_____

4.   List three of the IP filters that can be used.

_____

_____

_____

5.   List three of the port filters that can be used.

_____

_____

_____

Lab 8.3.3.1: Configure WEP on AP and Client

Estimated Time: 20 minutes

Number of Team Members: Students work in teams of two

Objectives

In this lab, students demonstrate an understanding of the role of a Wired Equivalent Privacy (WEP) key in network security. Additionally, students learn how to enable WEP on an AP and on the client PC.

Scenario

The purpose of WEP is to protect the privacy of transmitted data. WEP keys encrypt the data signals the access point transmits and to decrypt the data signals the access point receives (and includes data transmitted and received by the client).

Topology

Figure 8-21 shows the topology used in this lab.

Figure 8-21   Lab Topology

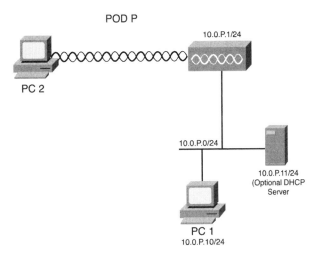

Note: The topology figures and lab examples contain **P** values. The **P** value in the addressing and naming scheme refers to *your* assigned Pod number.

The following are examples of determining **P** values:

- Pod2 is looking at a topology figure and is trying to determine the **P** values in the figure. In this scenario, the **P** values equal **2**. 10.0.**P**.12 becomes 10.0.**2**.12, 172.30.**P**.2 becomes 172.30.**2**.2, and so on.

- Pod1 is looking at a topology figure and is trying to determine the **P** values in the figure. In this scenario, the **P** values equal **1**. 10.0.**P**.12 becomes 10.0.**1**.12, 172.30.**P**.2 becomes 172.30.**1**.2, and so on.

In both examples, the **P** values are directly related to the Pod number of the team.

Preparation

The students should read and understand Chapter 8 from the *Fundamentals of Wireless LANs Companion Guide* prior to the lab.

All access points and PCs are properly set up according to the topology prior to the lab. Ensure an existing wireless connection is present from PC2 to the AP.

Tools and Resources

Each team of students requires the following equipment to complete this lab:

- Cisco Aironet access points

- PCs with the Cisco Aironet client adapter and utility properly installed

Step 1: Configuring WEP on the Access Point

To configure WEP on the access point, complete the following steps:

1. Verify connectivity from the wireless client (PC2) to the AP.

2. Open a web browser on the PC1 and type the IP address of the access point to configure in the browser address bar.

3. Go to the **Security** Setup page of the access point, as shown in Figure 8-22, and click the **Encryption Manager** option to display the Encryption Manager Page, shown in Figure 8-23.

Figure 8-22   Security Setup Page

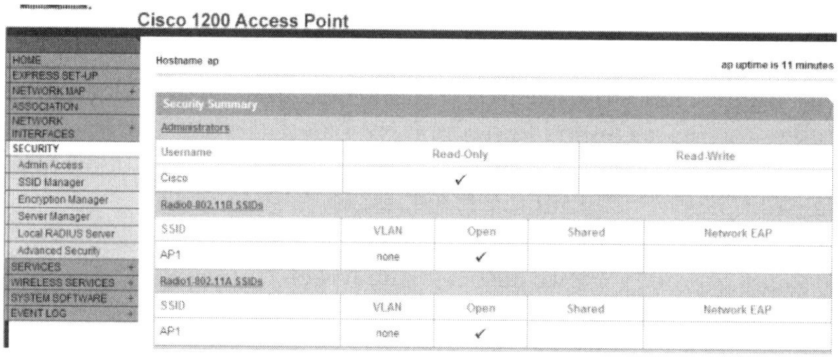

Figure 8-23   Encryption Manager Page

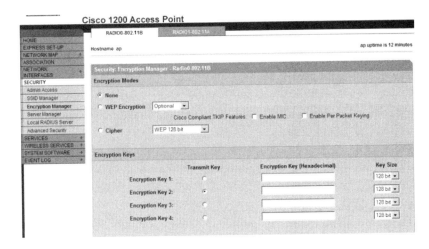

Step 2: Configuring WEP (Continued)

WEP keys can be entered in ASCII or hexadecimal on most equipment. Cisco Aironet equipment requires WEP keys to be entered in hexadecimal. 40-bit WEP keys are 10 hexadecimal characters long. 128-bit WEP keys are 26 hexadecimal characters long. To configure WEP, follow the steps below:

1.   Check the radio button WEP Encryption Mode for WEP Encryption.

2.   Use the pull down Menu to select **Mandatory.**

3.   Select the **Transmit Key**.

4.   Enter the **Encryption Key** (for lab purposes, this is **12345678909876543210123456)**

5.   Select the **Key Size** to be **128 bit.**

6.   Click the **Apply-All** button to apply these options.

7.   After WEP is configured on the access point with a **Mandatory** option, all the clients become disassociated to this access point.

Step 3: Verifying the WEP Configuration

View the **Security > Encryption Manager** page, shown in Figure 8-24. The WEP settings should be configured, and the Encryption Key field should be stored in the access point. However, the Encryption Key field should be encrypted with asterisk symbols to prevent unauthorized users from viewing the Encryption Key.

Figure 8-24   Encryption Manager Page

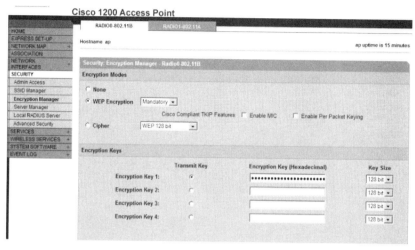

1.   What is the advantage of using hexadecimal versus decimal digits?

_____

2.   Are the letters in the Encryption Key field case sensitive?

_____
_____
_____

3.   What encryption option allows client devices that can communicate with the access point either with or without WEP?

_____

Step 4: Configuring WEP on PC2 Using the Client Adapter Utility

To configure the WEP settings on the wireless client adapter, complete the following steps:

1.   Open the Aironet client utility by clicking on the **ACU** icon.

2.   Click **Profile Manager** to edit the WEP settings.

3.   Under the Profile Management section, choose the profile being used for this lab, and click **Edit**.

4.   Go to the **Network Security** tab of the profile that is being used for the lab, as shown in Figure 8-25.

Figure 8-25   Network Security Tab

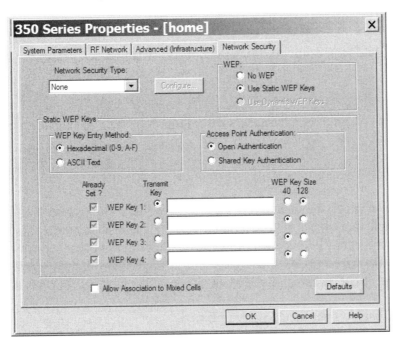

5.   Configure the following settings for WEP:

• Select the WEP setting: Use Static WEP keys

• Select the Static WEP key entry method: Hexadecimal

• Select the Access Point Authentication: Open authentication

• Select and enter the Transmit key (for lab purposes, this is 1234567890987654321 0123456).

• Select the WEP key Size: 128 bits

• Click the **OK** button to apply the WEP settings to the client.

• The client should reassociate to the access point after WEP is enabled properly on the access point and the client adapter utility.

a.   How many WEP keys can be stored on the Cisco client adapter?

_____

b.   What happens if a device receives a packet that is not encrypted with the appropriate key?

_____

c.   What is the more secure authentication method, shared key or open?

_____

Lab 8.3.3.2: Configure an AP as a Repeater Using WEP

Estimated Time: 30 minutes

Number of Team Members: Students work in teams of two

Objectives

Students extend the coverage of a basic service set topology by implementing an access point as a repeater using WEP.

Scenario

You can configure an access point as a repeater to extend the wireless infrastructure range or to overcome an obstacle that blocks radio communication. The repeater forwards traffic between wireless users and the wired LAN by sending packets to either another repeater or to an access point connected to the wired LAN. The data is sent through the route that provides the best performance for the client. In this lab, the Root AP is Pod1. The repeater AP is Pod2.

WEP must now be enabled per the security policy.

Topology

Figure 8-26 shows the topology used in this lab.

Figure 8-26   Lab Topology

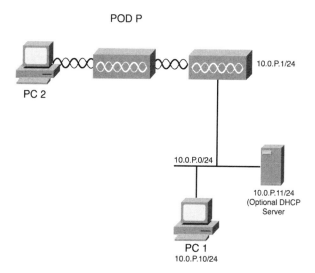

Note: The topology figures and lab examples contain **P** values. The **P** value in the addressing and naming scheme refers to *your* assigned Pod number.

The following are examples of determining **P** values:

- Pod2 is looking at a topology figure and is trying to determine the **P** values in the figure. In this scenario, the **P** values equal **2**. 10.0.**P**.12 becomes 10.0.**2**.12, 172.30.**P**.2 becomes 172.30.**2**.2, and so on.

- Pod1 is looking at a topology figure and is trying to determine the **P** values in the figure. In this scenario, the **P** values equal **1**. 10.0.**P**.12 becomes 10.0.**1**.12, 172.30.**P**.2 becomes 172.30.**1**.2, and so on.

In both examples, the **P** values are directly related to the Pod number of the team.

Preparation

The instructor should have a working wired network. PC1 should be connected to the wired network. Table 8-6 lists the settings for the APs in this lab.

Table 8-6 Lab AP Settings

Team	Access Point Name	SSID	Address
1	Pod1 (root)	AP1	10.0.1.1/24
2	Pod2 (repeater)	AP1	10.0.1.2/24

Tools and Resources

Each team needs the following equipment to complete this lab:

- 2 access points

- A PC or laptop

- Console cable

Additional Materials

Consult the following URLs for more information concerning the topics covered in this lab:

http://www.cisco.com/en/US/products/hw/wireless/ps430/products_installation_and_configuration_guide_book09186a0080147d69.html

Step 1: Configuring the Repeater AP

1. Make sure the first AP is configured and operational and clients can connect to the AP1. Pod1 is the root AP and should have an SSID of "AP1". Pod2 becomes the repeater AP. The repeater AP does not require any Ethernet cables when configured in repeater mode.

2.   Enter global configuration mode. Enter interface configuration mode for the radio. The 5-GHz radio is radio 1. Turn the interface off.

```
Pod2(config)#interface dot11Radio 1
Pod2(config-if)#shutdown
```

3.   Enter interface configuration mode for the 2.4-GHz radio.

```
Pod2(config)#interface dot11Radio 0
Pod2(config-if)#
```

4.   Create the SSID that the repeater uses to associate to a root access point; in the next step, designate this SSID as an infrastructure SSID. If you created an infrastructure SSID on the root access point, create the same SSID on the repeater.

```
Pod2(config-if)#ssid AP1
Pod2(config-if-ssid)#
```

5.   Designate the SSID as an infrastructure SSID. The repeater uses this SSID to associate to the root access point. Infrastructure devices must associate to the repeater access point using this SSID unless you also enter the **optional** keyword at the end of the command.

```
Pod2(config-if-ssid)#infrastructure-ssid
Pod2(config-if-ssid)#
*Mar  1 01:12:54.406: %LINK-5-CHANGED: Interface Dot11Radio0, changed state to reset
*Mar  1 01:12:54.424: %LINK-3-UPDOWN: Interface Dot11Radio0, changed state to up
Pod2(config-if-ssid)#
```

6.   Exit SSID configuration mode and return to radio interface configuration mode.

```
Pod2(config-if-ssid)#exit
Pod2(config-if)#
```

7.   Set the access point's role in the wireless LAN to repeater.

```
Pod2(config-if)#station-role repeater
```

8.   If Aironet extensions are disabled, enable Aironet extensions.

```
Pod2(config-if)#dot11 extension aironet
```

9.   MAC addresses can be entered for up to four parent access points. The repeater attempts to associate to MAC address 1 first; if that access point does not respond, the repeater tries the next access point in its parent list. (Optional) Enter the MAC address for the access point to which the repeater should associate.

```
Pod2(config-if)#parent 1 0987.1234.e345
```

(This should be the MAC address of Pod1 11.b radio.)

10.   Verify the configuration.

```
Pod2#show run
interface Dot11Radio0
 no ip address
 no ip route-cache
 !
 ssid AP1
    authentication open
    infrastructure-ssid
 !
 parent 1 0987.1234.e345
 speed basic-1.0 basic-2.0 basic-5.5 basic-11.0
 rts threshold 2312
 station-role repeater
```

Step 2: Verifying Connections on Pod1

After the repeater is set up, check the LEDs on top of the repeater AP. If the repeater is functioning correctly, the LEDs on the repeater and the root access point to which it is associated behave like this:

- The status LED on the root access point is steady green, indicating that at least one client device is associated with it (in this case, the repeater).

- The status LED on the repeater access point is steady green when it is associated with the root access point and the repeater has client devices associated to it. The repeater's status LED flashes (steady green for 7/8 of a second and off for 1/8 of a second) when it is associated with the root access point but the repeater has no client devices associated to it.

- The repeater access point should also appear as associated with the root access point in the root access point's Association Table. On Pod1, verify that Pod2 is connected. Other wireless clients may also be associated.

Now check the detailed status of all clients:

```
Pod1#show dot11 associations all-clients
```

Step 3: Verifying Connections on Pod2

1. Move the wireless laptop out of range of Pod1 into the range of Pod2.

2. On Pod2, verify that the laptop is associated. There may also be other wireless clients associated.

3. Check the detailed status of all clients.

    ```
    Pod2#show dot11 associations all-clients
    ```

    Is the laptop associated? What information can be used to verify the connection?

Step 4: Configuring WEP on the Root and Repeater AP

1. In interface mode, check that the available encryption can be set. Then view the available key sizes.

    ```
    Pod2(config-if)#encryption ?
      key    Set one encryption key
      mode   encryption mode
      vlan   vlan
    PodP(config-if)#encryption key 1 size ?
      128bit  128-bit key
      40bit   40-bit keyCreate a WEP key and set the key properties
    ```

2. Create a WEP key and set up its properties.

    ```
    PodP(config-if)#encryption key 1 size 128 12345678901234567890123456 transmit-key
    ```

Step 5: Verifying Connections on Pod1

1. After the WEP is set up, check the LEDs on top of the repeater AP for correct operation.

2. The repeater access point should also appear as associated with the root access point in the root access point's Association Table. On Pod1, verify that Pod2 is connected. There can also be other wireless clients associated.

3. Check the detailed status of all clients.

    ```
    Pod1#show dot11 associations all-clients
    ```

Step 6: Verifying Connections on Pod2

1. Move the wireless laptop out of range of Pod1 into the range of Pod2.

2. On Pod2, verify that the laptop is associated. There may also be other wireless clients associated.

3. Check the detailed status of all clients.

    ```
    Pod2#show dot11 associations all-clients
    ```

    Are any laptops associated? Why?

Step 7: Configuring the 802.11a Radio as a Repeater (Optional)

Erase the configuration on Pod2. Return to Step 1 and configure the repeater topology using the 801.11a radio instead. In this case, disable the 11b radio. Make sure Pod1 is configured to accept the 5-GHz clients.

Lab 8.4.5.1: Configuring LEAP/EAP Using Local RADIUS Authentication

Estimated Time: 40 minutes

Number of Team Members: Students work in teams of two

Objectives

In this lab, students learn about the second generation of WLAN security and how to implement LEAP on a WLAN for secure client authentication.

The main steps to this lab are as follows:

1. Configure AP WEP Key or Cipher.

2. Configure RADIUS Server.

3. Configure Local RADIUS Server.

4. Configure users.

5. Configure and verify LEAP/EAP authentication on the AP.

6. Configuring LEAP/EAP on the client (PC2) via ACU.

7. Monitor the connection, login, and authentication statistics.

Topology

Figure 8-27 shows the topology used in this lab.

Figure 8-27   Lab Topology

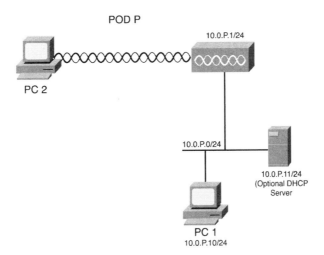

Note: The topology figures and lab examples contain **P** values. The **P** value in the addressing and naming scheme refers to *your* assigned Pod number.

Below are examples of determining **P** values:

* Pod2 is looking at a topology figure and is trying to determine the **P** values in the figure. In this scenario, the **P** values equal **2**. 10.0.**P**.12 becomes 10.0.**2**.12, 172.30.**P**.2 becomes 172.30.**2**.2, and so on.

* Pod1 is looking at a topology figure and is trying to determine the **P** values in the figure. In this scenario, the **P** values equal **1**. 10.0.**P**.12 becomes 10.0.**1**.12, 172.30.**P**.2 becomes 172.30.**1**.2, and so on.

In both examples, the **P** values are directly related to the Pod number of the team.

Scenario

One way to secure wireless LANs and improve network security is to use authentication for accessing the access point. Wireless clients can use Extensible Authentication Protocol (EAP) to authenticate to a wireless LAN. 802.1x local RADIUS authentication is available on the 1100 and 1200 APs. This allows LEAP/EAP to be used without requiring a Cisco Secure ACS Server. Furthermore, this feature provides a backup for ACS servers in an Enterprise network.

Preparation

Prior to this lab, the Cisco Aironet Access Point should be configured to allow clients to associate. The IP address, host name, and SSID should be configured on the AP. A PC should be installed with a Cisco Aironet Client Card, and it should already be associated to the access point.

Cable the equipment according to the Topology.

Update the Aironet Client Utility to version 6.0 or later.

Tools and Resources

Each team of students requires the following equipment to complete this lab:

* Cisco Aironet access point

* Hub or switch

* A wireless PC, laptop, or handheld (PC2) with a Cisco Aironet Client Adapter Card and utility properly installed and configured

* One wired PC (PC1)

Step 1: Configuring the AP WEP Keys or Cipher

1. To enable Cisco LEAP on the access point, WEP Encryption or a Cipher must be enabled.

2. From the **Security > Encryption Manager** page of the AP, shown in Figure 8-28, configure Encryption Key 1.

Figure 8-28   Encryption Manager Page

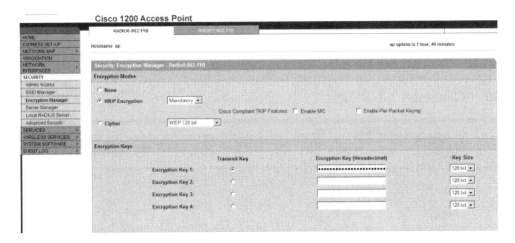

3. Click the WEP Encryption radio button and select **Mandatory**.

4. Click **Apply-All**.

   The **Cipher** option can be used for greater security. What options are available?

   _____

   _____

   _____

Step 2: Configuring RADIUS Server

Complete the following steps to configure the Backup RADIUS server from the **Security>Server Manager** page, shown in Figure 8-29.

Figure 8-29   Server Manager Page

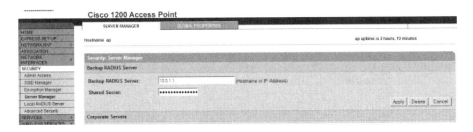

1. Enter the IP address of the Local RADIUS server in the Server Name/IP entry field. This is the IP address of the AP where the local RADIUS database is running (this should be 10.0.P.1, where P is the Pod number).

2. Enter the Shared Secret key of **secretkey**.

3. Click **Apply**.

Step 3: Configuring Local RADIUS Server

Complete the following steps to configure a Local RADIUS server from the **Security > Local RADIUS Server** page:

1. Click the **General Set-Up** tab to display the screen shown in Figure 8-30.

Figure 8-30   General Set-Up Page

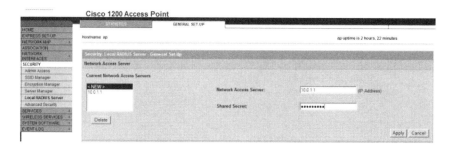

2. Enter the IP address of the Local RADIUS server in the Network Access Server entry field. This is the IP address of the AP where the local RADIUS database is running. This is 10.0.P.1 (where P is the Pod number).

3. Enter the Shared Secret key of **secretkey**.

4. Click **Apply**.

Step 4: Configuring Users

Complete the following steps to configure users from the **Security > Local RADIUS Server** page, shown in Figure 8-31:

Figure 8-31   Local RADIUS Server Page: Individual User Portion

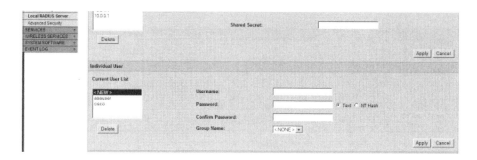

1.   Continue from the **General Set-Up** tab.

2.   Enter the users listed in Table 8-7.

Table 8-7   Individual Users for Local RADIUS Server

User	Username	Password
1	aaauser	aaapass
2	Cisco1	ciscopass

3.   Click **Apply**.

Step 5: Configuring Authentication on AP

To enable Cisco LEAP on the access point, complete the following steps to configure the Authentication Method:

1.   On the **Security > SSID Manager** page of the access point, as shown in Figure 8-32, create a new SSID of AP**P** (where **P** is the Pod number).

Figure 8-32   SSID Manager

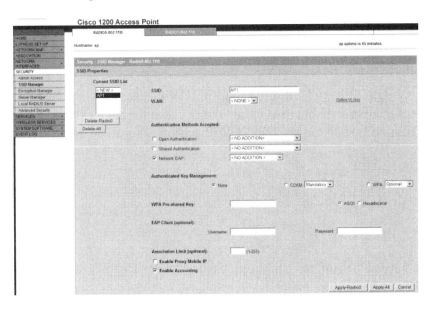

2.   Check the **Network EAP** box.

3.   Click the **Apply-All** button.

Step 6: Verifying the LEAP Configuration

From the **Security** Home page of the AP, shown in Figure 8-33, verify that Network EAP is checked and the only SSID is AP**P** (where **P** is the Pod number). The default, tsunami SSID, should be deleted for security. Also, verify the server-based security is configured correctly.

Figure 8-33   Security Summary

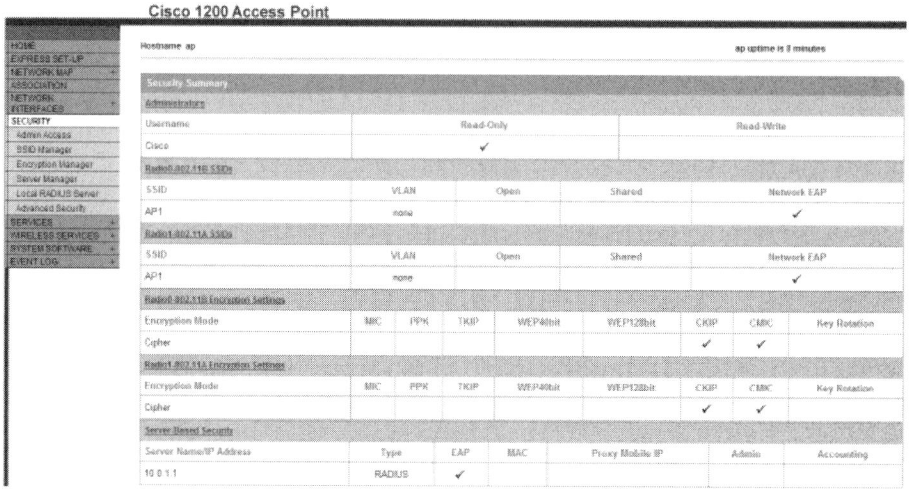

Step 7: Configuring LEAP on the ACU

To enable the EAP in the Aironet Client Utility, complete the following steps:

1.   On PC2, configure the TCP/IP settings for the **Wireless Network Connection** if a DHCP server is not available. Otherwise, when the client authenticates, the wireless PC will not be able to communicate via IP. The TCP/IP settings should be as follows:

   - IP address of 10.0.P.12

   - Subnet mask of 255.255.255.0

   - Gateway of 10.0.P.254

2.   Go to the **Network Security** tab in the Aironet Client Utility on PC2, as shown in Figure 8-34, and each of the wireless client computers.

3.   Select **LEAP** from the **Network Security Type:** drop-down list, and click **Configure**.

Figure 8-34   Network Security Tab

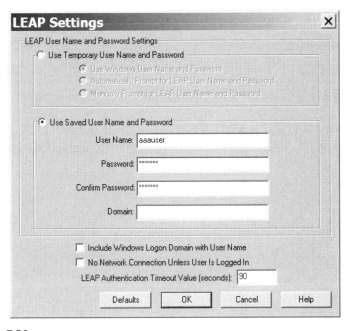

4.   Click **Use Saved User Name and Password** to result in the dialog box shown in Figure 8-35.

    a.   Enter **aaauser** for the **User Name.**

    b.   Enter **aaapass** for the **Password.**

    c.   Enter **aaapass** for the **Confirm Password.**

    d.   Uncheck the two checkboxes at the bottom of the LEAP Settings window.

Figure 8-35   LEAP Settings Window

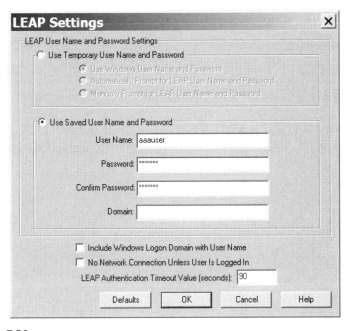

    e.   Click **OK**.

5. In the profile manager, select the profile that LEAP is configured on and click **OK**. If a save username and password was not configured, an authentication screen should come up asking for a user ID and password. Type in the following:

    a. The username for authentication is **aaauser**.
    b. The password for authentication is **aaapass**.

6. The ACM icon should change to green after the authentication is complete.

7. From PC1, PC2 or the ACS server, browse to the AP **Association** page to verify the connection.

    What are the three authentication states?

    _____

    _____

    _____

Step 8: Verifying the Wireless Connection

1. From the **Association** page of the AP, shown in Figure 8-36, verify the association state in the State column. This should display all the connected clients.

Figure 8-36   Association Page

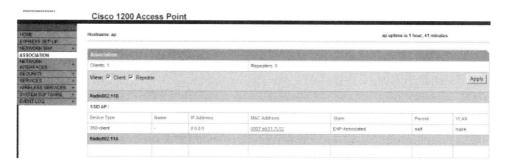

2. From the **Event Log** page of the AP, check the association logs.

3. From the **Security > Local RADIUS Server** page of the AP, click the **Statistics** tab, shown in Figure 8-37. Verify the User Information for authentication successes, failures, and blocks.

Figure 8-37   Local RADIUS Server Statistics Page

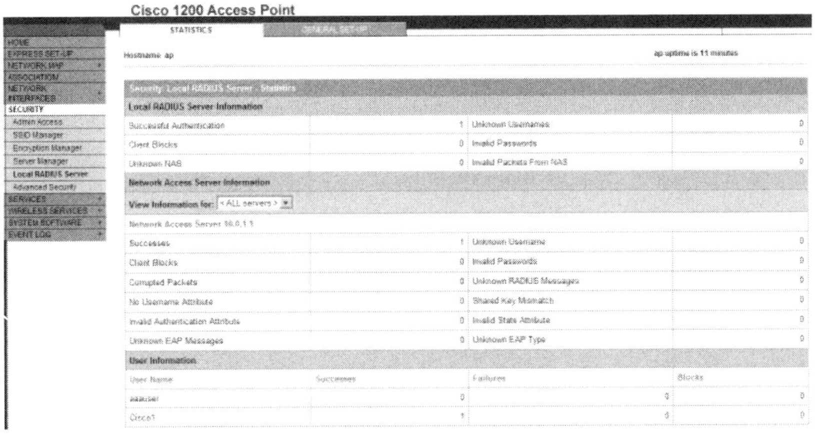

Lab 8.4.5.2: Configuring LEAP/EAP Using Cisco Secure ACS (Optional)

Estimated Time: 60 minutes

Number of Team Members: Students can work in teams of two

Objectives

In this lab, students learn about the second generation of WLAN security and how to implement LEAP on a WLAN for secure client authentication using Cisco Secure ACS.

Topology

Figure 8-38 shows the topology used in this lab.

Figure 8-38   Lab Topology

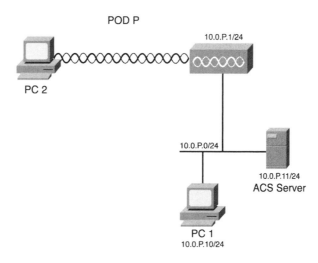

The topology figures and lab examples contain **P** values. The **P** value in the addressing and naming scheme refers to *your* assigned Pod number.

The following are examples of determining **P** values:

- Pod2 is looking at a topology figure and is trying to determine the **P** values in the figure. In this scenario, the **P** values equal **2**. 10.0.**P**.12 becomes 10.0.**2**.12, 172.30.**P**.2 becomes 172.30.**2**.2, and so on.

- Pod1 is looking at a topology figure and is trying to determine the **P** values in the figure. In this scenario, the **P** values would equal **1**. 10.0.**P**.12 becomes 10.0.**1**.12, 172.30.**P**.2 becomes 172.30.**1**.2, and so on.

In both examples, the **P** values are directly related to the Pod number of the team.

Scenario

One way to secure wireless LANs and improve network security is to use authentication for accessing the access point. Wireless clients can use EAP to authenticate though a wireless LAN. EAP can authenticate through digital certificates, such as public key infrastructure (PKI) or passwords and usernames. EAP can pass authentication information onto an authentication, authorization, and accounting (AAA) RADIUS server, such as a Cisco Access Control Server (ACS).

The Network Authentication Process can be summarized in four main stages:

1. The client adapter uses the username and password to start the authentication process.

2. The access point communicates with the EAP-compliant RADIUS server to authenticate the username and password.

3. If the username and password are valid, the RADIUS server and the client adapter negotiate a dynamic, session-based WEP key. The key, which is unique for the authenticated client, provides the client with secure network access.

4. The client and access point use the WEP key for all data transmissions during the session.

Preparation

Prior to this lab, the Cisco Aironet access point should be configured to allow clients to associate. The IP address, host name, and SSID should be configured on the AP. A PC should be installed with a Cisco Aironet Client Card, and it should already be associated to the access point.

Cable the equipment according to the network topology diagram shown in Figure 8-38.

A Windows 2000 Server running ACS 2.6 or above must be available.

The Aironet Client Utility must be updated to version 6.0 or later.

Tools and Resources

Each team of students requires the following equipment and software to complete this lab:

- Cisco Aironet access point

- Hub or switch

- A wireless PC, laptop, or handheld (PC2) with a Cisco Aironet Client Adapter Card and utility properly installed and configured

- Windows 2000 Server running Cisco Secure ACS 2.6 or above (an evaluation copy of Cisco Secure ACS can be downloaded from the following link: http://www.cisco.com/ cgi-bin/tablebuild.pl/acs-win-3des)

- One wired PC (PC1)

Step 1: Adding a AAA Client

Follow these steps to include the AP as a **AAA Client** in Cisco Secure ACS:

1. After properly loading the TACACS software on the Windows Server computer, on the ACS main menu, click **Network Configuration**.

2. Click **Add New Access Server**, or it may display **Add Entry**, as shown in Figure 8-39.

Figure 8-39   Network Configuration Page

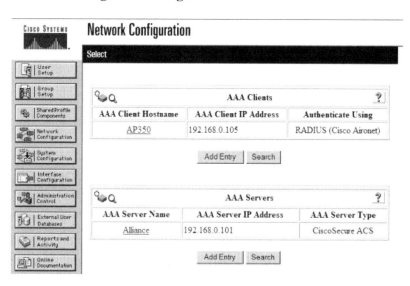

Step 2: Configuring AAA Client

1. In the **Network Access Server Hostname** box, type the system name of the access point. Enter **PodP** (where **P** is the Pod number).

2. In the **Network Access Server IP address** box, type the access point IP address. Enter **10.0.P.1** (where P is the Pod number).

3. In the **Key** box, type the shared secret that the AP and Cisco Secure ACS use to encrypt the data. For correct operation, the identical key, which is case sensitive, must be configured on the AP. For simplicity of the lab, use the word **secretkey**.

4. From the **Authenticate Using** list box, click the network security protocol. Select **RADIUS (Cisco Aironet)**, as shown in Figure 8-40.

Figure 8-40   Authenticate Using List Box

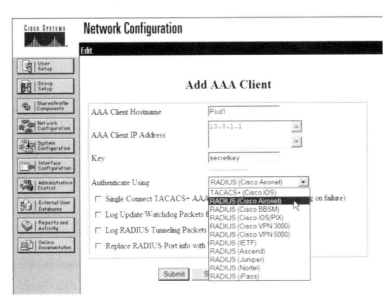

5.   Each access point in the class must be added to this list if it is using LEAP.

6.   Remote Access Services must be started on the RADIUS server for LEAP to work properly. To save the changes and apply them immediately, click the **Submit + Restart** button.

Note: It is important to click **Submit + Restart;** otherwise, the authentication will not work properly.

Step 3: Creating a User Account in the Access Control Server (ACS)

1.   Click the **User Setup** button located on the left side of the ACS Home page.

2.   Type the user name **aaauser** in the **User:** field box, as shown in Figure 8-41, and then click the **Add/Edit** button beneath this box.

3.   Type the user password **aaapass** in the **Password** box, and then type **aaapass** in the **Confirm Password** box, as shown in Figure 8-42.

4.   Click the **Submit** button to add this entry to the user list.

5.   Additional users can be added to this database list for each wireless PC client.

Figure 8-41   User Setup Page

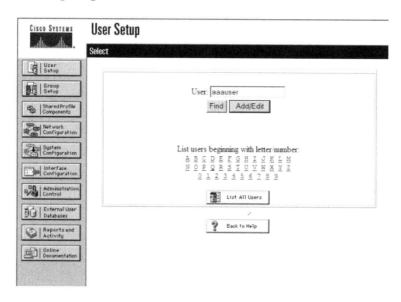

Figure 8-42   User Setup Page

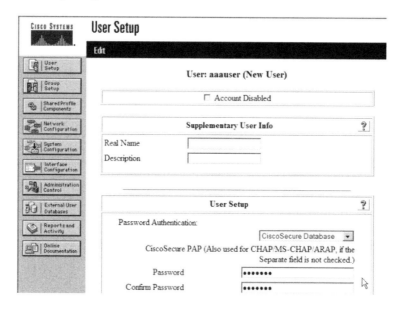

Step 4: Configuring the AP WEP Keys or Cipher

To enable Cisco LEAP on the access point, WEP Encryption or a Cipher must be enabled.

1.   From the **Security > Encryption Manager** page of the AP, shown in Figure 8-43, configure Encryption Key 1.

2.   Click the **WEP Encryption** radio button.

Figure 8-43   Encryption Manager Page

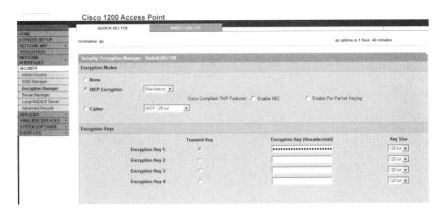

3.   Select **Mandatory**.

4.   Click **Apply-All**.

The **Cipher** option can be used for greater security. What options are available?

_____

_____

_____

Step 5: Configuring Authentication on AP

To enable Cisco LEAP on the access point, complete the following steps to configure the Authentication Method:

1.   On the **Security > SSID Manager** page of the access point, shown in Figure 8-44, create a new SSID of AP**P** (where **P** is the Pod number).

2.   Check the **Network EAP** box.

3.   Check the **Enable Accounting** box.

4.   Click the **Apply-All** button.

Figure 8-44   SSID Manager Page

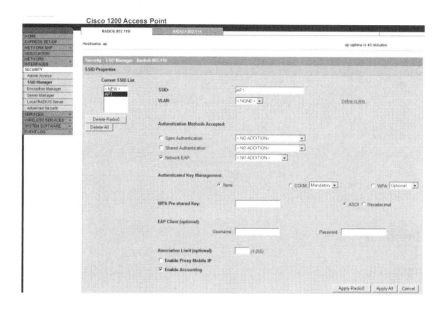

Step 6: AP RADIUS Configuration

To enable Cisco LEAP on the access point, complete the following steps to configure a RADIUS server from the **Security** > **Server Manager** page, shown in Figure 8-45.

Figure 8-45   Server Manager Page

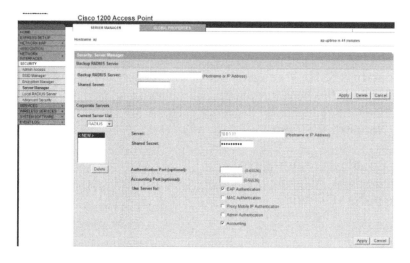

1.   Enter the IP address of the RADIUS server in the **Server:** entry field. This is the IP address of the Windows Server where the ACS software is running. (This should be 10.0.P.11, where P is the Pod number.)

2.   Enter the port number the RADIUS server uses for authentication. This defaults to port **1645** if the field is left empty.

3. Enter the shared secret used by the RADIUS server in the Shared Secret entry field. This was configured as **secretkey** on ACS. The shared secret on the access point must match the shared secret on the RADIUS server.

4. Check the **EAP Authentication** and **Accounting** boxes.

5. Click the **Apply** button.

6. From the **Security** Home page of the AP, shown in Figure 8-46, verify that Network EAP is checked and the only SSID is AP**P** (where **P** is the Pod number). The default, tsunami SSID, should be deleted for security. Also verify the server-based security is configured correctly, as shown.

Figure 8-46 Security Home Page

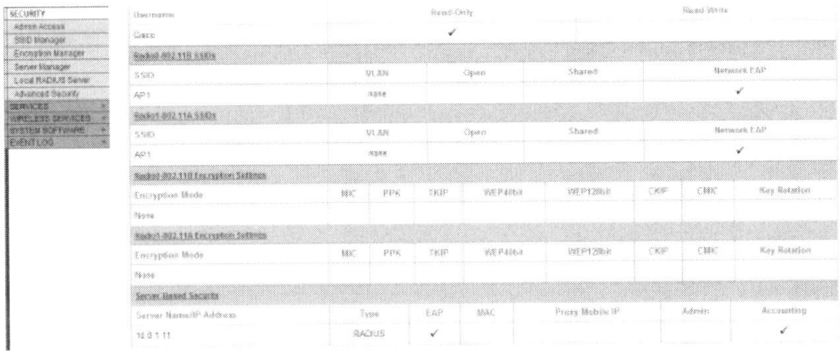

Step 7: Configuring LEAP on the ACU

To enable the EAP in the Aironet Client Utility, complete the following steps:

1. On PC2, configure the TCP/IP settings for the **Wireless Network Connection** if a DHCP server is not available. Otherwise, when the client authenticates, the wireless PC will not be able to communicate via IP. The TCP/IP Settings should be as follows:

   • IP address of 10.0.P.12 (where P is the Pod number)

   • Subnet mask of 255.255.255.0

   • Gateway of 10.0.P.254 (where P is the Pod number)

2. Go to the **Network Security** tab in the Aironet Client Utility on PC2 and each of the wireless client computers, as shown in Figure 8-47.

3. Select the **LEAP** from the **Network Security Type:** drop-down list, and click **Configure** to display the LEAP Settings window shown in Figure 8-48.

Figure 8-47   Aironet Client Utility: Network Security Tab

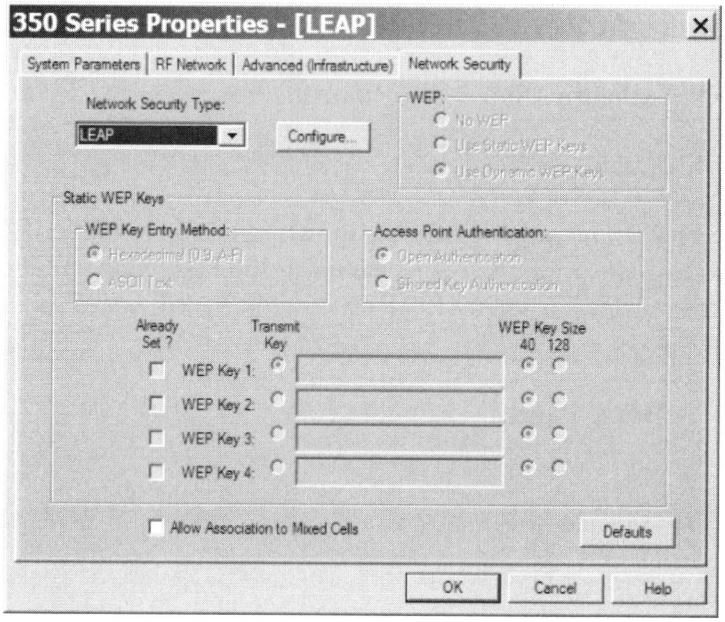

Figure 8-48   LEAP Settings Window

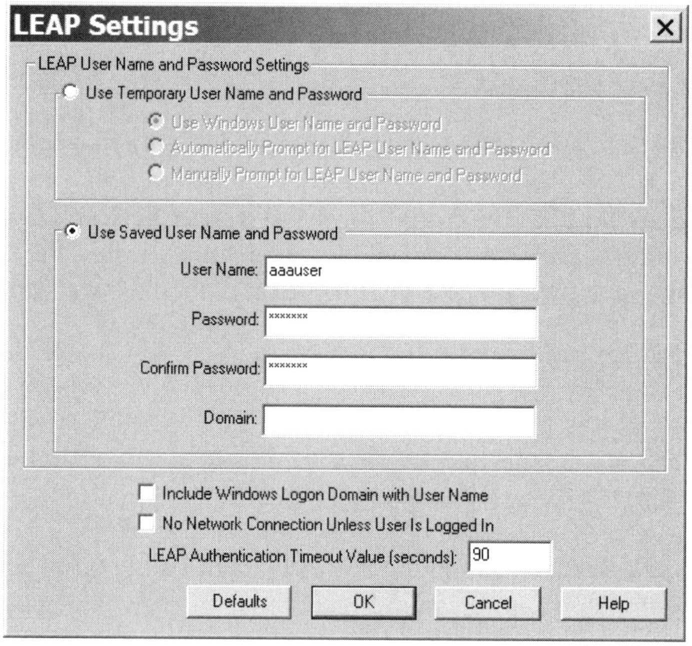

a.   Click **Use Saved User Name and Password.**
b.   Enter **aaauser** for the User Name.
c.   Enter **aaapass** for the Password.
d.   Enter **aaapass** for the Confirm Password.
e.   Uncheck the two checkboxes at the bottom of the LEAP Settings window.

4.   Click **OK**.

5.   In the profile manager, select the profile that LEAP is configured on and click **OK**. If a save username and password was not configured, an authentication screen should come up asking for a user ID and password. Type in the following:

   a.   The username for authentication is **aaauser**.
   b.   The password for authentication is **aaapass**.

6.   From PC1, PC2, or the ACS Server, browse to the AP **Association** page to verify the connection.

   What are the three authentication states?

   _____

   _____

   _____

Step 8: Verifying Connection

From the **Association** page of the AP, shown in Figure 8-49, verify the association state. This should display all the connected clients.

Figure 8-49   Association Page

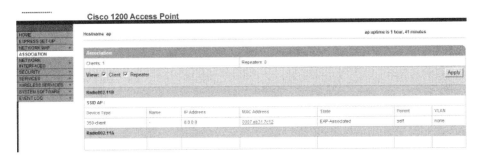

Step 9: Monitoring LEAP login on ACS (Optional)

1.   Click the **Reports and Activity** button located on the left side of the ACS Home page, shown in Figure 8-50.

2.   Click the **RADIUS Accounting** link.

3.   On the right-hand side, select the **RADIUS Accounting active.csv** link, as shown in Figure 8-51.

Figure 8-50   Reports and Activity Page

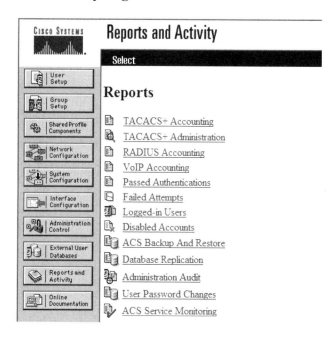

Figure 8-51   Select a RADIUS Accounting File

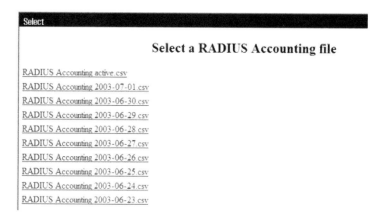

4.   Fill in the information found in the accounting file here:

a.   Time

_____

b.   User-Name

_____

c.   Group-Name

_____

d.   Calling-Station-Id

_____

e.   Acct-Status-Type

_____

f.   Acct-Session-Id

_____

g.   Framed-IP-Address

_____

h.   NAS-Port

_____

i.   NAS-IP-Address

_____

Lab 8.5.4.1: Configure Enterprise Security on AP

Estimated Time: 30 minutes

Number of Team Members: Students work in teams of two

Objectives

In this lab, students demonstrate an understanding of the role of enterprise wireless network security. Additionally, students configure MIC, TKIP, and BKR on an AP.

Scenario

The purpose of WEP is to protect the privacy of transmitted data. However, WEP has inherent security weaknesses. Many mechanisms are available to provide additional security for WEP.

Topology

Figure 8-52 shows the topology used in this lab.

Figure 8-52   Lab Topology

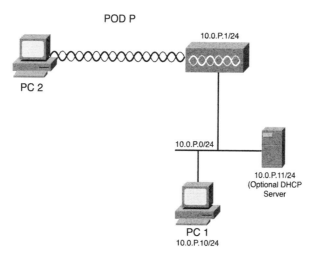

Note: The topology figures and lab examples contain **P** values. The **P** value in the addressing and naming scheme refers to *your* assigned Pod number.

The following are examples of determining **P** values:

- Pod2 is looking at a topology figure and is trying to determine the **P** values in the figure. In this scenario, the **P** values equal **2**. 10.0.**P**.12 becomes 10.0.**2**.12, 172.30.**P**.2 becomes 172.30.**2**.2, and so on.

- Pod1 is looking at a topology figure and is trying to determine the **P** values in the figure. In this scenario, the **P** values would equal **1**. 10.0.**P**.12 becomes 10.0.**1**.12, 172.30.**P**.2 becomes 172.30.**1**.2, and so on.

In both examples, the **P** values are directly related to the Pod number of the team.

Preparation

The AP and PCs should be properly set up according to the topology prior to the lab. Ensure an existing wireless connection is present from PC2 to the AP. The student should also be familiar with the following terms and concepts:

- **Temporal Key Integrity Protocol (TKIP)**—TKIP is a suite of algorithms surrounding WEP that is designed to achieve the best possible security on legacy hardware built to run WEP. TKIP adds four enhancements to WEP:

2. A per-packet key mixing function to defeat weak-key attacks

3. A new IV sequencing discipline to detect replay attacks

4. A cryptographic message integrity Check (MIC), called Michael, to detect forgeries such as bit flipping and altering packet source and destination

5. An extension of IV space, to virtually eliminate the need for rekeying

- **Message Integrity Check (MIC)**—MIC prevents attacks on encrypted packets called bit-flip attacks. During a bit-flip attack, an intruder intercepts an encrypted message, alters it slightly, and retransmits it, and the receiver accepts the retransmitted message as legitimate. The MIC, implemented on both the access point and all associated client devices, adds a few bytes to each packet to make the packets tamper proof.

- **Cisco Key Integrity Protocol (CKIP)**—Cisco WEP key permutation technique based on an early algorithm presented by the IEEE 802.11i security task group.

- **Cisco Message Integrity Check (CMIC)**—Like TKIP's Michael, the Cisco message integrity check mechanism is designed to detect forgery attacks.

- **Broadcast key rotation**—Broadcast key rotation allows the access point to generate the best possible random key and update all key-management capable clients periodically.

Tools and Resources

Each team of students requires the following equipment and knowledge to complete this lab:

- One AP and a wired PC

- Wireless PC with the ACU

Table 8-8 lists some of the WEP key restrictions. This is important when configuring various security options.

Table 8-8   WEP Key Restrictions

Security Configuration	WEP Key Restriction on AP
CCKM or WPA authenticated key management	Cannot configure a WEP key in key slot 1
LEAP or EAP authentication	Cannot configure a WEP key in key slot 4
Cipher suite with 40-bit WEP	Cannot configure a 128-bit key
Cipher suite with 128-bit WEP	Cannot configure a 40-bit key
Cipher suite with TKIP	Cannot configure any WEP keys
Cipher suite with TKIP and 40-bit WEP or 128-bit WEP	Cannot configure a WEP key in key slot 1 and 4
Static WEP with MIC or CMIC	AP and client devices must use the same WEP key as the transmit key, and the key must be in the same key slot on both access point and clients
Broadcast key rotation	Keys in slots 2 and 3 are overwritten by rotating broadcast keys

Step 1: Configuring and Verifying WEP on the AP

To configure WEP on the access point, complete the following steps:

1.   Verify connectivity from the wireless client (PC2) to the AP.

2. Open a web browser on the PC1 and type the IP address of the access point to configure in the browser address bar.

3. Go to the **Security Setup** page of the access point and click the **Encryption Manager** option to display the screen shown in Figure 8-53.

Figure 8-53   Security Encryption Manager Page

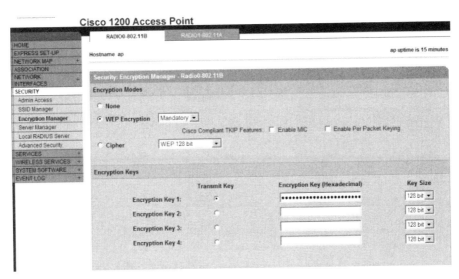

4. Check the radio button WEP Encryption Mode for **WEP Encryption.**

5. Use the pull down menu to select **Mandatory.**

6. Select the **Transmit Key.**

7. Enter the **Encryption Key** (for the purposes of this lab, enter **12345678909876543210123456).**

8. Select the **Key Size** to be **128 bits.**

9. Click the **Apply-All** button to apply these options.

10. After WEP is configured on the access point with a **Mandatory** option, all the clients become disassociated to this access point.

11. View the **Security>Encryption Manager** page. The WEP settings should be configured, and the Encryption Key field should be stored in the access point. However, the Encryption Key field should be encrypted with asterisk symbols to prevent unauthorized users from viewing the Encryption Key.

Step 2: Configuring and Verifying WEP on the Client

1. Open the Aironet Client Utility by clicking on the **ACU** icon.

2. Click **Profile Manager** to edit the WEP settings.

3. Under the Profile Management section, choose the profile being used for this lab, and click **Edit**.

4. Go to the **Network Security** tab of the profile that is being used for the lab, as shown in Figure 8-54.

Figure 8-54   Network Security Tab

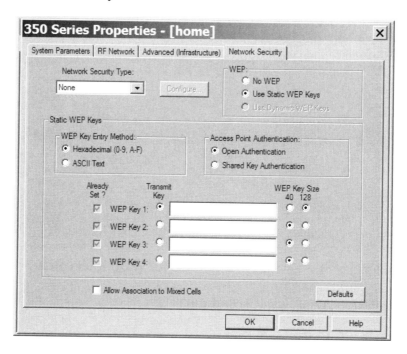

5. Configure the following settings for WEP:

   a. Select the WEP setting: **Use Static WEP Keys**.
   b. Select the Static WEP key entry method: **Hexadecimal**.
   c. Select the Access Point Authentication: **Open Authentication**.
   d. Select and enter the Transmit Key (for the purposes of this lab, enter **12345678909876543210123456**).
   e. Select the WEP Key Size: **128 bits**.
   f. Click the **OK** button to apply the WEP settings to the client.

Step 3: Enabling MIC and TKIP

After WEP is configured correctly, additional measures should be configured to secure the wireless link.

From the **Security > Encryption Manager** page, shown in Figure 8-55, enable Cisco Compliant TKIP features.

Figure 8-55   Encryption Manager Page

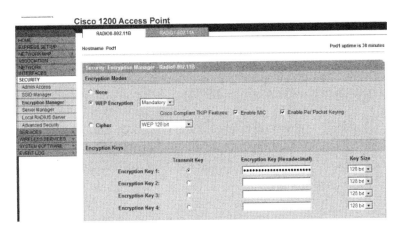

1.   Check the Enable MIC and Enable Per Packet Keying (PPK).

2.   Click Apply-All.

3.   From the Network Interfaces > Radio0-802.11b Settings tab, verify that the Aironet Extensions are enabled.

4.   Check the 802.11a interface, if applicable.

5.   From the Security page, shown in Figure 8-56, verify that MIC and PPK are enabled.

Figure 8-56   Security Page

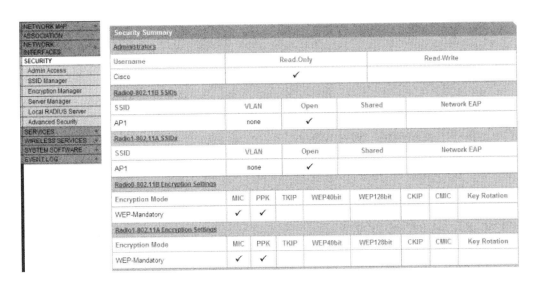

a.   What does MIC do to protect WEP?

_____

b. What attack does MIC prevent?

_____

c. Why do the Aironet extensions have to be used?

_____

Step 4: Enabling Broadcast Key Rotation (BKR)

When enabled, the AP provides a dynamic broadcast WEP key and changes it at the selected interval. Broadcast key rotation (BKR) is an excellent alternative to TKIP if the wireless LAN supports wireless client devices that are not Cisco devices, or that cannot be upgraded to the latest firmware for Cisco client devices.

1. Remove MIC and PPK configured from the previous step.

2. Check the **Enable Rotation with Interval** radio button, and enter a value of 90 seconds, as shown in Figure 8-57.

Figure 8-57 Enable Rotation with Interval Radio Button

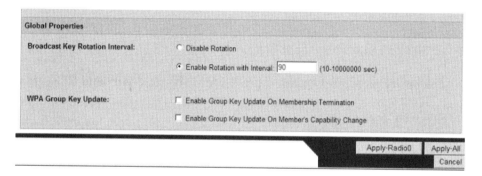

3. Click **Apply-All**.

4. From the **Security** page, shown in Figure 8-58, verify that Key Rotation is enabled.

Figure 8-58 Key Rotation Is Enabled

Radio0-802.11B Encryption Settings								
Encryption Mode	MIC	PPK	TKIP	WEP40bit	WEP128bit	CKIP	CMIC	Key Rotation
WEP-Mandatory								✓
Radio1-802.11A Encryption Settings								
Encryption Mode	MIC	PPK	TKIP	WEP40bit	WEP128bit	CKIP	CMIC	Key Rotation
WEP-Mandatory								✓

5. Verify connectivity from PC2 to the AP.

Step 5: Enabling a Cipher

1. From the **Security > Encryption Manager** page, remove Key Rotation configured from the previous step (see Figure 8-59).

Figure 8-59   Encryption Manager Page

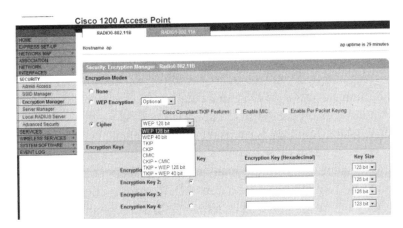

2. Check the **Cipher** radio button.

3. Choose **TKIP** from the drop-down menu.

4. Click **Apply-All.**

5. From the **Security** page, verify that TKIP is enabled, as shown in Figure 8-60.

Figure 8-60   Verify TKIP Is Enabled

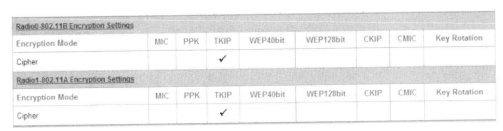

6. Verify the wireless connection from PC2 and the AP.

7. Return to task 3 and choose other Cipher options. Verify the settings from the **Security** page.

Step 6: Understanding Ciphers and Key Management (Optional Challenge)

From the **Security>SSID Manager** page, check the **Authenticated Key Management** options, as shown in Figure 8-61.

Figure 8-61   Authenticated Key Management

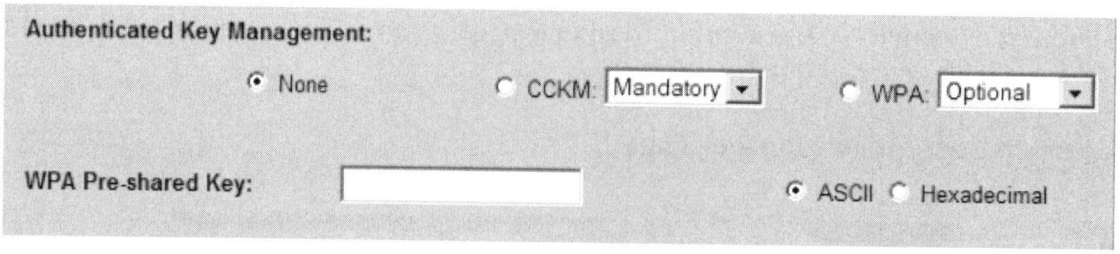

Using Cisco Centralized Key Management (CCKM), authenticated client devices can roam from one AP to another without any perceptible delay during reassociation. An AP on the network provides Wireless Domain Services (WDS) and creates a cache of security credentials for CCKM-enabled client devices on the subnet. The WDS access point's cache of credentials dramatically reduces the time required for reassociation when a CCKM-enabled client device roams to a new AP. When a client device roams, the WDS access point forwards the client's security credentials to the new AP, and the reassociation process is reduced to a two-packet exchange between the roaming client and the new AP. Roaming clients reassociate so quickly that no perceptible delay occurs in voice or other time-sensitive applications.

Wi-Fi Protected Access (WPA) is a standards-based, interoperable security enhancement that strongly increases the level of data protection and access control for existing and future wireless LAN systems. It is derived from and is forward-compatible with the upcoming IEEE 802.11i standard. WPA leverages Temporal Key Integrity Protocol (TKIP) for data protection and 802.1X for authenticated key management.

WPA key management supports two mutually exclusive management types: WPA and WPA-Pre-shared key (WPA-PSK). Using WPA key management, clients and the authentication server authenticate to each other using an EAP authentication method, and the client and server generate a pairwise master key (PMK). Using WPA, the server generates the PMK dynamically and passes it to the AP. Using WPA-PSK, a pre-shared key must be configured on both the client and the AP, and that pre-shared key is used as the PMK. Table 8-9 lists the Cipher suites compatible with CCKM and WPA.

More information on WPA can be found here:

http://www.weca.net/OPenSection/protected_access.asp

http://www.wi-fiplanet.com/tutorials/article.php/2148721

Table 8-9   Cipher Suites Compatible with WPA and CCKM

Authenticated Key Management Types	Compatible Cipher Suites
CCKM	encryption mode cipher wep128 encryption mode cipher wep40 encryption mode cipher ckip encryption mode cipher cmic encryption mode cipher ckip-cmic encryption mode cipher tkip encryption mode cipher tkip wep128 encryption mode cipher tkip wep40
WPA	encryption mode cipher tkip encryption mode cipher tkip wep128 encryption mode cipher tkip wep40

Explore the different Cipher settings.

Lab 8.5.4.2: Configuring Site-to-Site Wireless Link Using Enterprise Security

Estimated Time: 45 minutes

Number of Team Members: Students work in teams of two

Objectives

Configure a site-to-site bridged network using enterprise security features.

Scenario

A remote location located several miles away requires connectivity to the existing wired network. The connection can be bridged wirelessly with the use of two BR350s. The company's security policy mandated a minimum of 128-bit WEP security for all wireless connections.

Topology

Figure 8-62 shows the topology used in this lab.

Figure 8-62   Lab Topology

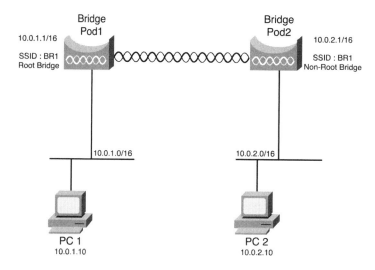

Preparation

Use the settings listed in Table 8-10 for this lab.

267

Table 8-10   Lab Device Settings

Device Name	Label	SSID	Address
BPod1	BR1	BR1	10.0.1.1/16
BPod2	BR2	BR1	10.0.2.1/16

Tools and Resources

Each team requires the following equipment to complete this lab:

- Two wired LAN segments that will be bridged together

- Two Cisco BR350

- PC with FTP server loaded and a file to transfer in the root directory of the FTP server

Step 1: Cable and Power the Bridge

1. Attach two rubber duck antennas to the RP-TNC connectors.

2. Plug the RJ-45 Ethernet cable into the Ethernet port on the back of the bridge. Plug the other end of the Ethernet cable into the Cisco Aironet power injector TO AP/BRIDGE end.

3. Connect the power cable into the inline power injector and to the receptacle.

Step 2: Connecting to the Bridge

Connect a nine-pin, male-to-female, straight-through serial cable to the COM port on a computer and to the RS-232 serial port on the bridge. (This cable ships with the bridge.)

1. Open a terminal emulator.

2. Enter the following settings for the connection:

- Bits per second (baud rate): 9600

- Data bits: 8

- Parity: none

- Stop bits: 1

- Flow control: Xon/Xoff

3. Press = to display the bride's home page. If the bridge has not been configured before, the Express Setup page appears as the home page. (Go to Step 3.)

4.   If the bridge is already configured, the Summary Status page appears as the home page. When the Summary Status screen appears, type :**resetall**, and press **Enter**.

Enter **yes** to confirm Resetting All parameters to factory defaults:

```
YES
00:02:12 (FATAL): Rebooting System due to Resetting Factory Defaults
*** Restarting System in 5 seconds...
```

5.   Type **yes**, and press **Enter** to confirm the command.

6.   Power cycle the bridge by removing the power.

Step 3: Connecting to the BR350 via Express Setup

1.   Plug a second RJ-45 Ethernet cable into the power injector end labeled TO NETWORK. Plug the other end of the Ethernet cable into the Ethernet port on a switch or hub. Then, connect PC1 to the switch. A crossover cable can be used to connect directly from the inline power injector to PC1/PC2.

2.   Configure PC1 to 10.0.0.2/24.

3.   Open a web browser and enter the default bridge address, http://10.0.0.1, and press **Enter**.

4.   Either of the following pages appears:

   • The **Summary Status** page, also known as the **Home** page

   • The **Express Setup** page, shown in Figure 8-63

Figure 8-63   Express Setup Page

5. If the Express Setup page does not appear, from the Summary Status page, click the Setup hyperlink, as shown in Figure 8-64. This brings up the Setup page.

Figure 8-64   Setup Hyperlink

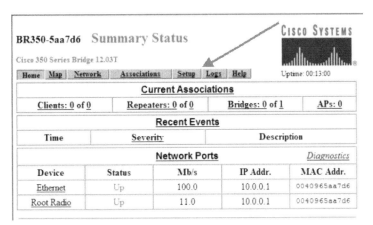

6. Click the **Express Setup** link, as shown in Figure 8-65. This brings up the Express Setup page.

Figure 8-65   Express Setup Link

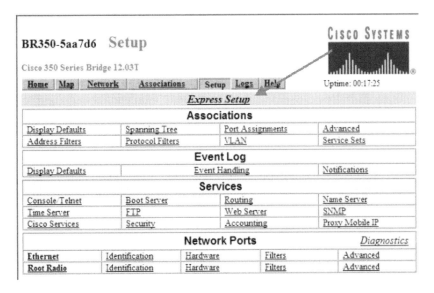

Step 4: Configuring the Bridge Settings

1. Configure the settings listed in Table 8-11 using the Express Setup page, as shown in Figure 8-66.

Table 8-11   Bridge Settings

Parameter	BPod1	BPod2
System Name:	BPod1	BPod2
Configuration Server Protocol:	None	None
Default IP address:	10.0.1.1	10.0.2.1
Default Gateway:	10.0.1.254	10.0.1.254
Service Set ID:	BR1	BR1
Role in Radio Network:	Root Bridge	Non-Root Bridge w/o Clients

Figure 8-66   Express Setup Page

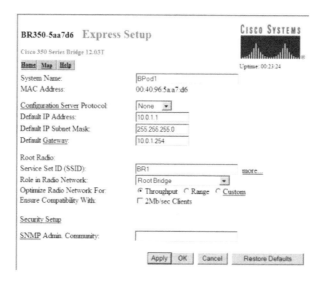

2.   Click **Apply**. The connection drops.

3.   Configure the PCs:

• PC1 with an IP address of 10.0.1.10/24

• PC2 with an IP address of 10.0.2.10/24

4.   Reconnect using the browser. Enter **10.0.P.1** and connect.

5.   Verify the settings.

a.   What roles can the bridge serve in the network?

_____

_____

_____

b.   Why would the BR350 be used in Root Access Point mode, compared to using a 1200 or 1100 AP?

_____

_____

_____

Step 6: Testing the Connection

Verify client PCs are configured with the appropriate IP address. The only wireless devices on this topology are the two wireless multifunction bridges used for the point-to-point connection.

1.   After the wireless bridge link is configured properly, ping from PC1 to BPod2. Then, ping from PC1 to PC2.

Were these successful?

_____

2.   Test Layer 7 connectivity by browsing to BPod2 from PC1.

3.   Configure FTP or web services on PC1 and PC2. Transfer a file from PC1 to PC2 and vice versa. Calculate the download performance across the wireless link.

a.   What was the download speed in Mbps?

_____

b.   What is the distance limitation between two wireless bridges?

_____

c.   What is the distance limitation between an AP and a Bridge?

_____

d.   Why are 2 bridges able to connect at longer distances?

_____

Step 7: Configuring WEP on Both Bridges

Follow these steps to set up WEP keys and enable WEP:

1.   On the Summary Status page, click **Setup.**

2.   On the Setup page, click **Security**.

3. On the Security Setup page, click **Radio Data Encryption (WEP)**.

4. From the **Root Radio Data Encryption** page.

5. Before WEP can be enabled, a WEP key must be entered in at least one of the Encryption Key fields.

6. Use the Key Size pull-down menu, shown in Figure 8-67, to select the **128-bit** encryption for the WEP Key 1.

Figure 8-67   Key Size Pull-Down Menu

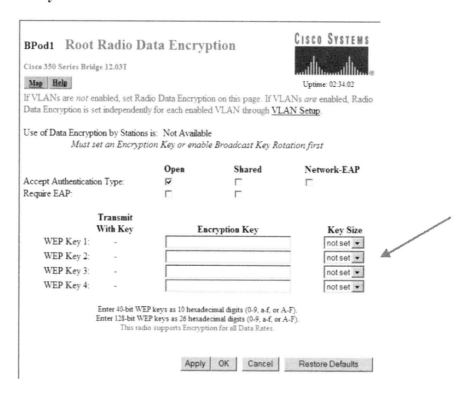

7. Click in the Encryption Key field and enter a WEP key.

    How many digits must be entered for 128-bit WEP? Record the key below.

    _____

    _____

8. Click **Apply** to save the WEP Key.

9. From the drop-down box that appears next to the **Use of Data Encryption by Stations is**, as shown in Figure 8-68, select **Full Encryption**.

Figure 8-68   Use of Data Encryption by Stations Is Pull-Down Menu

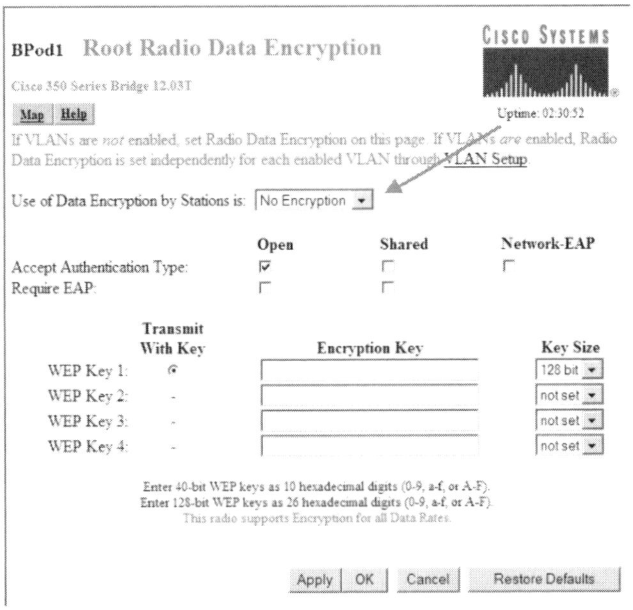

10.   Click **OK**, which returns the bridge to the Security Setup page.

11.   Repeat the same steps on the other bridge.

Note: The characters typed for the key contents appear only when typing. After you click **Apply** or **OK**, the key contents cannot be viewed. Select **Not set** from the Key Size pull-down menu to clear a key.

Table 8-12 shows a sample WEP key configuration on the Root and Non-Root device.

Table 8-12   WEP Key Setup Example

Bridge (Root)			Non-Root Device	
Key Slot	Transmit?	Key Contents	Transmit?	Key Contents
1	x	12345678901234567890abcdef	-	12345678901234567890abcdef
2	-	09876543210987654321fedcba	x	09876543210987654321fedcba
3	-	not set	-	not set
4	-	not set	-	not set

Because the bridge's WEP key 1 is selected as the transmit key, WEP key 1 on the other device must contain the same contents.

274

Step 8: Retesting the Connection

1. After the wireless bridge link is configured with WEP, ping each PC to test end-to-end connectivity between the two PCs.

   Was this successful? If not, what should be checked?

2. Configure FTP services on PC1 and PC2. Calculate the download performance across the wireless link.

   a. What was the download speed in Mbps? Did WEP have an impact on performance?

   b. What other enhancements can be used to improve WEP security?

   c. What technology can be used at Layer 3 to improve security of the wireless link?

Step 9: Enabling Enterprise Security

After WEP is configured correctly, additional measures should be configured to secure the wireless link. Follow these steps to set up TKIP, MIC, and BKR.

1. From the Setup Page, click the **Root Radio: Advanced** link, as shown in Figure 8-69.

Figure 8-69   Root Radio Advanced Link

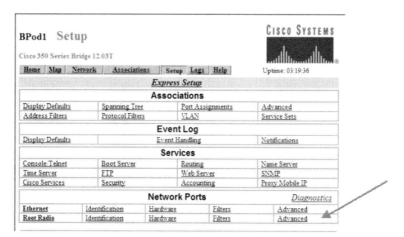

2. From the **Root Radio Advanced** page, select **MMH** from the drop-down list for the **Enhanced MIC verification for WEP** setting, as shown in Figure 8-70.

Figure 8-70   Select MMH from the Drop-Down List

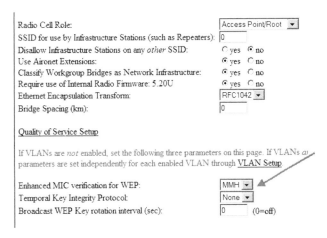

3.   Verify the Use Aironet Extensions is selected as **yes**.

4.   Click the **Apply** button. The wireless link is lost with the other bridge.

5.   Configure the other bridge with the same security setting.

6.   The link should be re-established.

7.   From the Root Radio: Advanced page, select **Cisco** from the drop-down list for the Temporal Key Integrity Protocol, as shown in Figure 8-71.

Figure 8-71   Select Cisco **from the Drop-Down List**

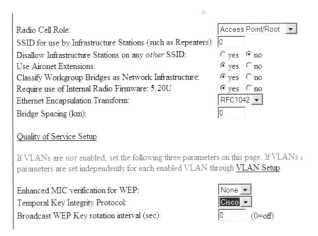

8.   Verify the Use Aironet Extensions is selected as **yes**.

9.   Click the **Apply** button. The wireless link is lost with the other bridge.

10.   Now configure the other bridge with the same security setting.

11.   The link should be re-established.

  a.   What attack does TKIP prevent?

  _____

  b.   Why do the Aironet extensions have to be used?

  _____

12.   From the Root Radio Advance page, enter a value of **90 seconds** as the **Broadcast WEP Key rotation interval**, as shown in Figure 8-72.

Figure 8-72   Enter a Value of 90 Seconds as the Broadcast WEP Key Rotation Interval

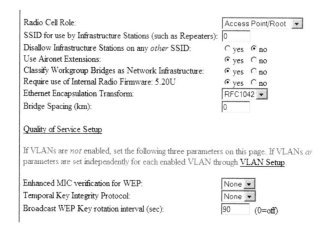

13.   Click the **Apply** button. The wireless link is lost with the other bridge.

14.   Configure the other bridge with the same security setting.

15.   The link should be re-established.

  What attack does BKR prevent?

  _____

Lab 8.6.2: Configure VLANs on the AP

Estimated Time: 40 minutes

Number of Team Members: Students work in teams of two

Objective

Students extend VLANs into a WLAN.

Scenario

VLANs can be extended into a WLAN by adding IEEE 802.11Q tag awareness to the AP. Frames destined for different VLANs are transmitted by the access point wirelessly on different SSIDs with different WEP keys. Only the clients associated with that VLAN receive those packets. Conversely, packets coming from a client associated with a certain VLAN are 802.11Q tagged before they are forwarded onto the wired network.

The basic wireless components of a VLAN consist of an AP and a client associated to it using wireless technology. The AP is physically connected through a trunk port to the network VLAN switch on which the VLAN is configured. The physical connection to the VLAN switch is through the access point's Ethernet port. A router is also necessary to route between the different VLANs. Up to 16 SSIDs can be configured on the AP, hence 16 VLANs are supported. Configuring the AP to support VLANs is a three-step process:

Create SSIDs and assign authentication settings to SSIDs.

Assign SSIDs to VLANs and enable the VLAN on the radio and Ethernet ports.

Topology

Figure 8-73 shows the topology used in this lab.

Figure 8-73   Lab Topology

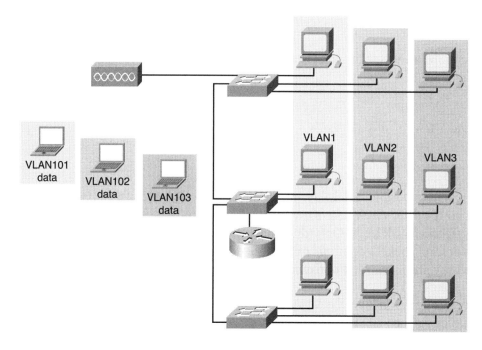

Preparation

Reset the AP to the default configuration.

Table 8-13 shows the settings for the VLAN IDs and corresponding SSIDs.

Table 8-13   VLAN ID/SSID Settings

Team	Access Point Name	SSID	VLAN	Authentication	Bridge Group	BVI Address
1	PodP	management voice data guest	10 101 102 103	Network EAP Shared Network EAP Open	1 101 102 103	10.0.P.1/24

Tools and Resources

Each team needs the following equipment to complete this lab:

- One access point

- Two PCs or laptops

- Console cable

Additional Materials

Consult the following URL for additional information about the topics covered in this lab:

http://www.cisco.com/en/US/products/hw/wireless/ps430/products_installation_and_configuration_guide_book09186a0080147d69.html

Step 1: Configuring the System Name and BVI Address

From the **Express Set-Up** page, as shown in Figure 8-74, configure the System Name and BVI address.

Figure 8-74   Express Setup Page

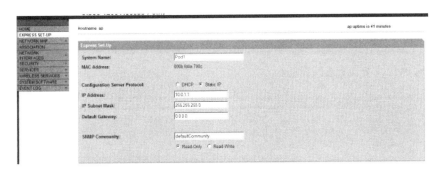

Step 2: Defining the SSIDs and Authentication Type

From the **Security > SSID Manager** page, shown in Figure 8-75, configure the 802.11b radio management, voice, data, and guest SSIDs and authentication type according to Table 8-13.

Figure 8-75   SSID Manager Page

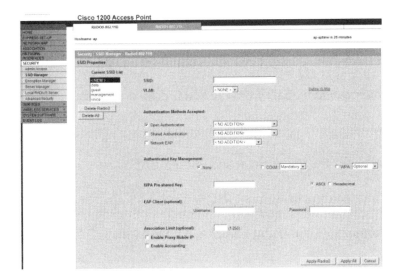

1.   Enter the *management* SSID in the SSID: box.

2.   Select the authentication method.

3.   Click **Apply-All**.

4.   Repeat the steps for the voice, data, and guest SSIDs.

     Why is VLAN ID 10 used for the management VLAN instead of VLAN ID 1?

Step 3: Defining the VLANs

From the **Services > VLAN** page, as shown in Figure 8-76, configure the 802.11b radio for management, voice, data, and guest VLANs according to the settings in Table 8-13.

Figure 8-76   Services > VLAN Page

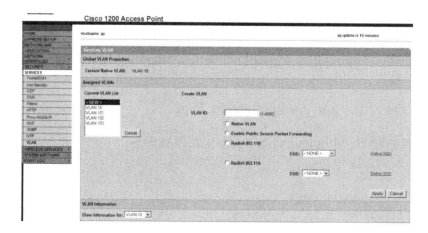

1.   Enter VLAN ID *10* in the VLAN ID: box. Because this is the management VLAN, check the **Native VLAN** box. Also, check the **Radio0-802.11B**.

2.   Choose the *management* SSID from the **SSID** drop down box.

3.   Click **Apply**.

4.   Repeat the steps for the voice, data, and guest VLANs.

Step 4: Verifying the Configuration via GUI

From the **Security** home page, shown in Figure 8-77, verify the VLAN configuration.

Figure 8-77   Security Home Page

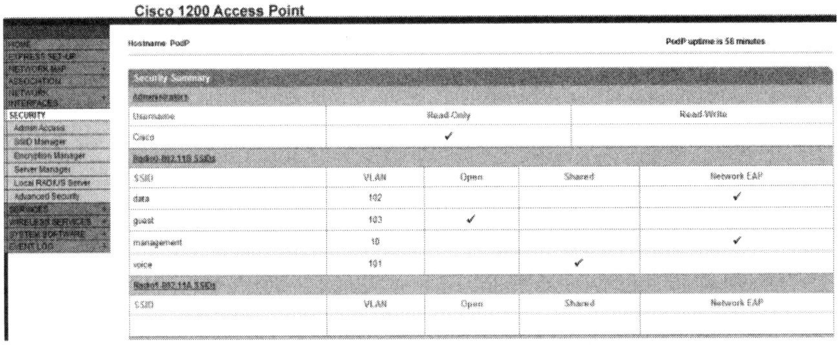

Step 5: Verifying the Configuration via IOS CLI

1.   Telnet or console into the AP.

2.   Verify the configuration via IOS CLI:

```
PodP#show run
sh run
Building configuration...
Current configuration : 3167 bytes
!
version 12.2
no service pad
service timestamps debug datetime msec
service timestamps log datetime msec
service password-encryption
!
hostname PodP
!
enable secret 5 $1$N46P$W9Eb.bK3xvfZ1XgDmRXDZ1
!
username Cisco password 7 01300F175804
ip subnet-zero
!
!
bridge irb
!
!
interface Dot11Radio0
 no ip address
 no ip route-cache
 !
 ssid data
    vlan 102
    authentication network-eap eap_methods
 !
 ssid guest
    vlan 103
    authentication open
 !
 ssid management
    vlan 10
    authentication network-eap eap_methods
 !
 ssid voice
    vlan 101
    authentication shared
 !
 speed basic-1.0 basic-2.0 basic-5.5 basic-11.0
 rts threshold 2312
 station-role root
!
interface Dot11Radio0.10
 encapsulation dot1Q 10 native
 no ip route-cache
```

```
  bridge-group 1
  bridge-group 1 subscriber-loop-control
  bridge-group 1 block-unknown-source
  no bridge-group 1 source-learning
  no bridge-group 1 unicast-flooding
  bridge-group 1 spanning-disabled
!
interface Dot11Radio0.101
  encapsulation dot1Q 101
  no ip route-cache
  bridge-group 101
  bridge-group 101 subscriber-loop-control
  bridge-group 101 block-unknown-source
  no bridge-group 101 source-learning
  no bridge-group 101 unicast-flooding
  bridge-group 101 spanning-disabled
!
interface Dot11Radio0.102
  encapsulation dot1Q 102
  no ip route-cache
  bridge-group 102
  bridge-group 102 subscriber-loop-control
  bridge-group 102 block-unknown-source
  no bridge-group 102 source-learning
  no bridge-group 102 unicast-flooding
  bridge-group 102 spanning-disabled
!
interface Dot11Radio0.103
  encapsulation dot1Q 103
  no ip route-cache
  bridge-group 103
  bridge-group 103 subscriber-loop-control
  bridge-group 103 block-unknown-source
  no bridge-group 103 source-learning
  no bridge-group 103 unicast-flooding
  bridge-group 103 spanning-disabled
!
interface Dot11Radio1
  no ip address
  no ip route-cache
  speed basic-6.0 9.0 basic-12.0 18.0 basic-24.0 36.0 48.0 54.0
  rts threshold 2312
  station-role root
  bridge-group 1
  bridge-group 1 subscriber-loop-control
  bridge-group 1 block-unknown-source
  no bridge-group 1 source-learning
  no bridge-group 1 unicast-flooding
  bridge-group 1 spanning-disabled
!
interface FastEthernet0
  no ip address
  no ip route-cache
  duplex auto
  speed auto
!
interface FastEthernet0.10
  encapsulation dot1Q 10 native
  no ip route-cache
  bridge-group 1
  no bridge-group 1 source-learning
  bridge-group 1 spanning-disabled
!
interface FastEthernet0.101
  encapsulation dot1Q 101
  no ip route-cache
  bridge-group 101
  no bridge-group 101 source-learning
  bridge-group 101 spanning-disabled
!
interface FastEthernet0.102
  encapsulation dot1Q 102
  no ip route-cache
  bridge-group 102
  no bridge-group 102 source-learning
  bridge-group 102 spanning-disabled
!
interface FastEthernet0.103
  encapsulation dot1Q 103
  no ip route-cache
```

```
 bridge-group 103
 no bridge-group 103 source-learning
 bridge-group 103 spanning-disabled
!
interface BVI1
 ip address 10.0.P.1 255.255.255.0
 no ip route-cache
!
ip http server
ip http help-path http://www.cisco.com/warp/public/779/smbiz/
prodconfig/help/eag/ivory/1100
bridge 1 route ip
!
!
line con 0
line vty 0 4
 login local
line vty 5 15
 login
!
end
PodP#
```

Step 6: Configuring PCs and Connect to the AP

1. Configure two wireless PCs.

- PC 1 with Open Authentication with an SSID of guest

- PC2 with Shared Authentication with an SSID of voice

2. Verify the connection via the **Association** page.

Note: Cisco recommends not using shared keys due to inherent security flaws with the technology.

Step 7: Configuring 802.11a VLANs (Optional)

1. Create the SSIDs for the 802.11a radio and apply to the existing VLANs.

2. Verify the settings afterwards via the **Security** home page, as shown in Figure 8-78.

Figure 8-78   Security Home Page

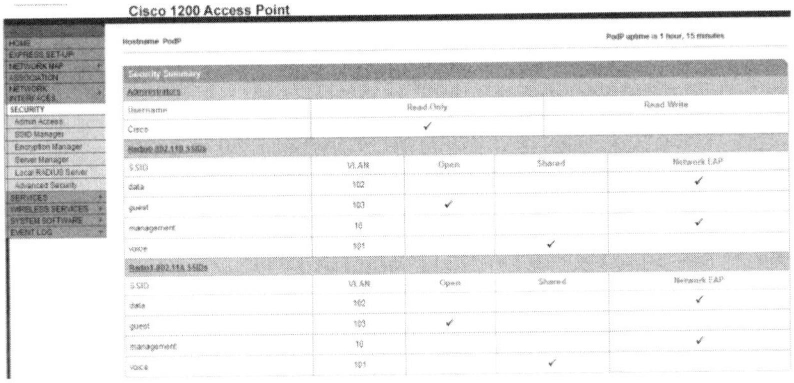

3. Verify the setting via IOS CLI.

4. Return to Step 6 and configure 2 802.11a clients. Verify the connections.

5. Save the configuration to a text file.

Chapter 9

Applications, Design, and Site Survey Preparation

Lab 9.3.9: WLAN Design

Estimated Time: Time needed for this lab can vary

Number of Team Members: Students work individually or in small groups

Objectives

In this lab, students identify various applications of wireless LANs. The students then choose one application and detail a WLAN design for it. The detailed design should use all the following to present their findings:

- Drawings

- Configurations

- Topologies

- Issues

- Advantages

- Disadvantages

- Challenges

- Any other useful information

Scenario

The four main design requirements for a WLAN solution are as follows:

- It must have high availability.

- It must be scalable.

- It must be manageable.

- It must be an open architecture allowing integration with third-party equipment.

Along with the design requirements, there are a few WLAN design basics:

- The same principles apply to all WLAN designs.

- Get to know the customer and the customer's needs.

- Design the WLAN to meet those needs.

Preparation

The student must read and understand the material presented in Chapter 9 from the *Cisco Networking Academy Program Fundamentals of Wireless LANs Companion Guide* prior to beginning this lab.

Tools and Resources

The following tools and resources are helpful with this lab:

- Online Internet research

- Industry site visits or contacts

- Trade journals

Step 1: Identifying Customer Industry

Identify the customer's industry for which the team will design the wireless LAN application. Some common industries are as follows:

- Retailing

- Warehousing

- Healthcare

- Hotel/Hospitality

- Education

- Wireless Office

- Transportation

- Government and Military

- Internet service provider

Provide a brief summary of the business.

_____

_____

_____

_____

Step 2: Collecting Customer Data

When dealing with data collection, consider the following questions:

- What are the needs of the customer?

- What applications are used over the WLAN?

- What bandwidth do these applications require?

Notes

_____

_____

_____

_____

_____

Step 3: Determining Customer Load and Coverage

The following questions should be answered when dealing with load and coverage:

- What is the total number of potential wireless clients on the network?

- How big of an area has to be covered by the wireless LAN?

A diagram or sketch of the coverage area is required with this section.

Notes

_____

_____

_____

_____

_____

Step 4: Determining Customer Bandwidth and Throughput

The following should be dealt with in regards to bandwidth and throughput:

- What actual bandwidth speed is required by the wireless networking application used?

- How can this bandwidth requirement be achieved with the chosen access point configuration?

  - Cell size

  - Channels

  - Data rate settings

  - High speed technologies such as 802.11a or 802.11g

Note this information on the diagram you created in Step 3.

Notes

_____

_____

_____

_____

_____

Step 5: Considering the Demands of Mobile Users

When dealing with WLANs, the demands of mobile users must be considered:

- Will the users need to roam about the coverage area?

- Will they require seamless roaming?

- What kind of design can be used in the topology to accomplish these objectives?

Notes

_____
_____
_____
_____
_____

Step 6: Determining Power Consumption of Wireless Clients

What kind of power settings is to be used on the wireless clients to conserve power when and if they need to be mobile and roam about the facility?

Notes

_____
_____
_____
_____
_____

Step 7: Determining Potential Interference to the WLAN

The following steps must be taken when dealing with potential interference to the WLAN:

1. Identify the typical sources of radio frequency (RF) interference for the type of industry for which the WLAN application is being designed.

2. Locate each type of RF interference and note a possible option or solution for this type of interference.

Note the sources of RF interference on the diagram that you created in Step 3.

Step 8: Considering Encryption Requirements and Methods

Encryption must also be considered depending on the client and the industry for which the WLAN is being designed:

*   What are the data security and privacy requirements of the customer?

*   What methods will be used to ensure their privacy and security requirements for the wireless LAN?

    *   No encryption

    *   40-bit encryption

    *   128-bit encryption

Note the advantages and disadvantages of each.

_____
_____
_____
_____
_____

Step 9: Assessing Fire Code and Safety for the WLAN Coverage Area

What are the fire and safety risks usually associated with the industry coverage area that has been chosen? List each risk and identify the available options and solutions for each of them.

Notes

_____
_____
_____
_____
_____

Lab 9.5.5: Link Status Meter and Preferences

Estimated Time: 5 minutes

Number of Team Members: Students work in teams of two

Objectives

In this lab, students operate the Link Status Meter (LSM) utility for the wireless client adapter. Students then learn how to set the Preferences options for the Aironet Client Utilities (ACU).

Scenario

Step 1 explains how to use the LSM utility to determine the performance of the RF link between the client adapter and its associated access point.

Step 3 explains how to set optional preferences for the ACU.

Preparation

The student must read and understand the material presented in Chapter 9 from the *Fundamentals of Wireless LANs Companion Guide* prior to beginning the lab.

Tools and Resources

The following equipment is required to complete this lab:

- Cisco Aironet access point properly operating and configured

- PC or laptop with a Cisco Aironet Wireless client adapter and utility properly installed

Step 1: Using the Link Status Meter to Determine the Signal Strength

1. Open the Aironet Client Utility screen.

2. Click the **Link Status Meter** button. The Link Status Meter screen appears.

    Data pertaining to the performance of the RF link can be accessed from the ACU and LSM. However, each utility displays them differently. This data is represented by histograms in the ACU and is depicted graphically in the LSM.

3. The Link Status Meter screen, shown in Figure 9-1, provides a graphical display of the following:

- **Signal strength**—The strength of the radio signal from the client adapter at the time packets are being received. It is displayed as a percentage along the vertical axis.

- **Signal quality**—The quality of the radio signal from the client adapter at the time packets are being received. It is displayed as a percentage along the horizontal axis.

Figure 9-1   Link Status Screen

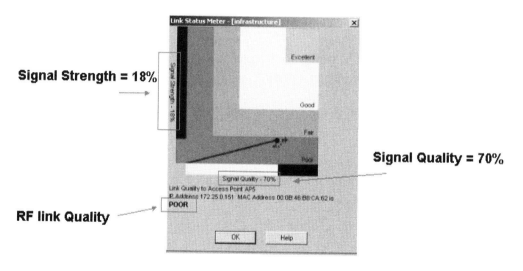

a.   What is the signal strength of the PC to the access point (%)?

_____

b.   What is the signal quality of the PC to the access point (%)?

_____

c.   What is the quality of the overall RF link?

_____

Step 2: Setting ACU Preferences

1.   Open the ACU screen.

2.   Click **Preference** on the ACU screen to display the screen shown in Figure 9-2.

Figure 9-2   ACU Screen

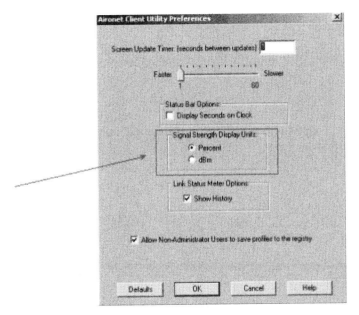

What units are the signal strength and signal quality expressed in?

_____

_____

3.   Click the **Percent** or the **dBm** option to change the Signal Strength Display Units. Choose the opposite of whatever the current setting is.

4.   Click the **OK** button to save the changes.

5.   Click on the **Site Survey** button on the ACU screen.

What units are the signal strength and signal quality expressed in now?

_____

_____

6.   Click on the **Preference** button and change the preferences to the settings preferred.

7.   Click the **OK** button to save the changes.

Lab 9.6.2: Using the Bridge Range Calculation Utility

Estimated Time: 15 minutes

Number of Team Members: Students work in teams of two or individually

Objectives

The student learns how to use the Cisco Bridge Range Calculation Utility to determine bridge distances based on the following:

- Type of bridge

- Antenna

- Cables

- Splitter

- Other applicable wireless connectors

Scenario

Cisco makes it easy to calculate bridge distances by using the Cisco distance calculations spreadsheet that is available from Cisco.com.

These values are for line-of-sight and provide a 10dB fade margin, which helps ensure that the calculations work.

Preparation

The student should download the Cisco Bridge Range Calculation Utility at the following link:

http://www.cisco.com/application/vnd.ms-excel/en/us/guest/products/ps458/c1225/ ccmigration_09186a00800a912a.xls

Step 1: Using the Cisco Bridge Range Calculation Worksheet

The Cisco Bridge Range Calculation Worksheet is shown in Figure 9-3.

Figure 9-3   Cisco Bridge Range Calculation Worksheet

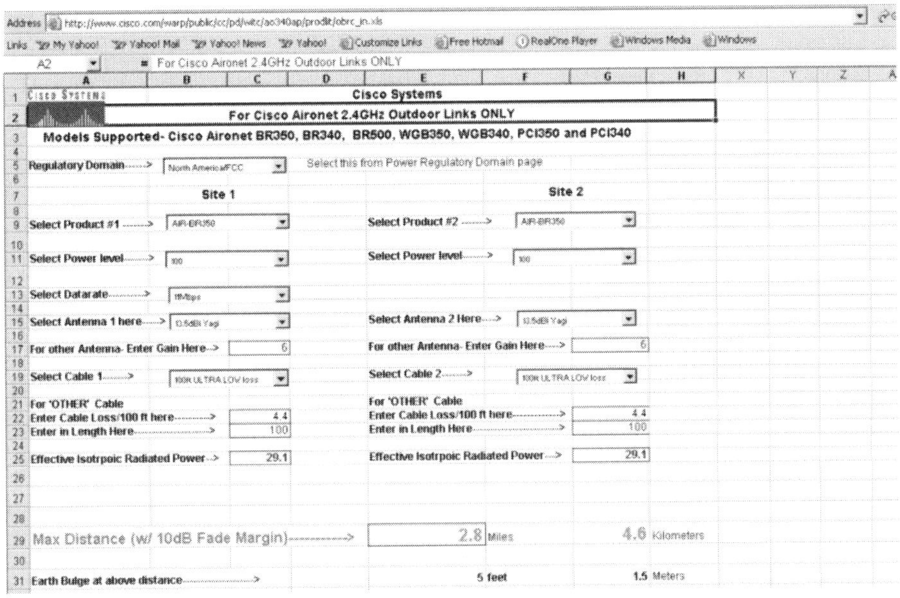

1.   Download, install, and open the Cisco Bridge Range Calculation Utility.

2.   Select the product line being used. If using access points outdoors, the same procedures can be followed.

3.   Select the proper antenna for both sites.

4.   For other non-Cisco antennas, enter the gain in dBi. If the gain is provided in dBd, simply add 2.14 to the number to convert to dBi.

5.   Select the cable used on both sites:

      If using something other than standard Cisco antennas, enter in the length and cable loss per 100 feet In the appropriate place. For Cisco cables, this is 6.7dB/100 feet at 2.4 Ghz.

      If a different cable is being used, contact the cable vendor for this information.

6.   Add any other losses due to splitters, connectors, and so forth into the miscellaneous Column.

7.   The example in Figure 9-4 uses the following:

      • 20dBm, or 2.4 GHz, for the transmitter power

      • 13.5 dBi yagis antennas

      • 2 cables of 20 feet each

Figure 9-4   Calculation Example

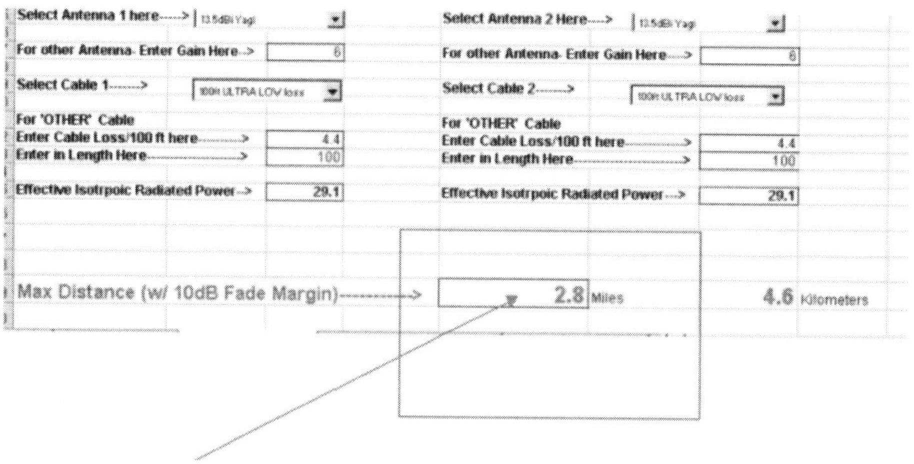

8.   The Bridge Range Calculation Utility gives a maximum distance of approximately 2.8 miles.

    a.   What is the maximum distance when changing the data rate to 5.5 Mbps?

_____

    b.   What is the maximum distance when changing the data rate to 2 Mbps?

_____

    c.   What is the maximum distance when changing the data rate to 1 Mbps?

_____

    d.   What is an easy way to extend the maximum distance while using the same power settings and antenna?

_____

Chapter 10

Site Survey and Installation

Lab 10.2.7.1: Site Survey Active Mode

Estimated Time: 20 minutes

Number of Team Members: Students work in teams of two

Objective

In this lab, the student determines the best placement and coverage, or overlap, for the wireless access points. This is done through the use of the wireless client adapter site survey utility.

Scenario

A site survey provides detailed information about all of the following:

- Where the access points are to be located

- How they will be mounted

- How they will be connected to the network

- Where any cabling or power may need to be installed

The Aironet Client Utility (ACU) site survey tool operates at the radio frequency (RF) level and determines the best placement and coverage, or overlap, for access points.

During the site survey, the current status of the network is read from the client adapter and displayed four times per second so network performance can be accurately gauged.

The feedback received helps to eliminate areas with low RF signal levels that can result in a loss of connection between the client adapter and its associated access point.

The site survey tool can operate in two modes:

- **Passive mode**—This is the default site survey mode. It does not initiate any RF network traffic. It simply listens to the traffic that the client adapter hears and displays the results.

- **Active mode**—This mode causes the client adapter to actively send or receive low-level RF packets to or from its associated access point. It then provides information on the success rate. It also allows parameters to be set governing how the site survey is performed.

Preparation

The student must read and understand the material presented in Chapter 10, "Site Survey and Installation" in the *Fundamentals of Wireless LANs Companion Guide* prior to the lab.

Perform the site survey when the RF link is functioning with all other systems and noise sources operational.

Execute the site survey entirely from the mobile station.

When using the active mode, conduct the site survey with all variables set to operational values.

Tools and Resources

The following tools and resources are required for this lab:

- An access point with a valid IP address

- PC or laptop with a client adapter and client utilities installed

Step 1: Using Active Mode

Follow Steps 1 through 3 to activate the site survey active mode and obtain current information about the client adapter's ability to transmit and receive RF packets.

From the Client Utility Site Survey Passive Mode screen click the **Setup** button, as shown in Figure 10-1. The Site Survey Active Mode Setup screen looks like the example shown in Figure 10-2.

Figure 10-1   Client Utility Site Survey Passive Mode

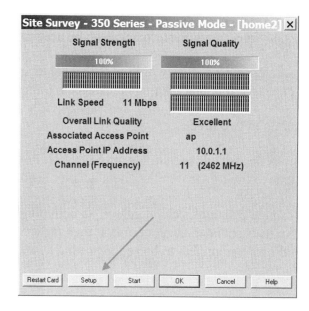

Figure 10-2   Client Utility Site Survey Active Mode

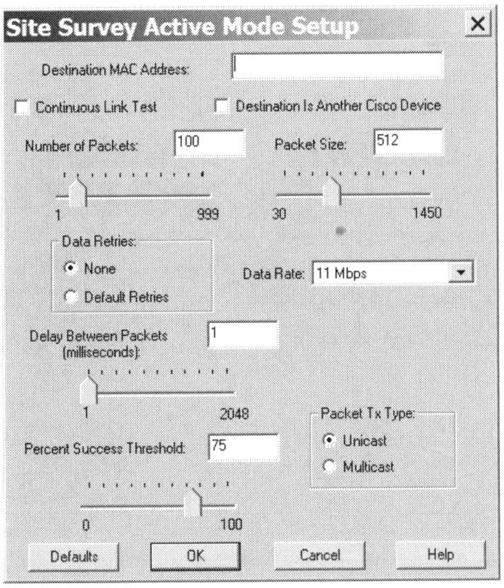

Step 2: Using Passive Mode

After setting any parameters, click **OK** to save the settings. The Site Survey Passive Mode screen appears.

Note the information on the Passive Mode screen:

1.   What is the signal strength?

    _____

2.   What is the signal quality?

    _____

3.   What is the link speed?

    _____

4.   What is the overall link quality?

    _____

Step 3: Running Site Survey Test

Click the **Start** button, as shown in Figure 10-3, to run the site survey test.

Figure 10-3   Run the Site Survey Test

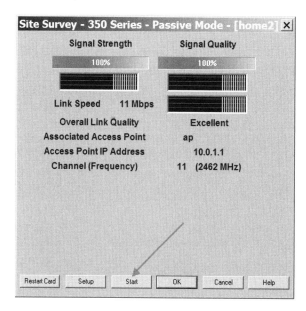

The Site Survey Active Mode screen, shown in Figure 10-4, appears.

Figure 10-4   Site Survey Active Mode Screen

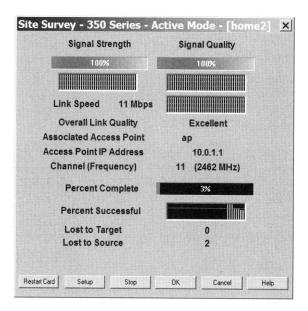

Position the Laptop PC in various locations relative to the access point.

Note the changes in the indicator field values listed below:

1.   What is the signal strength?

2. What is the signal quality?

_____

3. What is the link speed?

_____

4. What is the overall link quality?

_____

5. How many packets were lost to target?

_____

6. How many packets were lost to source?

_____

When the Stop button is clicked or the Percent Complete reaches 100%, the active mode changes back to the passive mode, as shown in Figure 10-5.

Figure 10-5   Site Survey Passive Mode Screen

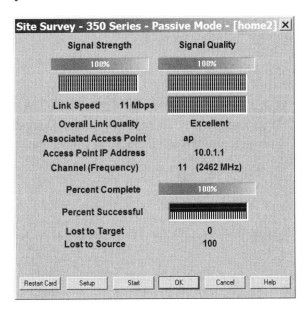

Click **OK** or **Cancel** to exit the site survey application.

Lab 10.2.7.2: Survey the Facility

Estimated Time: Actual time varies depending on the size of the site

Number of Team Members: Students work in teams of two

Objective

In this lab, students perform a site survey of an assigned location. Students should include all the following in site survey results:

- Channel selections

- Data rates

- Antenna selection

- Scenario

A site survey provides detailed information about the following:

- Where the access points are to be located

- How they will be mounted

- How they will be connected to the network

- Where any cabling or power may need to be installed

By providing the customer with a detailed site survey report, the IT manager can turn the necessary portions over to a local contractor. The contractor can then install the network cabling and power cabling needed to provide the wireless LAN (WLAN) connectivity to the network, as shown in Figure 10-6.

Figure 10-6   WLAN

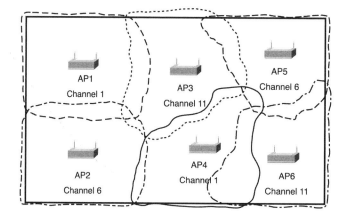

Preparation

The student should perform all the following in preparation for this lab:

- Read through the lab prior to conducting the site survey.

- Perform the site survey when the RF link is functioning with all other systems and noise sources operational.

- Execute the site survey entirely from the mobile station.

- Conduct the site survey with all variables set to operational values for use in the active mode.

- Obtain a site map and permission to use the areas that are to be surveyed in advance.

Tools and Resources

The following tools and resources are required for this lab:

- An access point with a valid IP address

- A PC with a client adapter and client utilities installed

- A site map of the area you are surveying

- An optional site survey kit for performing the site survey at an extended site other than the classroom

Step 1: Beginning the Site Survey in a Corner of the Facility

The easiest way to start a site survey is to pick one area of the facility that needs coverage. Choose a corner and place the access point (AP) in that corner. Survey the coverage of that AP and make a note of where the furthest point of coverage is from it. Then move the AP to the furthest coverage point, as shown in Figure 10-7.

Note: If the AP is placed in the corner, as much as 75% of your coverage cell might be wasted covering an area outside the building that does not need coverage.

Figure 10-7   Move the APs to the Furthest Coverage Point

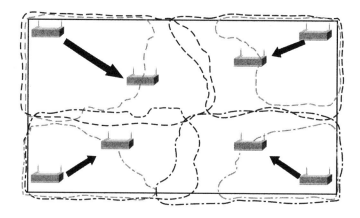

Sketch the actual site that is surveyed in the space provided below. Indicate where the AP is located. Draw the pattern of coverage.

Step 2: Planning for Overlap

After the AP has been moved, survey its coverage. It might be necessary to move the AP several times to find the best placement.

After you decide on the best location for that AP, move to a different corner of the facility and repeat the process. In a more advanced survey, repeating the process four times might provide coverage only around the perimeter of the facility.

Now fill in the holes in coverage. This is where experience and judgment comes into play. Some engineers might elect to survey the perimeter and then fill in the center.Remember, if seamless coverage is needed, the coverage cells must overlap. For a standard survey, 15% overlap is usually sufficient to provide for smooth, transparent handoffs.

Figure 10-8   Patterns of Coverage

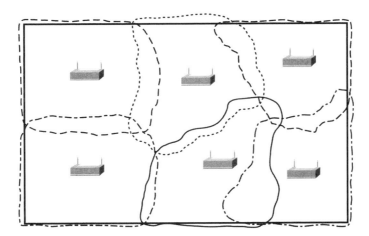

Sketch the actual site that is surveyed in the space provided below. Indicate where the APs will be located. Draw the patterns of coverage, as shown in Figure 10-8.

Step 3: Surveying from the Middle

Survey the first two areas and fill in the middle. Another approach is to survey the first two access points and find the coverage areas.

Place an AP at the edge of the first AP cell, survey the coverage, and then move the AP out further to utilize its entire cell, as shown in Figure 10-9. This allows the size of the cell to be roughly judged. Then survey the new location to determine feasibility, and adjust as necessary.

Figure 10-9   Move the AP to Utilize the Entire Cell

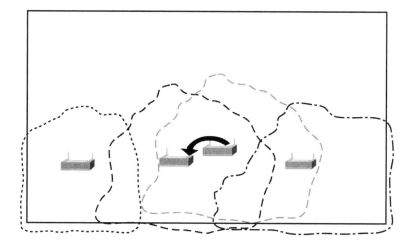

After the AP location is decided, continue this process until the entire facility is covered.

Step 4: Determining Channel Selection

When surveying, take into account the fact that there are only three nonoverlapping channels when using 802.11b and 802.11g. To maximize the data rate, use these nonoverlapping channels, which ensures that the APs do not interfere with each other, as shown in Figure 10-10.

As the WLAN is being designed, survey using the channel on which the AP is intended to operate.Part of the surveying duties is to test for interference. If every AP is surveyed using the same channel but not the actual channel the AP will be using, verifying that no interference exists on the channel that the AP is to use is difficult.

Figure 10-10   Use Nonoverlapping Channels

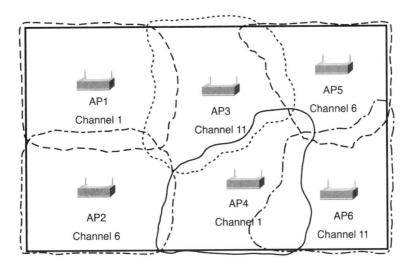

Sketch the actual site that is surveyed in the space provided below. Indicate where the APs will be located and the channels to be used. Draw the patterns of coverage.

Step 5: Surveying the Data Rates

After the minimum data rate that the customer will use has been determined, survey at that data rate. The data rate that is chosen drastically affects the results of the site survey. In the example shown in Figure 10-11, the same area is surveyed at two different data rates. If the survey is done at 2 Mbps, it takes 6 access points to cover the facility. If the survey is done at 5.5 Mbps, it might take 12 access points to cover the facility.**Figure 10-11   The Same Area Is Surveyed at Two Different Data Rates**

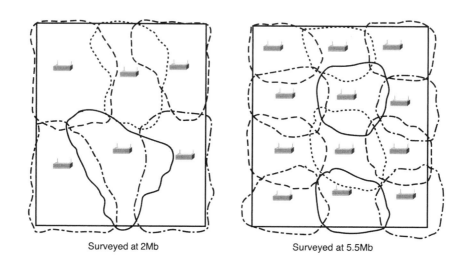

Surveyed at 2Mb   Surveyed at 5.5Mb

Step 6: Determining Antenna Choice, Power Level, and Cell Size

The student may elect to use a different antenna to obtain more coverage from the access points, use smaller antennas, and add more access points. Another possibility is changing the power levels on one or more of the access points to change the size of the coverage cell or cells, as shown in Figure 10-12. Finally, the student may elect to use a combination of these options to get the coverage they need.

Figure 10-12   Change the Size of the Coverage Cell

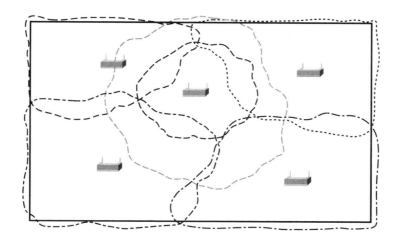

Lab 10.3.6: Mounting and Installation

Estimated Time: Actual time varies depending on the amount of supplies and tools

Number of Team Members: Students work in teams of two

Objectives

The objective of this lab is to explore wireless installation options and methods for the following:

- BR350
- AP1200

Scenario

Proper installation techniques are required to complete a safe and professional installation. Students should demonstrate proficiency using drywall or concrete anchors and wood screws. Proper routing and anchoring of Ethernet cables can be covered as well.

Tools and Resources

The following equipment is required to complete this lab:

- Cordless drill and screwdriver
- 1200 AP
- 1200 AP mounting brackets
- BR350 mounting kit
- Tie wraps
- Wood blocks
- Available flat surface and drop ceiling for practice mounting
- Ceiling enclosure (optional)

Additional Resources

Consult the following URLs for additional help with this lab:

http://www.chatsworth.com/zone/wireless.htm

http://www.nema-enclosures.cc/

http://www.nema.org/index_nema.cfm/606/

http://ulstandardsinfonet.ul.com/scopes/2043.html

Caution: It is important to keep the following items in mind while performing this lab:

- Always consult the instructor before drilling in any surface.

- Never drill additional holes in antennas, APs, or bridges, as this voids the warranty.

- Make sure any electrical power is turned off.

- Always have a person hold the ladder when in use.

- Always create a buffer zone with bright markers or cones.

Step 1: Mounting AP on Surface

The 1200 AP can be mounted on the following surfaces:

- Horizontal or vertical flat surfaces, such as walls or ceilings

- Suspended ceilings

The 1200 AP meets Underwriters Laboratories (UL) 2043 certification, and has an extended operating temperature of (-20 to 55°C or -4 to 131°F). Keep this in mind when deciding where to mount the AP.

The access point ships with a detachable mounting bracket, shown in Figure 10-13, and the necessary mounting hardware. Because it is detachable, you can use the mounting bracket as a template to mark the positions of the mounting holes for the installation. Then, install the mounting bracket and attach the access point when ready. The mounting bracket provides a professional look to the installation.

Figure 10-13   Mounting Bracket

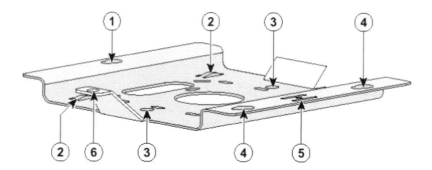

311

Mounting on a Horizontal or Vertical Surface

Perform the following steps to mount the access point on a horizontal or vertical surface, as shown in Figure 10-14.

Figure 10-14   Mounted Access Point

1. Use the mounting bracket as a template to mark the locations of the four mounting holes.

2. Drill one of the following sized holes at the locations marked:

    -   3/16 in. (4.7 mm) if using wall anchors

    -   1/8 in. (6.3 mm) if not using wall anchors

3. Install the anchors in the wall, if using them. Otherwise, go to Step 4.

4. Secure the mounting bracket to the surface using the #8 fasteners.

5. Attach the access point to the mounting bracket.

Note: You can make the installation more secure by mounting it to a stud or major structural member and using the appropriate fasteners. On a vertical surface, mount the bracket with its security hasp facing down, as shown in Figure 10-15.

Figure 10-15   Mounting Bracket and Hardware

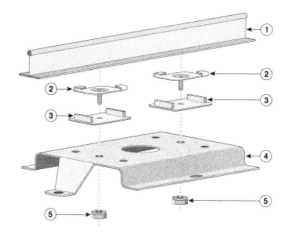

Mounting on a Suspended Ceiling

To comply with NEC code, a #10-24 grounding lug is provided on the mounting bracket.

Perform the steps that follow to mount the access point on a suspended ceiling or as directed by the instructor.

1. Determine the location where to mount the access point.

2. Attach two caddy fasteners to the suspended ceiling T-rail.

3. Use the mounting bracket to adjust the distance between the caddy fasteners so they align with the holes in the mounting bracket.

4. Use a standard screwdriver to tighten the caddy fastener studs in place on the suspended ceiling T-rail. Do not over tighten.

5. Install a plastic spacer on each caddy fastener stud. The spacer's legs should contact the suspended ceiling T-rail.

6. Attach the mounting bracket to the caddy fastener studs, and start a Keps nut on each stud.

7. Use a wrench or pliers to tighten the Keps nuts. Do not over tighten.

8. Attach the access point to the mounting bracket.

Attaching the Access Point to the Mounting Bracket

Perform the following steps to attach the access point to the mounting bracket:

1. Line up the three mounting pins on the access point with the large ends of the keyhole-shaped holes on the mounting bracket.

2.   Insert the access point into the keyhole-shaped holes, and maintain a slight pressure to hold it in place.

3.   Slide the access point's mounting pins into the small ends of the keyhole-shaped holes on the mounting bracket, and push the connector end of the access point. You will hear a click when the locking detent contacts the access point and locks it into place.

4.   Attach and adjust the antenna(s) or antenna cables.

5.   Connect the Ethernet cable to the access point's Ethernet port.

6.   Insert the 1200 series power module cable connector into the access point's 48 VDC power port (if using a local power source).

Securing the Access Point to the Mounting Bracket

The security hasp on the mounting bracket allows the access point to lock to the bracket, making it more secure. When the access point is properly installed on the mounting bracket, the holes in the security hasps line up so a padlock can be installed.

Known compatible padlocks are Master Lock models 120T or 121T.

Other AP Mounting Options

The AP can be mounted using nylon or metal tie wraps. Also, you can attach wood blocks to steel beams. You can attaché ¾-inch plywood to concrete walls to provide a buffer against moisture. Attaching a mounting bracket to wood is much easier than mounting directly to steel or concrete.

Step 2: Mounting Bridge Indoors

Mount the bridge or access point to a wall using the mounting kit and the mounting template, shown in Figure 10-16. The kit contains the following parts:

- Four #6 plastic wall anchors

- Four #8 x 0.88" sheet-metal screws

1.   If the original mounting template cannot be found, create a mounting template to drill four holes in the wall. Take the BR350 and trace the outline of the bridge and the holes on a separate piece of cardstock or paper. Or, check it with the one shown in Figure 10-16.

2.   Mark the holes on the wall.

3.   Drill the holes. The holes should be 3/16 in. (0.48 cm) in diameter and 1 in. (2.54 cm) deep.

Figure 10-16   Mounting Template

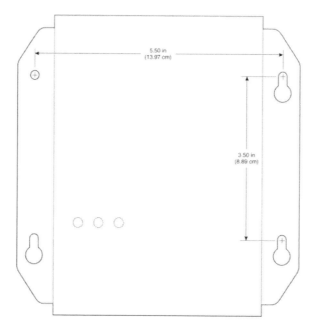

4.   Tap the wall anchors into the holes.

5.   Drive three screws into the wall anchors corresponding to the keyholes in the mounting template, leaving a small gap between the screw head and the anchor.

6.   Position the case's keyholes over the screws and pull down to lock it in place.

7.   Drive the remaining screw into the fourth wall anchor and tighten all mounting screws.

8.   Connect the Ethernet cable to the access point or bridge.

9.   If the access point or bridge has removable antennas, connect the antennas or antenna cables to the access point or bridge.

Step 4: Using Enclosures to Mount APs and Bridges

You can use enclosures to mount APs and bridges indoors and outdoors. Many types and styles of enclosures exist. Figure 10-17 shows a sample wall enclosure.

Figure 10-17   Wall Enclosure

Alternative AP Installation in Drop Ceiling (Optional)

Using a ceiling-mounted enclosure, as shown in Figure 10-18, the Cisco 350, 1100, or 1200 with the standard dipole (rubber duck) can be safely installed in a drop-ceiling grid. This saves time and cost of installing other antennas.

Figure 10-18   Ceiling Mounted Enclosure

Ceiling-mounted enclosures from Chatsworth include the following:

- AAT-CAP-35 - Faceplate for Cisco 350

- AAT-CAP-11 -Faceplate for Cisco 1100

- AAT-CAP-12 – Faceplate for Cisco 1200

Consult with the local, state, and federal guidelines for the proper enclosure. Table 10-1 lists NEMA Rating levels.

Table 10-1   NEMA Rating Levels

NEMA	Use	Protection Against
1	Indoor	Hand contact with enclosed equipment. Low-cost enclosure but suitable for clean and dry environments.
2	Indoor	Limited amounts of falling dirt and water.
3	Outdoors	Windblown dust, rain, and sleet; ice that forms on the enclosure.
3R	Outdoors	Falling rain and sleet; ice that forms on the enclosure.
4	Indoor	Windblown dust and rain, splashing water, and hose-directed water; ice that forms on the enclosure.
4X	Indoor/ Outdoors	Corrosion, windblown dust and rain, splashing water, and hose-directed water; ice that forms on the enclosure.
6	Indoor/ Outdoors	Occasional temporary submersion.

NEMA	Use	Protection Against
6P	Indoor/ Outdoors	Occasional prolonged submersion. Corrosion protection.
12	Indoor/Outdoors	Dust, falling dirt, and dripping noncorrosive liquids.
13	Indoor	Dust, spraying of water, oil, and noncorrosive coolant.

Lab 10.4.2.1: Request for Proposal

Estimated Time: Time varies depending on the scope of the project

Number of Team Members: Students work in teams of two

Objective

The objective of this lab is to prepare a request for proposal (RFP) for a fictitious business for adding a WLAN to its business network.

Scenario

An RFP lists a customer's design requirements and the types of solutions a network design must include. Organizations send an RFP to vendors and design consultants. They use the responses they receive to help select a suitable vendor or supplier.

Preparation

The instructor will compile a list of approved fictitious businesses used for the RFP.

Tools and Resources

The following tools and resources are helpful with this lab:

- Online Internet research

- Vendor literature and site contacts

- Trade journals and publications

Additional Materials

A variety of technology RFPs are available at the following URL:

http://networkcomputing.telezoo.com/asp/vrfp/showvendorrfp.asp?idcats=722&history=^709^722&techname=Wireless

Step 1: Preparing an RFP

Prepare an RFP that lists the design requirements of the business selected and the types of solutions for the network design. The RFP must include all of the following:

- Business goals for the project

- Scope of the project

- Information on the existing network and applications

- Information on new applications

- Technical requirements including the following:

  - Scalability

  - Availability

  - Performance

  - Security

  - Manageability

  - Usability

  - Adaptability

  - Affordability

- Warranty requirements for products

- Environmental or architectural constraints that could affect implementation

- Training and support requirements

- Preliminary schedule with milestones and deliverables

- Legal contractual terms and conditions

Lab 10.4.2.2: RFP Response

Estimated Time: Time varies depending on the scope of the project

Number of Team Members: Students work in teams of two

Objective

In this lab, students prepare a response to a request for proposal (RFP) for the addition of a WLAN to an existing wired LAN. Compete against other student teams by responding to the same RFP.

Scenario

In Lab 10.4.2.1, an RFP was prepared for a fictitious business seeking to add a WLAN to its existing network.

The instructor has reviewed those RFPs and has decided that each team will respond to the RFP.

Organizations send an RFP to vendors and design consultants. They then use the responses they receive to weed out suppliers that cannot meet requirements.

RFP responses help organizations compare all of the following presented by competing suppliers:

- Designs

- Product capabilities

- Pricing

- Service

- Support alternatives

Despite the fact that a response to an RFP must stay within the guidelines specified by the customer, use ingenuity to ensure that the response highlights the benefits of the design.

Base the response on an analysis of the customer's business and technical goals, and the flow and characteristics of network traffic. Write the response so the reader can easily recognize that the design satisfies critical selection criteria.

When writing the response, be sure to consider the competition. Try to predict what other vendors or design consultants might propose, and then call attention to the aspects of this solution that are likely to be superior to competing designs.

In addition, pay attention to the customer's business style. Remember the importance of understanding the customer's biases and any office politics or project history that could affect the perception of the proposed design.

Preparation

The instructor will choose one RFP prepared from Lab 10.4.2.1. All the student groups will use this RFP. All student teams must respond to the same RFP chosen by the instructor.

Tools and Resources

The following tools and resources are helpful with this lab:

- Online Internet research sites

- Vendor literature, trade journals, and publications

- Response requirements

Step 1: Creating a Design Based on the RFP Criteria

The RFP states that the response must include some or all of the following topics:

- A network topology for the new design

- Information on the protocols, technologies, and products that form the design

- An implementation plan

- A training plan

- Support and service information

- Prices and payment options

- Qualifications of the responding vendor or supplier

- Recommendations from other customers for whom the supplier has provided a solution

- Legal contractual terms and conditions

Lab 10.4.2.3: Review of RFP Response

Estimated Time: Actual times vary depending on the scope of the project

Number of Team Members: The instructor reviews the responses with the class

Objective

In this lab, students review the response written to the RFP created in Lab 10.4.2.1, and determine whether the response created in Lab 10.4.2.2 meets the requirements of the RFP. Students shall rank the responses according to how well they addressed the RFP.

Scenario

Organizations use the responses they receive to eliminate suppliers that cannot meet requirements. RFP responses help organizations compare all of the following presented by competing suppliers:

- Design

- Product capabilities

- Pricing

- Service and support alternatives

- Security

Use the comparison chart in Table 10-2 for the responses to rank them prior to this lab.

Tools and Resources

Comparison chart for ranking the RFP responses:

Table 10-2   Comparison Chart

Team	Design	Product Capabilities	Pricing	Service and Support	Training	Security
TEAM 1						
TEAM 2						
TEAM 3						
TEAM 4						

Team	Design	Product Capabilities	Pricing	Service and Support	Training	Security
TEAM 5						
TEAM 6						
TEAM 7						
TEAM 8						
TEAM 9						
TEAM 10						

Step 1: Ranking the RFP Responses

Review the responses to the RFP and determine if it meets the guidelines set in the RFP. Rank each response; use the following criteria to help rank the RFPs:

- Business goals for the project

- Scope of the project

- Information on the existing network and applications

- Information on new applications

- Technical requirements, including scalability, availability, performance, security, manageability, usability, adaptability, and affordability

- Warranty requirements for products

- Environmental or architectural constraints that could affect implementation

- Training and support requirements

- Preliminary schedule with milestones and deliverables

- Legal contractual terms and conditions

Step 2: Assigning a Weighting System

Assign a weight to each criterion. Assigning a weight to each criterion makes allowances to a team's total score based upon the importance of an individual criterion's impact on the project.

For example, a team might score very high on its design and low on support. But which of the criterion is more important to the project's success? Should each of these criteria be given the same weighted score? If training is more important to the organization, assign a higher weight to it; if the pricing is of higher importance to the organization, assign a higher weight to the pricing category.

Have the class rank the criterion in order of importance to the project using Table 10-3. As an example, a multiplier based upon criterion importance is placed next to each criterion.

Table 10-3   Criterion Ranking

Team	Designs (3X)	Product Capabilities (5X)	Pricing (4X)	Service and Support (3X)	Training (2X)	Security (5X)
TEAM 1						
TEAM 2						
TEAM 3						
TEAM 4						
TEAM 5						
TEAM 6						
TEAM 7						
TEAM 8						
TEAM 9						
TEAM 10						

The ranking system can be based upon how well each of the teams addressed the projects criterion; for example, the following can be used:

- 1 – Poor

- 2 – Satisfactory

- 3 – Above Average

- 4 – Excellent

The score takes the ranking number and multiplier to assign a weighted score to the team. For example, consider the score for TEAM 1 in Table 10-4

Table 10-4   TEAM 1 Score

Team	Designs (3X)	Product Capabilities (5X)	Pricing (4X)	Service and Support (3X)	Training (2X)	Security (5X)
TEAM 1	6	15	16	9	6	10

TEAM 1 scored as follows:

- Designs – 2, the weighted score becomes 2 times 3 equaling 6

- Product Capabilities – 3, the weighted score becomes 3 times 5 equaling 15

- Pricing – 4, the weighted score becomes 4 times 4 equaling 16

- Service – 3, the weighted score becomes 3 times 3, equaling 9

- Training – 3, the weighted score becomes 3 times 2 equaling 6

- Security – 2, the weighted score becomes 2 times 5 equaling 4

TEAM 1's total score becomes 6 + 15 + 16 + 9 + 9 + 4 = 59.

Score each team. The team with the largest numerical score wins the contract.

Chapter 11

Troubleshooting Management, Monitoring, and Diagnostics

Lab 11.1.4: Basic Troubleshooting on AP

Estimated Time: 10 minutes

Number of Team Members: Students work in teams of two

Objective

In this lab, students use basic troubleshooting procedures for problems with an access point (AP).

Scenario

Troubleshooting networks, including WLANs, is more important than ever. Networks continue to add services as time goes on, and with each added service comes more variables involved in implementing networks. This adds to the complexity of troubleshooting the networks as well. So, organizations increasingly depend on network administrators and network engineers having strong troubleshooting skills.

Tools and Resources

The following tools and resources are required for this lab:

- Access point properly installed and configured on a wired LAN

- PC with a properly installed wireless NIC and client utility

Step 1: Checking the Top Panel Indicators

1. If the access point is not communicating, check the three indicators on the top panel, as shown in Figure 11-1. These indicators can quickly assess the status of the unit.

Figure 11-1   Top Panel Indicators

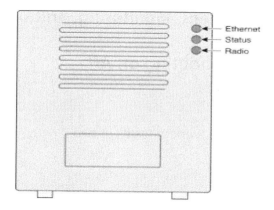

The indicator lights have the following meanings:

The Ethernet indicator signals traffic on the wired LAN, or Ethernet infrastructure. This indicator blinks green when a packet is received or transmitted over the Ethernet infrastructure.

a.   Is the Ethernet Indicator light blinking on your access point?

_____

The Status indicator signals operational status. Blinking green indicates that the access point is operating normally but is not associated with any wireless devices. Steady green indicates that the access point is associated with a wireless client.

b.   Is the status of the access point associated or not associated?

_____

The Radio indicator blinks green to indicate radio traffic activity. The light is normally off, but it blinks green whenever a packet is received or transmitted over the access point's radio.

c.   Is there radio traffic on your access point?

_____

Step 2: Checking the Basic Settings

1.   Check the Service Set Identifier (SSID) of the access point and client, shown in Figure 11-2. Mismatched basic settings are the most common causes of lost connectivity with wireless clients. Wireless clients attempting to associate with the access point must use the same SSID as the access point.

Figure 11-2   Check the SSID

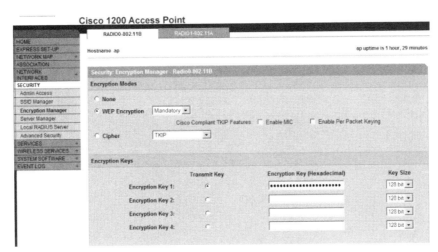

2.   Verify authentication is set to **Open** on the access point and client. A shared key exposes the Wired Equivalent Protocol (WEP) key unnecessarily due to weaknesses in design.

Step 3: Checking the WEP Key

1.   The WEP key used to transmit data must be set up exactly the same on the access point and any wireless devices with which it associates. Make sure to enter the key in hexadecimal on the client and access point. The Encryption Manager page is shown in Figure 11-3, and the Network Security tab of the Properties window is shown in Figure 11-4.

Figure 11-3   Encryption Manager Page

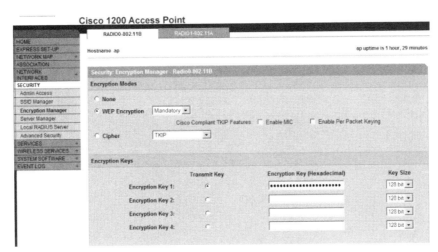

Figure 11-4   **Network Security Tab**

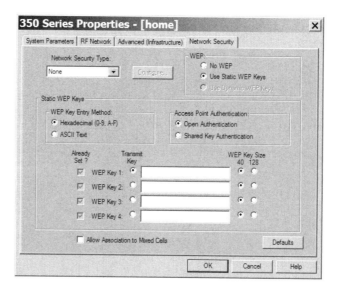

2.   If a possibility exists that the access point WEP key and the Client Adapter WEP key are not congruent to each other, reset the WEP setting to the default configuration or overwrite the current WEP key.

3.   If the password that allows the access point to be configured is unknown, or if major changes to the configuration need to be made, the configuration may need to be completely reset.

Lab 11.2.6: Troubleshooting TCP/IP Issues

Estimated Time: 20 minutes

Number of Team Members: Students work in teams of two

Objectives

In this lab, standard TCP/IP commands are utilized to troubleshoot connectivity problems between the wireless client and the access point (AP).

Scenario

Basic troubleshooting for TCP/IP on Windows machines combines facts gathered from the perspective of all of the following:

- The router

- The switch

- The bridge

- The access point

- The Windows client or server

Check to see if it is possible to connect using IP addresses. Use an IP address as a target for the standard TCP/IP commands such as **ping, tracert**, and **telnet.** You can verify the basic IP setup with the **winipcfg** utility for Windows 95 and 98, and the **ipconfig** utility for Windows NT, 2000, and XP.

Preparation

The student should read and understand the material presented in Chapter 11, "Troubleshooting Management, Monitoring, and Diagnostics" of the *Fundamentals of Wireless LANs Companion Guide* prior to the lab.

Tools and Resources

The following tools and resources help with this lab:

- AP configured on a wired network

- PC with wireless client adapter and utility properly installed

- A NeoTrace Express freeware program, which can be downloaded at the following URL: http://www.networkingfiles.com/PingFinger/Neotraceexpress.htm

Additional Materials

Microsoft: http://www.microsoft.com/technet/treeview/default.asp?url=/technet/prodtechnol/winxppro/proddocs/tcpip_utils.asp

Step 1: Pinging to Confirm Network Connectivity

Use the **ping** command to confirm basic network connectivity on IP networks. For IP, the **ping** command sends Internet Control Message Protocol (ICMP) Echo messages. ICMP is the Internet protocol that reports errors and provides information relevant to IP packet addressing. If a station receives an ICMP Echo message, it sends an ICMP Echo Reply message back to the source.

It is a good idea to use the **ping** command when the network is functioning properly to see how the command works under normal conditions, and to have something to compare against when troubleshooting.

From the PC, ping the access point and examine the results:

```
C:\>ping 172.25.0.149

Pinging 172.25.0.149 with 32 bytes of data:

Reply from 172.25.0.149: bytes=32 time<10ms TTL=249
Reply from 172.25.0.149: bytes=32 time<10ms TTL=249
Reply from 172.25.0.149: bytes=32 time<10ms TTL=249
Reply from 172.25.0.149: bytes=32 time<10ms TTL=249

Ping statistics for 172.25.0.149:
    Packets: Sent = 4, Received = 4, Lost = 0 (0% loss),
Approximate round trip times in milli-seconds:
    Minimum = 0ms, Maximum =  0ms, Average =  0ms
C:\>
```

Step 2: Using the Tracert Tool to Determine Route Used

The **tracert** tool on a Windows host reports each router a TCP/IP packet crosses on its way to a destination. It does essentially the same thing as the **trace** command in the Cisco IOS Software. The syntax for the **tracert** command is as follows:

```
tracert [-d [-h maximum_hops] [-j host-list] [-w timeout] target_name
```

The following is an explanation of the command's parameters:

- **d**—Specifies to not resolve addresses to host names (use recommended in test networks to avoid DNS delays)

- **h** *maximum_hops*—Specifies the maximum number of hops to search for the target

- **j** *host-list*—Specifies loose source route along the host list

- **w** *timeout*—Specifies the number of milliseconds specified by *timeout* to wait for each reply

- *target_name*—Specifies the name or IP address of the target host

Errors that can occur include the asterisk (*) and the 'request timed out' message. These messages indicate a problem with the router or a problem elsewhere on the network. The error might relate to a forwarded packet or one that timed out.

Another common error is a report of 'destination network unreachable.' This error usually indicates that network filtering is happening, likely from a firewall. It might also indicate a routing problem, such as a failed network link.

From the PC, perform a tracert to http://www.cisco.com.

```
C:\>tracert www.cisco.com
Tracing route to www.cisco.com [198.133.219.25] over a maximum of 30 hops:
  1   <10 ms   <10 ms   <10 ms   sjc8-00-gw1.cisco.com [171.71.88.2]
  2   <10 ms   <10 ms   <10 ms   sjc2-dtb-gw1.cisco.com [171.71.240.105]
  3   <10 ms   <10 ms   <10 ms   sjc5-sbb4-gw1.cisco.com [171.71.241.153]
  4   <10 ms   <10 ms   <10 ms   sjc12-rbb-gw4.cisco.com [171.71.241.254]
  5   <10 ms   <10 ms   <10 ms   sjck-rbb-gw2.cisco.com [171.69.7.229]
  6   <10 ms   <10 ms   <10 ms   sj-wall-1.cisco.com [171.69.7.182]
  7   <10 ms   <10 ms   <10 ms   sjce-dirty-gw1.cisco.com [128.107.240.197]
  8   <10 ms   <10 ms   <10 ms   sjck-sdf-ciod-gw2.cisco.com [128.107.239.102]
  9   <10 ms   <10 ms   <10 ms   www.cisco.com [198.133.219.25]
Trace complete.
```

Step 3: Using the ipconfig Utility to Determine TCP/IP Configuration

The command syntax for **ipconfig** and **winipcfg** is as follows:

```
ipconfig [/all | /renew [adapter] | /release [adapter]]
```

The **ipconfig** command applies to Windows 2000 and later releases, while the **winipcfg** command applies to pre-Windows 2000 releases. The following are the parameters of the command:

- **all**—Produces a full display. Without this switch, **ipconfig** displays only the IP address, subnet mask, and default gateway values for each network card.

- **/renew** [*adapter*]—Renews dynamic host configuration protocol (DHCP) configuration parameters. This option is available only on systems running the DHCP Client service. To specify an adapter name, type the adapter name that appears when you use **ipconfig** without parameters.

- **/release** [*adapter*]—Releases the DHCP configuration. This option disables TCP/IP on the local system and is available only on DHCP clients.

With no parameters, the **ipconfig** utility presents all of the current TCP/IP configuration values to the user, including IP address and subnet mask.

To check the local host configuration, enter a DOS window on the host and enter the **ipconfig /all** command. This command shows your TCP/IP address configuration, including the address of the Domain Name System (DNS) server. If any of the IP addresses are incorrect, or if no IP address is displayed, determine the correct IP address and edit it or enter it for the local host.

Complete the information in Table 11-1.

Table 11-1   TCP/IP Configuration Settings

TCP/IP Setting	Information
Host Name	
Primary DNS Suffix	
Node Type	
IP Routing Enabled	
WINS Proxy Enabled	
DNS Suffix Search List	
Connection-specific DNS Suffix	
Description	
Physical Address	
DHCP Enabled	
Autoconfiguration Enabled	
IP Address	
Subnet Mask	
Default Gateway	
DHCP Server	
DNS Servers	
Primary WINS Server	
Secondary WINS Server	
Lease Obtained	
Lease Expires	

Step 4: Using Telnet to Test Layer 7 Connectivity

1.   Test Layer 7 connectivity from your host PC to the access point by establishing a Telnet connection to the access point:

```
C:\>telnet 10.0.P.1
User Access Verification
Username:
Password:
AP1200#
```

     a.   Was the telneting successful?

_____

     b.   Which command will be used for testing in the situations in Table 11-2?

Table 11-2   Situations and Commands

Situation	Command
Host cannot access other hosts through access point or bridge.	
Host cannot access certain networks by the way of AP or bridge.	
Users can access some hosts, but not others.	
Some services are available and others are not.	
Users cannot make any connections when one parallel path is down.	
Certain protocols are blocked and others are not	

Step 5: Finding and Downloading Freeware Software Utilities for telnet, trace, and ping

Freeware utilities are available for download over the Internet that allow telnet, trace, and ping in a Graphical User Interface (GUI) environment. One such program is NeoTrace Express. You can download it at the following URL site:

http://www.networkingfiles.com/PingFinger/Neotraceexpress.htm

vxUtil is another great free utility for the PocketPC, which can be downloaded from http://www.cam.com/vxutil.html.

The utilities include the following:

- DNS Audit

- DNS Lookup

- Finger

- Get HTML

- Info

- IP Subnet Calculator

- Password Generator

- Ping

- Ping Sweep

- Port Scanner

- Quote

- Time Service

- Trace Route

- Whois

Perform an Internet search to find two other TCP/IP utilities. Record them here. Share with the class.

_____

_____

Lab 11.5.6.1: Configure Syslog on AP

Estimated Time: 25 minutes

Number of Team Members: Students work in teams of two

Objective

In this lab, students configure and use syslog logging to monitor network events.

Scenario

A network security administrator should always log significant events on the AP to the syslog server. A syslog server should be located on a secure internal network to ensure log integrity. The syslog server can be a dedicated server or another server running syslog services.

A syslog server is a basic application that allows Aironet AP and bridge event information to be viewed from a Windows system. It includes all the following features:

- Receiving syslog messages via either TCP or UDP

- Full reliability because messages can be sent via TCP

- Ability to receive syslog messages from devices

Topology

Figure 11-5 shows the topology used in this lab.

Figure 11-5   Lab Topology

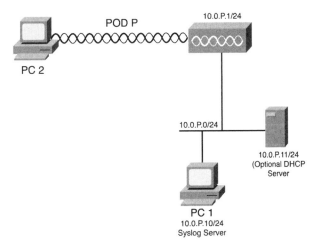

Note: The topology figures and lab examples contain **P** values. The **P** value in the addressing and naming scheme refers to *your* assigned Pod number.

Examples of determining **P** values follow:

- Pod2 is looking at a topology figure and is trying to determine the **P** values in the figure. In this scenario, the **P** values equal 2. 10.0.P.12 becomes 10.0.2.12, 172.30.P.2 becomes 172.30.2.2, and so on.

- Pod1 is looking at a topology figure and is trying to determine the **P** values in the figure. In this scenario, the **P** values equal 1. 10.0.P.12 becomes 10.0.1.12, 172.30.P.2 becomes 172.30.1.2, and so on.

In both examples, the **P** values are directly related to the Pod number of the team.

Preparation

The student should read and understand material presented in Chapter 11 from the *Fundamentals of Wireless LANs Companion Guide* prior to this lab.

Numerous syslog servers are available on the Internet. This lab assumes that Kiwi Syslog Daemon is used. This is a freeware utility that you can download at http://www.kiwisyslog.com. Download the syslog server and install the executable file.

Tools and Resources

The following tools and resources are required for this lab:

- A properly set up wired LAN

- A properly set up and installed AP

- A PC acting as the syslog server with a static IP address

- A PC with a properly installed wireless client adapter and utility

Additional Materials

Further information about the objectives covered in this lab can be found at the following website:

http://www.kiwisyslog.com

Command List

Table 11-3 lists and describes the commands used in this lab exercise. Refer to this list if you need assistance during the lab.

Table 11-3   Lab Command Descriptions

Command	Description
configure terminal	Enters global configuration mode
logging on	Enables message logging
logging host	Logs messages to a syslog server host
show logging	Verifies the log settings and entries
show running-config	Verifies the active configuration in DRAM.
copy running-config startup-config	Saves the active configuration into Flash
service timestamps log uptime	Enables log timestamps
service sequence-numbers	Enables sequence numbers

Step 1: Downloading and Installing the Kiwi Syslog Software

1.   Go to the http://www.kiwisyslog.com/software_downloads.htm site and download the free edition of the kiwi syslog software.

2.   Install the executable file.

Step 2: Setting Up the Kiwi Syslog Daemon

Click the **Kiwi Syslog Daemon** icon on the desktop to bring up the syslog screen, as shown in Figure 11-6.

Step 3: Enabling Logging on the Access Point

1.   Open the AP browser menu and go to the **EVENT LOG**>**Notification Options** page.

2.   Enable the **Events Generate Syslog Messages** utility on the AP, as shown in Figure 11-7.

3.   Type in the Syslog Server Host IP address. This should be 10.0.P.10.

4.   Set the Syslog Facility logging level. You can use the default, Local7.

      What other selections are available?

      _____

5.   Click the **Apply** button to begin logging events to the Kiwi Syslog.

Figure 11-6   Kiwi Syslog Screen

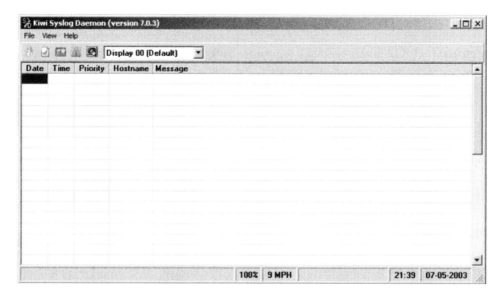

Figure 11-7   Enable Event Generate Syslog Messages

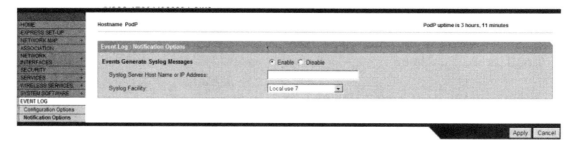

Step 4: Viewing the Kiwi Syslog Event Log

1.   Generate events to the syslog by logging into the access point that is being monitored. Figure 11-8 shows the event log.

2.   Have the wireless users log onto the AP.

3.   Have the wireless users log off the AP.

4.   These changes trigger a logged event on the syslog. What is the message that was displayed on the syslog?

Figure 11-8   Event Log

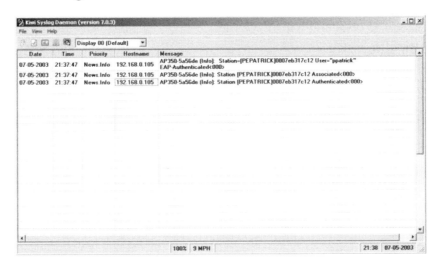

Step 5: Enabling Logging on the Access Point

1.   Erase the configuration and reload the AP.

2.   Configure the AP according to the topology.

3.   Enable the access point using the Cisco IOS with the following command:

```
PodP(config)#logging on
```

4.   To send the logging messages to a syslog server located on PC1, use the following command (where **P** is the Pod number):

```
PodP(config)#logging host 10.0.P.10
```

5.   View the available messaging levels for syslog:

```
PodP(config)#logging trap ?
  <0-7>           Logging severity level
  alerts          Immediate action needed         (severity=1)
  critical        Critical conditions             (severity=2)
  debugging       Debugging messages              (severity=7)
  emergencies     System is unusable              (severity=0)
  errors          Error conditions                (severity=3)
  informational   Informational messages          (severity=6)
  notifications   Normal but significant conditions (severity=5)
  warnings        Warning conditions              (severity=4)
  <cr>
```

6.   Configure the syslog message level to debugging.

```
PodP(config)#logging trap debugging   (or 7)
```

7.   Enable the service timestamps on the access point using the following command:

```
PodP(config)#service timestamps log uptime
```

8.   Enable the service sequence numbers on the access point logging using the following command:

```
PodP(config)#service sequence-numbers
```

Step 6: Verifying the Configuration

1.   Verify the configuration on the AP:

```
PodP#show running-config
Building configuration...

Current configuration : 2552 bytes
!
version 12.2
no service pad
service timestamps debug datetime msec
service timestamps log uptime
service password-encryption
service sequence-numbers
!
hostname PodP
!
logging trap debugging
logging 10.0.1.10
!
[output omitted]
```

2.   Use the **show logging** command to view the entries:

```
PodP#show logging
Syslog logging: enabled (0 messages dropped, 2 messages rate-limited, 0 flushes, 0
overruns)
    Console logging: level debugging, 312 messages logged
    Monitor logging: level debugging, 0 messages logged
    Buffer logging: level debugging, 314 messages logged
    Logging Exception size (4096 bytes)
    Count and timestamp logging messages: disabled
    Trap logging: level informational, 316 message lines logged
Log Buffer (4096 bytes):
*Mar  4 04:44:28.924: %DOT11-6-DISASSOC: Interface Dot11Radio0, Deauthenticatin
 Station 0007.8592.e4ea Reason: Previous authentication no longer valid
*Mar  4 04:47:55.076: %DOT11-6-ASSOC: Interface Dot11Radio0, Station csawyer 00
9.b74c.b479 Associated KEY_MGMT[NONE]
*Mar  4 04:51:36.967: %DOT11-4-MAXRETRIES: Packet to client 0009.b74c.b479 reac
ed max retries, remove the client
*Mar  4 04:51:36.968: %DOT11-6-DISASSOC: Interface Dot11Radio0, Deauthenticatin
 Station 0009.b74c.b479 Reason: Previous authentication no longer valid
*Mar  4 05:36:44.416: %DOT11-6-ASSOC: Interface Dot11Radio0, Station KDEVIAEN-W
K02 00d0.59c8.ca3f Reassociated KEY_MGMT[NONE]
 --More--
[output omitted]
```

3.   To clear the log, use the following command:

```
PodP#clear logging
Clear logging buffer [confirm]
PodP#
```

4.   Issue the **show log** command again to view the clear log:

```
PodP#show log
Syslog logging: enabled (0 messages dropped, 2 messages rate-limited, 0 flushes,
 0 overruns)
    Console logging: level debugging, 312 messages logged
    Monitor logging: level debugging, 0 messages logged
    Buffer logging: level debugging, 314 messages logged
    Logging Exception size (4096 bytes)
    Count and timestamp logging messages: disabled
    Trap logging: level informational, 316 message lines logged

Log Buffer (4096 bytes):
PodP#
```

Step 7: Viewing the Kiwi Syslog Event Log

1. Generate events to the syslog by establishing a wireless connection to the AP. Also, log· into the AP via telnet or SSH.

2. The login triggers logged events on the syslog server located on PC1.

    What is the message that was displayed on the syslog?

    _____

    _____

Lab 11.5.6.2: Configure SNMP on AP

Estimated Time: 20 minutes

Number of Team Members: Students work in teams of two

Objective

In this lab, students install and configure the Kiwi Syslog Daemon to listen for SNMP logs. Students configure the contact and location of the SNMP agent and test the configuration.

Scenario

SNMP is an application layer protocol that facilitates the exchange of management information between network devices. It is part of the TCP/IP protocol suite. SNMP uses User Datagram Protocol (UDP) port 161 for most requests and responses. SNMP traps use UDP port 162.

Topology

Figure 11-9 shows the topology used in this lab.

Figure 11-9   Lab Topology

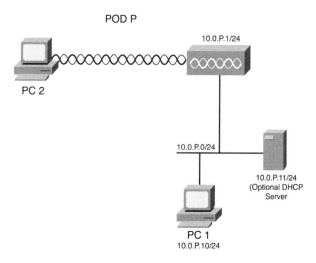

Note: The topology figures and lab examples contain **P** values. The **P** value in the addressing and naming scheme refers to *your* assigned Pod number.

Examples of determining **P** values follow:

- Pod2 is looking at a topology figure and is trying to determine the **P** values in the figure. In this scenario, the **P** values equals 2. 10.0.P.12 becomes 10.0.2.12, 172.30.P.2 becomes 172.30.2.2, and so on.

- Pod1 is looking at a topology figure and is trying to determine the **P** values in the figure. In this scenario, the **P** values equals 1. 10.0.P.12 becomes 10.0.1.12, 172.30.P.2 becomes 172.30.1.2, and so on.

In both examples, the **P** values are directly related to the Pod number of the team.

Preparation

Table 11-4 documents the basic settings to be applied to the AP for each team.

Table 11-4   AP Setup

Team	Access Point Name	SSID	Address
1	Pod1	AP1	10.0.1.1/24
2	Pod2	AP2	10.0.2.1/24

Tools and Resources

The following tools and resources are required for this lab:

- One AP 1200

- A wired PC (PC1) acting as the SNMP server

- A wireless PC or laptop with ACU

Command List

Table 11-5 lists and describes the commands used in this lab exercise. Refer to this list if assistance is needed during the lab exercise:

Table 11-5   Lab Command Descriptions

Command	Description
no snmp-server	Disables SNMP
show snmp	Monitors SNMP status
snmp-server community	Defines the community access string
snmp-server contact	Sets the system contact string
snmp-server enable traps snmp	Enables the sending of traps, and specifies the type of notification to be sent

Command	Description
snmp-server host	Configures the recipient of an SNMP trap operation
snmp-server location	Sets the system location string

Step 1: Downloading and Installing the Software

1. Go to the following website and download Kiwi Syslog Daemon Standard version software: http://www.kiwisyslog.com/software_downloads.htm.

2. Install the program on PC1.

Step 2: Setting Up and Executing the Kiwi Syslog Daemon

1. Click the **Setup** icon located in the upper-left corner of the syslog program window. The setup window then appears, as shown in Figure 11-10.

Figure 11-10   Syslog Program Window

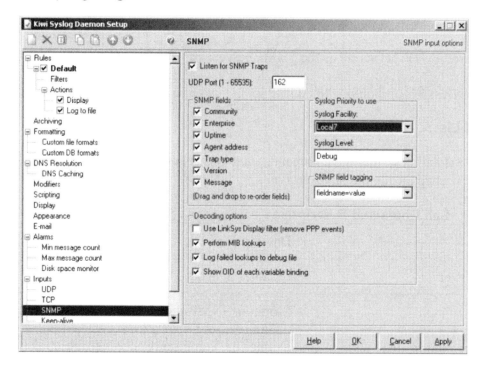

2. Configure SNMP on Kiwi Syslog Daemon by checking the **Listen for SNMP Traps** box.

3. Click the **OK** button to save the changes.

What UDP port does SNMP Trap Watcher listen on?

Step 2: Using the Web Browser to Set Up SNMP

1. Ensure the AP is configured according to Table 11-4. Ping from PC1, located at 10.0.P.10 to the AP to ensure connectivity.

2. Browse to the **SERVICES > SNMP** page of the AP, shown in Figure 11-11.

Figure 11-11   Services > SNMP Page

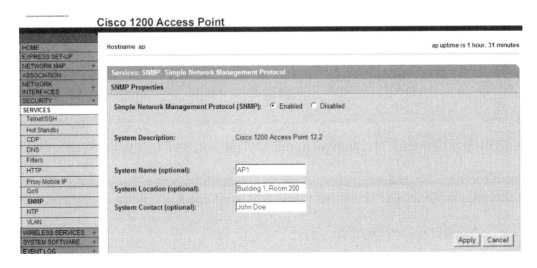

3. Click the Enabled radio button to enable SNMP on the AP.

4. Set a System Name (this is optional, but useful).

5. Set a System Location (this is optional, but useful)

6. Set a System Contact (this is optional, but useful)

7. Complete the following information for your access point:

    System Name:

    _____

    System Location:

    _____

    System Contact:

    _____

6.   Click the **Apply** button.

Step 3: Creating a Public Community String

Create a public community string with Read Only, as shown in Figure 11-12. In a production environment, it is important to configure a unique string for increase security. SNMP Read Only provides monitoring via an SNMP management application.

Figure 11-12   Public Community String with Read Only

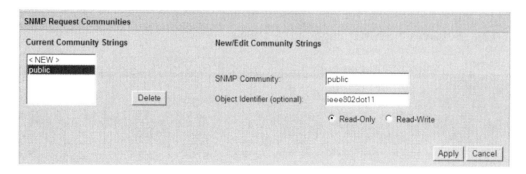

Step 4: Creating a Private Community String

Follow the three steps listed here to create a private community string that permits SNMP read-write access monitoring and management via SNMP management applications.

1.   Click **<NEW>** in Current Community Strings.

2.   Create a private1234 community string with Read-Write, as shown in Figure 11-13.

Figure 11-13   Private Community String

3.   Click the **Apply** button to create the string.

Step 5: Setting SNMP Trap Destinations

1.   Set an **SNMP Trap Destination** by entering the IP address of PC1 located at 10.0.P.10, as shown in Figure 11-14.

Figure 11-14   SNMP Trap Destination

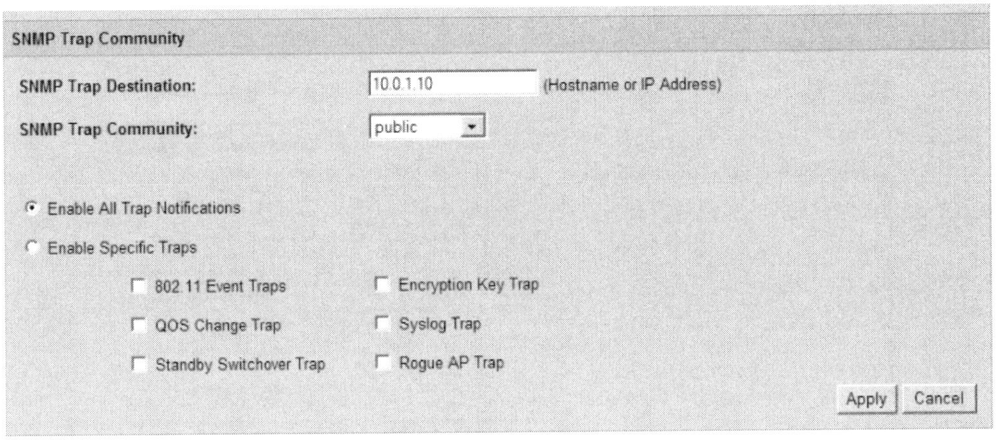

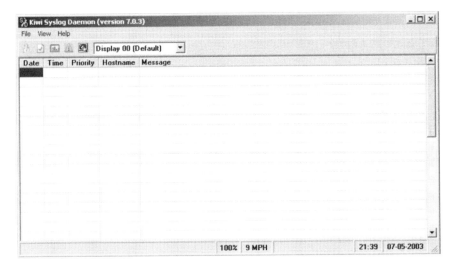

2.   Set the SNMP Trap Community to **public**.

3.   Select **Enable All Trap Notifications**.

4.   Click the **Apply** button.

Step 6: Test the Configuration

1.   Click the **Kiwi Syslog Daemon** icon on the desktop to bring up the syslog application. The Kiwi Syslog Daemon, shown in Figure 11-15, can be customized or the defaults can be used.

Figure 11-15   Kiwi Syslog Daemon

2.   Have a wireless user connect to the bridge.

3.   Have the wireless user disconnect from the bridge.

4.   View the main logging screen on Kiwi, shown in Figure 11-16.

Figure 11-16   Kiwi Syslog Daemon with Entries

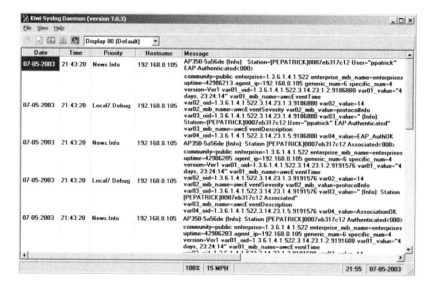

Step 7: Setting the System Contact and Location of the SNMP Agent via IOS CLI

Before beginning this step, reset the AP back to factory configuration. Configure the AP according to Table 11-4.

1.   Configure the system contact and location:

```
PodP(config)#snmp-server contact [name] [phone]
PodP(config)#snmp-server location [location]
```

2.   What command would be used to verify this information on an AP?

Step 8: Enabling SNMP Traps

1.   Enable all the SNMP trap types at once:

```
PodP(config)#snmp-server enable traps snmp
```

2.   Specify the SNMP destination host the trap notifications will be sent to:

```
PodP(config)#snmp-server host 10.0.P.10 private udp-port 162
```

3.   If the default for an SNMP response is on port 162, what port is the request sent on?

Step 9: Testing the Configuration

1.   Exit out of the access point and log back in using the wrong password. After the failed attempts, log back into the access point. There are now entries of traps sent from the AP to the SNMP server. Check the SNMP application on PC1.

2.   Besides **startup-config** and **running-config**, where would information on the contact, location, and SNMP logging information for SNMP on the router be?

_____

Step 10: Disabling the SNMP Traps on the Access Point

To disable the SNMP traps on the AP, use the following commands:

```
PodP(config)#no snmp-server enable traps
PodP(config)#no snmp-server system-shutdown
PodP(config)#no snmp-server trap-auth
```

Note: By disabling SNMP trap notifications, which are not needed, the amount of free bandwidth can be increased, and unnecessary SNMP processing tasks can be eliminated.

Lab 11.5.6.3: Configure Syslog and SNMP on the Bridge

Estimated Time: 25 minutes

Number of Team Members: Students work in teams of two

Objective

In this lab, students configure and use syslog logging to monitor network events. Students also configure the contact and location of the SNMP agent and test the configuration.

Scenario

A network security administrator should always log significant events on the bridge to the syslog or SNMP server. A server should be located on a secure internal network to ensure log integrity. The server can be a dedicated server or another server running syslog services or SNMP.

Topology

Figure 11-17 shows the topology used in this lab.

Figure 11-17   Lab Topology

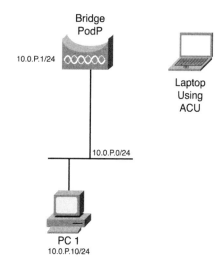

Note: The topology figures and lab examples contain **P** values. The **P** value in the addressing and naming scheme refers to *your* assigned Pod number.

The following are examples of determining **P** values:

- Pod2 is looking at a topology figure and is trying to determine the **P** values in the figure. In this scenario, the **P** values equals 2. 10.0.P.12 becomes 10.0.2.12, 172.30.P.2 becomes 172.30.2.2, and so on.

- Pod1 is looking at a topology figure and is trying to determine the **P** values in the figure. In this scenario, the **P** values equals 1. 10.0.P.12 becomes 10.0.1.12, 172.30.P.2 becomes 172.30.1.2, and so on.

In both examples, the **P** values are directly related to the Pod number of the team.

Preparation

The student should read and understand material presented in Chapter 11 from the *Fundamentals of Wireless LANs Companion Guide* prior to this lab.

Tools and Resources

The following tools and resources are required to complete this lab:

- One BR350

- A wired PC (PC1) acting as the syslog and syslog server with a static IP address

- A PC or laptop with a properly installed wireless client adapter and utility

Step 1: Downloading and Installing the Software

1. Go to the following website and download Kiwi Syslog Daemon Standard version software: http://www.kiwisyslog.com/software_downloads.htm.

2. Install the program on PC1.

Step 2: Setting Up and Executing the Kiwi Syslog Daemon

Click the **Kiwi Syslog Daemon** icon on the desktop to bring up the syslog application. The Kiwi Syslog Daemon, shown in Figure 11-18, can be customized or the defaults can be used.

Figure 11-18   Kiwi Syslog Daemon

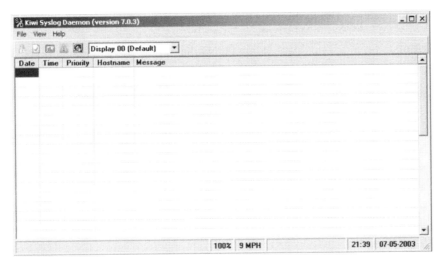

Step 3: Enabling Logging on the Bridge

1.   From the Setup page, click the **Event Log Notifications** link, as shown in Figure 11-19.

Figure 11-19   Kiwi Syslog Daemon: Setup Page

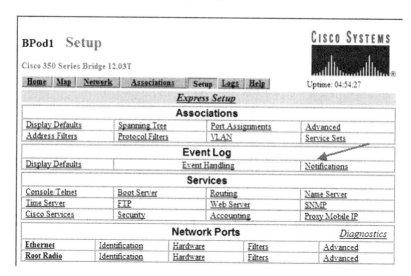

Figure 11-20 shows the Event Notifications Setup page.

Figure 11-20   Event Notifications Setup Page

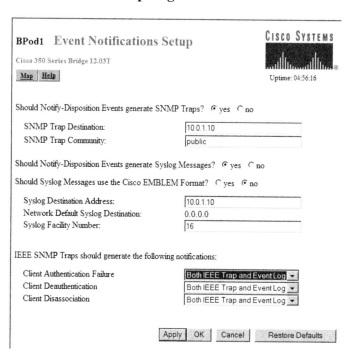

2.   Type in the Syslog and SNMP Destination Host IP address. This should be 10.0.P.10.

3.   Click the **Apply** button to begin logging events to the Kiwi Syslog.

4. From the Setup page, click on the **Services** SNMP link. The SNMP Setup page is shown in Figure 11-21.

Figure 11-21   SNMP Setup Page

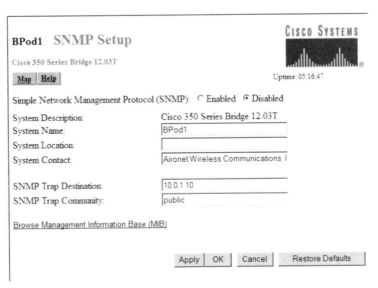

5. Click the **Enabled** radio button to enable SNMP.

6. Configure a system location and contact.

7. Click the **Apply** button to begin logging events to the SNMP Trap Watcher.

Step 4: Viewing Event Logs

Configuring logging is only half of the logging scenario. A security administrator must monitor the logs on a daily basis.

Generate events to the syslog by logging into the bridge that is being monitored.

1. Have a wireless user connect to the bridge.

2. Have the wireless user disconnect from the bridge.

3. View the messages in the Kiwi syslog window, as shown in Figure 11-22. The Host name should match the IP address of the bridge.

4. Click the **Setup** icon located in the upper-left corner of the syslog program window. The setup window then appears, as shown in Figure 11-23.

Figure 11-22   Kiwi Syslog Window

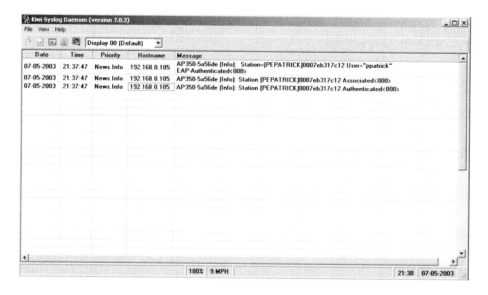

Figure 11-23   Syslog Program Window

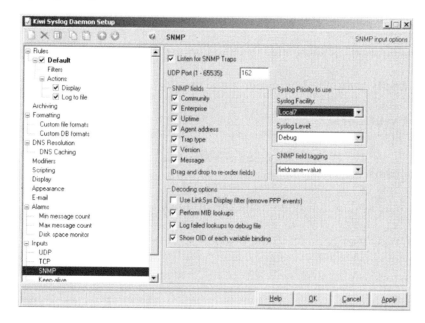

5. Configure SNMP on the Kiwi Syslog Daemon by checking the **Listen for SNMP Traps** box.

6. Click the **OK** button to save the changes.

7. Have a wireless user connect to the bridge.

8. Have the wireless user disconnect from the bridge.

9.   View the main logging screen on Kiwi, as shown in Figure 11-24.

Figure 11-24   Kiwi Main Logging Screen

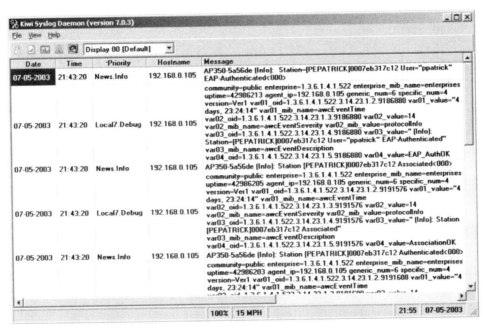

10.   Notice the SNMP messages contain much more information than the syslog messages. The Host name should match the IP address of the bridge.

11.   When using the Cisco WLAN Solutions engine or other enterprise-level SNMP applications, SNMP can be used for monitoring and management.

Chapter 12

Emerging Technologies

Lab 12.4.8.1: Wireless Case Study of a School

Estimated Time: Actual time of completion varies

Number of Team Members: Students work in teams of two

Objective

In this lab, students determine the feasibility of deploying a WLAN at a local school in the area.

Scenario

Connectivity to IT tools is often restricted to IT classrooms or computer labs. However, with the emergence of on-line curriculum and multimedia learning materials, the demand for student access from any part of the campus is growing. Productivity for professors, lecturers, and teachers is no different. A wireless network can enable teachers and students to gain access to information, productivity tools, and applications regardless of their environment or smart devices, such as laptops, PDAs, BlackBerries, and phones.

Step 1: Arranging the Visit

Locate a school in the area and make arrangements for a site visit. Then, schedule an interview with the person responsible for the school or district computer network.

1.   Name of the school:

   _____

2.   Person contacted:

   _____

Step 2: Documenting the Existing Network

Summarize the existing computer network available for student access at this school. A good place to start might be the access available in the library.

_____
_____
_____
_____
_____
_____

Step 3: Listing the Educational Initiatives Relating to WLANs

1. List any planned future enhancements to this network:

_____

_____

_____

_____

_____

2. How much of the future enhancements involve additional cabling? Are classrooms cabled for network access? Is there an outdoor study area that student's use that could benefit from a wireless hotspot? Record answers in the space provided.

_____

_____

_____

_____

_____

Step 4: Determining the User Needs

Determine how many additional users are expected to utilize the wired network and record this information in the space provided below.

This helps determine the amount of access points needed to service the users. For example, using the 2.4 GHz range, estimate one access point per 10 to 15 users and three access points per cell area for normal bandwidth users. This allows approximately 30 to 45 students per cell coverage. In the 5 GHz range, four access points can be co-located in one area and possibly up to 12, but heavy bandwidth users should stay with a wired network.

_____

_____

_____

_____

_____

Step 5: Preparing and Estimating

Prepare a rough estimate of the project cost in the space provided. Include labor, equipment, and supplies. Create a separate spreadsheet of WLAN devices and accessories to be ordered.

_____

_____

_____

_____

_____

Step 6: Developing a Proposed WLAN Solution for This School

The following information should be included in the WLAN solution for the school:

- Frequency range spectrum chosen and the reason

- Total number of access points

- Type of antenna

- How you will secure access to the WLAN

- Budget

- Installation schedule

- Total cost for the WLAN deployment

- Pros and cons of the WLAN solution

- Conclusion

Step 7: Presenting the Proposal

Present the proposal to the classroom in a PowerPoint presentation.

Lab 12.4.8.2: Wireless Case Study of an Organization

Estimated Time: Actual time of completion varies

Number of Team Members: Students work in teams of two

Objective

In this lab, students learn about the process of implementing a WLAN in an existing organization.

Scenario

A recent study of WLANs, conducted by NOP World-Technology, studied the perceived benefits of WLANs after implementation. The study found that WLANs increase productivity. End-users stay connected to the network an average of 1.75 hours longer each day, and report average daily timesavings of 70 minutes. Overall, WLANs create a productivity increase of 22%.

Preparation

The instructor can do some of the preliminary research involved in locating organizations in the area that have implemented or have plans to implement a WLAN.

Step 1: Locating an Organization That Has Implemented a WLAN

List the organization name and describe its core service or business:

_____

_____

_____

_____

_____

Step 2: Coordinating an Onsite Interview with the IT Manager

1. Who was contacted?

    _____

2. What is this person's primary responsibility?

    _____

    _____

3. Was a site survey performed?

    _____

4. What prompted the necessity of the WLAN?

_____

_____

_____

_____

_____

5. Describe the organization's wired network prior to adding a WLAN. For example, what routers, switches, workstations, servers, and applications were used?

_____

_____

_____

_____

_____

6. List the equipment that was added for the WLAN deployment.

_____

_____

_____

_____

_____

7. What methods are used to secure access onto the WLAN?

_____

_____

_____

_____

_____

8. What quantifiable results were achieved?

_____

_____

_____

_____

_____

Notes

Notes

Notes

Notes

Notes

Notes

Notes